Artificial Intelligence

Artificial Intelligence

Mia Williams

Larsen & Keller
www.larsen-keller.com

Artificial Intelligence
Mia Williams
ISBN: 978-1-64172-635-1 (Hardback)

 Larsen & Keller

Published by Larsen and Keller Education,
5 Penn Plaza,
19th Floor,
New York, NY 10001, USA

Cataloging-in-Publication Data

Artificial intelligence / Mia Williams.
        p. cm.
Includes bibliographical references and index.
ISBN 978-1-64172-635-1
1. Artificial intelligence. 2. Digital computer simulation. 3. Neural computers. 4. Fifth generation computers.
5. Electronic data processing. I. Williams, Mia.
Q335 .A78 2022
006.3--dc23

For more information regarding Larsen and Keller Education and its products, please visit the publisher's website www.larsen-keller.com

Table of Contents

This book is a culmination of my many years of practice in this field. I attribute the success of this book to my support group. I would like to thank my parents who have showered me with unconditional love and support and my peers and professors for their constant guidance.

The intelligence demonstrated by machines is referred to as artificial intelligence. It also refers to the machines that are capable of mimicking the cognitive functions of the human brain such as learning and problem-solving. It is broadly classified into three types of systems, namely, human inspired, analytical and humanized artificial intelligence. A few of the capabilities of artificial intelligence include understanding human speech, competing in strategic games and intelligent routing in content delivery networks. It is also used in various other fields such as medical diagnosis, art creation, proving mathematical theorems, online assistants, search engines as well as in customer targeting in online advertisements. This book presents the complex subject of artificial intelligence in the most comprehensible and easy to understand language. Most of the topics introduced herein cover new techniques and the applications of this field. Those with an interest in this field would find this book helpful.

The details of chapters are provided below for a progressive learning:

Chapter – What is Artificial Intelligence?

The intelligence demonstrated by machines is referred to as artificial intelligence or AI. Some of the types of AI are artificial general intelligence, superintelligence and artificial consciousness. This is an introductory chapter which will introduce briefly all the significant classifications of artificial intelligence.

Chapter – Algorithms, Tools and Frameworks

The rules which are followed during problem solving operations by a computer are known as algorithms. Some of the major types of algorithms are search algorithms, evolutionary algorithms and machine learning algorithms. A few of the tools and frameworks that are used in artificial intelligence are TensorFlow, Apache SystemML, Apache Mahout and Torch. This chapter closely examines these algorithms, tools and frameworks that are used within artificial intelligence.

Chapter – Applications

Artificial intelligence finds applications in numerous areas. A few of them are speech recognition, face recognition, computer vision, data mining and automation. The diverse applications of artificial intelligence in these fields have been extensively discussed in this chapter.

Chapter – Artificial intelligence: Problems, Approaches, Advantages and Disadvantages

There are various approaches related to artificial intelligence including cybernetics and brain simulation, cognitive simulation, logic-based, knowledge-based, embodied intelligence, statistical learning, etc. These diverse approaches of artificial intelligence as well as its problems, advantages and disadvantages have been thoroughly discussed in this chapter.

Chapter – Philosophy and Ethics

The philosophy of artificial intelligence is concerned with the issues related to the possibility of building an intelligent thinking machine. The ethics of artificial intelligence is a section of ethics of technology which deals specifically with artificially intelligent beings and robots. This chapter closely examines the key concepts of philosophy and ethics of artificial intelligence such as Turing test and computational theory of mind.

Mia Williams

1
What is Artificial Intelligence?

The intelligence demonstrated by machines is referred to as artificial intelligence or AI. Some of the types of AI are artificial general intelligence, superintelligence and artificial consciousness. This is an introductory chapter which will introduce briefly all the significant classifications of artificial intelligence.

Artificial intelligence (AI) is the simulation of human intelligence processes by machines, especially computer systems. These processes include learning (the acquisition of information and rules for using the information), reasoning (using rules to reach approximate or definite conclusions) and self-correction. Particular applications of AI include expert systems, speech recognition and machine vision.

AI can be categorized as either weak or strong. Weak AI, also known as narrow AI, is an AI system that is designed and trained for a particular task. Virtual personal assistants, such as Apple's Siri, are a form of weak AI. Strong AI, also known as artificial general intelligence, is an AI system with generalized human cognitive abilities. When presented with an unfamiliar task, a strong AI system is able to find a solution without human intervention.

Because hardware, software and staffing costs for AI can be expensive, many vendors are including AI components in their standard offerings, as well as access to Artificial Intelligence as a Service (AIaaS) platforms. AI as a Service allows individuals and companies to experiment with AI for various business purposes and sample multiple platforms before making a commitment. Popular AI cloud offerings include Amazon AI services, IBM Watson Assistant, Microsoft Cognitive Services and Google AI services.

While AI tools present a range of new functionality for businesses ,the use of artificial intelligence raises ethical questions. This is because deep learning algorithms, which underpin many of the most advanced AI tools, are only as smart as the data they are given in training. Because a human selects what data should be used for training an AI program, the potential for human bias is inherent and must be monitored closely.

Some industry experts believe that the term artificial intelligence is too closely linked to popular culture, causing the general public to have unrealistic fears about artificial intelligence and improbable expectations about how it will change the workplace and life in general. Researchers and marketers hope the label augmented intelligence, which has a more neutral connotation, will help people understand that AI will simply improve products and services, not replace the humans that use them.

Types of Artificial Intelligence

Arend Hintze, an assistant professor of integrative biology and computer science and engineering at Michigan State University, categorizes AI into four types, from the kind of AI systems that exist today to sentient systems, which do not yet exist. His categories are as follows:

- Type 1: Reactive machines - An example is Deep Blue, the IBM chess program that beat Garry Kasparov in the 1990s. Deep Blue can identify pieces on the chess board and make predictions, but it has no memory and cannot use past experiences to inform future ones. It analyzes possible moves - its own and its opponent - and chooses the most strategic move. Deep Blue and Google's AlphaGO were designed for narrow purposes and cannot easily be applied to another situation.

- Type 2: Limited memory - These AI systems can use past experiences to inform future decisions. Some of the decision-making functions in self-driving cars are designed this way. Observations inform actions happening in the not-so-distant future, such as a car changing lanes. These observations are not stored permanently.

- Type 3: Theory of mind - This psychology term refers to the understanding that others have their own beliefs, desires and intentions that impact the decisions they make. This kind of AI does not yet exist.

- Type 4: Self-awareness. In this category, AI systems have a sense of self, have consciousness. Machines with self-awareness understand their current state and can use the information to infer what others are feeling. This type of AI does not yet exist.

Examples of AI Technology

AI is incorporated into a variety of different types of technology. Here are examples:

- Automation: What makes a system or process function automatically. For example, robotic process automation (RPA) can be programmed to perform high-volume, repeatable tasks that humans normally performed. RPA is different from IT automation in that it can adapt to changing circumstances.

- Machine learning: The science of getting a computer to act without programming. Deep learning is a subset of machine learning that, in very simple terms, can be thought of as the automation of predictive analytics. There are three types of machine learning algorithms:

  ◦ Supervised learning: Data sets are labeled so that patterns can be detected and used to label new data sets.

  ◦ Unsupervised learning: Data sets aren't labeled and are sorted according to similarities or differences.

  ◦ Reinforcement learning: Data sets aren't labeled but, after performing an action or several actions, the AI system is given feedback.

- Machine vision: The science of allowing computers to see. This technology captures and analyzes visual information using a camera, analog-to-digital conversion and digital signal processing. It is often compared to human eyesight, but machine vision isn't bound by biology and can be programmed to see through walls, for example. It is used in a range of applications from signature identification to medical image analysis. Computer vision, which is focused on machine-based image processing, is often conflated with machine vision.

- Natural language processing (NLP): The processing of human - and not computer - language by a computer program. One of the older and best known examples of NLP is spam detection, which looks at the subject line and the text of an email and decides if it's junk. Current approaches to NLP are based on machine learning. NLP tasks include text translation, sentiment analysis and speech recognition.

- Robotics: A field of engineering focused on the design and manufacturing of robots. Robots are often used to perform tasks that are difficult for humans to perform or perform consistently. They are used in assembly lines for car production or by NASA to move large objects in space. Researchers are also using machine learning to build robots that can interact in social settings.

- Self-driving cars: These use a combination of computer vision, image recognition and deep learning to build automated skill at piloting a vehicle while staying in a given lane and avoiding unexpected obstructions, such as pedestrians.

AI Applications

Artificial intelligence has made its way into a number of areas. Here are six examples:

- AI in healthcare: The biggest bets are on improving patient outcomes and reducing costs. Companies are applying machine learning to make better and faster diagnoses than humans. One of the best known healthcare technologies is IBM Watson. It understands natural language and is capable of responding to questions asked of it. The system mines patient data and other available data sources to form a hypothesis, which it then presents with a confidence scoring schema. Other AI applications include chatbots, a computer program used online to answer questions and assist customers, to help schedule follow-up appointments or aid patients through the billing process, and virtual health assistants that provide basic medical feedback.

- AI in business: Robotic process automation is being applied to highly repetitive tasks normally performed by humans. Machine learning algorithms are being integrated into analytics and CRM platforms to uncover information on how to better serve customers. Chatbots have been incorporated into websites to provide immediate service to customers. Automation of job positions has also become a talking point among academics and IT analysts.

- AI in education: AI can automate grading, giving educators more time. AI can assess students and adapt to their needs, helping them work at their own pace. AI tutors can provide additional support to students, ensuring they stay on track. AI could change where and how students learn, perhaps even replacing some teachers.

- AI in finance: AI in personal finance applications, such as Mint or Turbo Tax, is disrupting financial institutions. Applications such as these collect personal data and provide financial advice. Other programs, such as IBM Watson, have been applied to the process of buying a home. Today, software performs much of the trading on Wall Street.

- AI in law: The discovery process, sifting through of documents, in law is often over-whelming for humans. Automating this process is a more efficient use of time. Start-ups are also building question-and-answer computer assistants that can sift pro-grammed-to-answer questions by examining the taxonomy and ontology associated with a database.

- AI in manufacturing: This is an area that has been at the forefront of incorporating robots into the workflow. Industrial robots used to perform single tasks and were separated from human workers, but as the technology advanced that changed .

Security and Ethical Concerns

The application of AI in the realm of self-driving cars raises security as well as ethical concerns. Cars can be hacked, and when an autonomous vehicle is involved in an accident, liability is un-clear. Autonomous vehicles may also be put in a position where an accident is unavoidable, forcing the programming to make an ethical decision about how to minimize damage.

Another major concern is the potential for abuse of AI tools. Hackers are starting to use sophisti-cated machine learning tools to gain access to sensitive systems, complicating the issue of security beyond its current state.

Deep learning-based video and audio generation tools also present bad actors with the tools neces-sary to create so-called deepfakes , convincingly fabricated videos of public figures saying or doing things that never took place .

Regulation of AI technology

Despite these potential risks, there are few regulations governing the use AI tools, and where laws do exist, the typically pertain to AI only indirectly. For example, federal Fair Lending regulations require financial institutions to explain credit decisions to potential customers, which limit the ex-tent to which lenders can use deep learning algorithms, which by their nature are typically opaque. Europe's GDPR puts strict limits on how enterprises can use consumer data, which impedes the training and functionality of many consumer-facing AI applications.

Categorization of AI

Artificial intelligence can be divided into two different categories: weak and strong. Weak artificial intelligence embodies a system designed to carry out one particular job. Weak AI systems include video games such as the chess example from above and personal assistants such as Amazon's Alexa and Apple's Siri. You ask the assistant a question, it answers it for you.

Strong artificial intelligence systems are systems that carry on the tasks considered to be hu-man-like. These tend to be more complex and complicated systems. They are programmed to handle situations in which they may be required to problem solve without having a person in-tervene. These kinds of systems can be found in applications like self-driving cars or in hospital operating rooms.

Special Considerations: Controversy over Artificial Intelligence

Since its beginning, artificial intelligence has come under scrutiny from scientists and the public alike. One common theme is the idea that machines will become so highly developed that humans will not be able to keep up and they will take off on their own, redesigning themselves at an exponential rate.

Another is that machines can hack into people's privacy and even be weaponized. Other arguments debate the ethics of artificial intelligence and whether intelligent systems such as robots should be treated with the same rights as humans.

Self-driving cars have been fairly controversial as their machines tend to be designed for the lowest possible risk and the least casualties. If presented with a scenario of colliding with one person or another at the same time, these cars would calculate the option that would cause the least amount of damage.

Another contentious issue many people have with artificial intelligence is how it may affect human employment. With many industries looking to automate certain jobs through the use of intelligent machinery, there is a concern that people would be pushed out of the workforce. Self-driving cars may remove the need for taxis and car-share programs, while manufacturers may easily replace human labor with machines, making people's skills more obsolete.

Computer science defines AI research as the study of "intelligent agents": Any device that perceives its environment and takes actions that maximize its chance of successfully achieving its goals. A more elaborate definition characterizes AI as "a system's ability to correctly interpret external data, to learn from such data, and to use those learnings to achieve specific goals and tasks through flexible adaptation."

A typical AI analyzes its environment and takes actions that maximize its chance of success. An AI's intended utility function (or goal) can be simple ("1 if the AI wins a game of Go, 0 otherwise") or complex ("Do mathematically similar actions to the ones succeeded in the past"). Goals can be explicitly defined, or induced. If the AI is programmed for "reinforcement learning", goals can be implicitly induced by rewarding some types of behavior or punishing others. Alternatively, an evolutionary system can induce goals by using a "fitness function" to mutate and preferentially replicate high-scoring AI systems, similarly to how animals evolved to innately desire certain goals such as finding food. Some AI systems, such as nearest-neighbor, instead of reason by analogy, these systems are not generally given goals, except to the degree that goals are implicit in their training data. Such systems can still be benchmarked if the non-goal system is framed as a system whose "goal" is to successfully accomplish its narrow classification task.

AI often revolves around the use of algorithms. An algorithm is a set of unambiguous instructions that a mechanical computer can execute. A complex algorithm is often built on top of other, simpler, algorithms. A simple example of an algorithm is the following (optimal for first player) recipe for play at tic-tac-toe:

1. If someone has a "threat" (that is, two in a row), take the remaining square. Otherwise,

2. If a move "forks" to create two threats at once, play that move. Otherwise,

3. Take the center square if it is free. Otherwise,

4. If your opponent has played in a corner, take the opposite corner. Otherwise,

5. Take an empty corner if one exists. Otherwise,

6. Take any empty square.

Many AI algorithms are capable of learning from data; they can enhance themselves by learning new heuristics (strategies, or "rules of thumb", that have worked well in the past), or can themselves write other algorithms. Some of the "learners" described below, including Bayesian networks, decision trees, and nearest-neighbor, could theoretically, (given infinite data, time, and memory) learn to approximate any function, including which combination of mathematical functions would best describe the world. These learners could therefore, derive all possible knowledge, by considering every possible hypothesis and matching them against the data. In practice, it is almost never possible to consider every possibility, because of the phenomenon of "combinatorial explosion", where the amount of time needed to solve a problem grows exponentially. Much of AI research involves figuring out how to identify and avoid considering broad range of possibilities that are unlikely to be beneficial. For example, when viewing a map and looking for the shortest driving route from Denver to New York in the East, one can in most cases skip looking at any path through San Francisco or other areas far to the West; thus, an AI wielding a pathfinding algorithm like A* can avoid the combinatorial explosion that would ensue if every possible route had to be ponderously considered in turn.

The earliest (and easiest to understand) approach to AI was symbolism (such as formal logic): "If an otherwise healthy adult has a fever, then they may have influenza". A second, more general, approach is Bayesian inference: "If the current patient has a fever, adjust the probability they have influenza in such-and-such way". The third major approach, extremely popular in routine business AI applications, are analogizers such as SVM and nearest-neighbor: "After examining the records of known past patients whose temperature, symptoms, age, and other factors mostly match the current patient, X% of those patients turned out to have influenza". A fourth approach is harder to intuitively understand, but is inspired by how the brain's machinery works: the artificial neural network approach uses artificial "neurons" that can learn by comparing itself to the desired output and altering the strengths of the connections between its internal neurons to "reinforce" connections that seemed to be useful. These four main approaches can overlap with each other and with evolutionary systems; for example, neural nets can learn to make inferences, to generalize, and to make analogies. Some systems implicitly or explicitly use multiple of these approaches, alongside many other AI and non-AI algorithms; the best approach is often different depending on the problem.

Learning algorithms work on the basis that strategies, algorithms, and inferences that worked well in the past are likely to continue working well in the future. These inferences can be obvious, such as "since the sun rose every morning for the last 10,000 days, it will probably rise tomorrow morning as well". They can be nuanced, such as "X% of families have geographically separate species with color variants, so there is an Y% chance that undiscovered black swans exist". Learners also work on the basis of "Occam's razor": The simplest theory that explains the data is the likeliest. Therefore, according to Occam's razor principle, a learner must be designed such that it prefers simpler theories to complex theories, except in cases where the complex theory is proven substantially better.

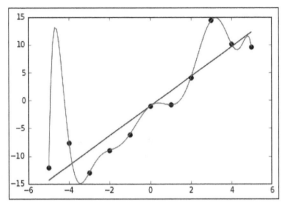

The blue line could be an example of overfitting a linear function due to random noise.

Settling on a bad, overly complex theory gerrymandered to fit all the past training data is known as overfitting. Many systems attempt to reduce overfitting by rewarding a theory in accordance with how well it fits the data, but penalizing the theory in accordance with how complex the theory is. Besides classic overfitting, learners can also disappoint by "learning the wrong lesson". A toy example is that an image classifier trained only on pictures of brown horses and black cats might conclude that all brown patches are likely to be horses. A real-world example is that, unlike humans, current image classifiers don't determine the spatial relationship between components of the picture; instead, they learn abstract patterns of pixels that humans are oblivious to, but that linearly correlate with images of certain types of real objects. Faintly superimposing such a pattern on a legitimate image results in an "adversarial" image that the system misclassifies.

A self-driving car system may use a neural network to determine which parts of the picture seem to match previous training images of pedestrians, and then model those areas as slow-moving but somewhat unpredictable rectangular prisms that must be avoided.

Compared with humans, existing AI lacks several features of human "commonsense reasoning"; most notably, humans have powerful mechanisms for reasoning about "naïve physics" such as space, time, and physical interactions. This enables even young children to easily make inferences like "If I roll this pen off a table, it will fall on the floor". Humans also have a powerful mechanism of "folk psychology" that helps them to interpret natural-language sentences such as "The city councilmen refused the demonstrators a permit because they advocated violence". (A generic AI has difficulty discerning whether the ones alleged to be advocating violence are the councilmen or the demonstrators). This lack of "common knowledge" means that AI often makes different mistakes than humans make, in ways that can seem incomprehensible. For example, existing self-driving cars cannot reason about the location nor the intentions of pedestrians in the exact way that humans do, and instead must use non-human modes of reasoning to avoid accidents.

Examples of AI

The machines haven't taken over. Not yet at least. However, they are seeping their way into our lives, affecting how we live, work and entertain ourselves. From voice-powered personal assistants like Siri and Alexa, to more underlying and fundamental technologies such as behavioral algorithms, suggestive searches and autonomously-powered self-driving vehicles boasting powerful predictive capabilities, there are several examples and applications of artificial intellgience in use today.

However, the technology is still in its infancy. What many companies are calling A.I. today, aren't necessarily so. Software engineer can claim that any piece of software has A.I. due to an algorithm that responds based on pre-defined multi-faceted input or user behavior. That isn't necessarily A.I.

A true artificially-intelligent system is one that can learn on its own. We're talking about neural networks from the likes of Google's DeepMind, which can make connections and reach meanings without relying on pre-defined behavioral algorithms. True A.I. can improve on past iterations, getting smarter and more aware, allowing it to enhance its capabilities and its knowledge.

That type of A.I., the kind that we see in wonderful stories depicted on television through the likes of HBO's powerful and moving series, Westworld, or Alex Garland's, Ex Machina, are still way off. We're not talking about that. At least not yet. Today, we're talking about the pseudo-A.I. technologies that are driving much of our voice and non-voice based interactions with the machines - the machine-learning phase of the Digital Age.

While companies like Apple, Facebook and Tesla rollout ground-breaking updates and revolutionary changes to how we interact with machine-learning technology, many of us are still clueless on just how A.I. is being used today by businesses both big and small. How much of an effect will this technology have on our future lives and what other ways will it seep into day-to-day life? When A.I. really blossoms, how much of an improvement will it have on the current iterations of this so-called technology?

A.I. and Quantum Computing

The truth is that, whether or not true A.I. is out there or is actually a threat to our existence, there's no stopping its evolution and its rise. Humans have always fixated themselves on improving life across every spectrum, and the use of technology has become the vehicle for doing just that. And although the past 100 years have seen the most dramatic technological upheavals to life than in all of human history, the next 100 years is set to pave the way for a multi-generational leap forward.

This will be at the hands of artificial intelligence. A.I. will also become smarter, faster, more fluid and human-like thanks to the inevitable rise of quantum computing. Quantum computers will not only solve all of life's most complex problems and mysteries regarding the environment, aging, disease, war, poverty, famine, the origins of the universe and deep-space exploration, just to name a few, it'll soon power all of our A.I. systems, acting as the brains of these super-human machines.

However, quantum computers hold their own inherent risks. What happens after the first quantum computer goes online, making the rest of the world's computing obsolete? How will existing architecture be protected from the threat that these quantum computers pose? Considering that the world lacks any formidable quantum resistant cryptography (QRC), how will a country like the United States or Russia protect its assets from rogue nations or bad actors that are hellbent on using quantum computers to hack the world's most secretive and lucrative information?

In a conversation with Nigel Smart, founder of Dyadic Security and Vice President of the International Association of Cryptologic Research, a Professor of Cryptology at the University of Bristol and an ERC Advanced Grant holder, he tells me that quantum computers could still be about 5 years out. However, when the first quantum computer is built, Smart tells me that:

> "All of the world's digital security is essentially broken. The internet will not be secure, as we rely on algorithms which are broken by quantum computers to secure our connections to web sites, download emails and everything else. Even updates to phones, and downloading applications from App stores will be broken and unreliable. Banking transactions via chip-and-PIN could be rendered insecure (depending on exactly how the system is implemented in each country)."

Clearly, there's no stopping a quantum computer led by a determined party without a solid QRC. While all of it is still what seems like a far way off, the future of this technology presents a Catch-22, able to solve the world's problems and likely to power all the A.I. systems on earth, but also incredibly dangerous in the wrong hands.

Applications of Artificial Intelligence in use Today

Beyond our quantum-computing conundrum, today's so-called A.I. systems are merely advanced machine learning software with extensive behavioral algorithms that adapt themselves to our likes and dislikes. While extremely useful, these machines aren't getting smarter in the existential sense, but they are improving their skills and usefulness based on a large dataset. These are some of the most popular examples of artificial intelligence that's being used today.

Siri

Everyone is familiar with Apple's personal assistant, Siri. She's the friendly voice-activated computer that we interact with on a daily basis. She helps us find information, gives us directions, add events to our calendars, helps us send messages and so on. Siri is a pseudo-intelligent digital personal assistant. She uses machine-learning technology to get smarter and better able to predict and understand our natural-language questions and requests.

Alexa

Alexa's rise to become the smart home's hub, has been somewhat meteoric. When Amazon first introduced Alexa, it took much of the world by storm. However, it's usefulness and its uncanny ability to decipher speech from anywhere in the room has made it a revolutionary product that can help us scour the web for information, shop, schedule appointments, set alarms and a million other things, but also help power our smart homes and be a conduit for those that might have limited mobility.

Tesla

If you don't own a Tesla, you have no idea what you're missing. This is quite possibly one of the best cars ever made. Not only for the fact that it's received so many accolades, but because of its predictive capabilities, self-driving features and sheer technological "coolness." Anyone that's into technology and cars needs to own a Tesla, and these vehicles are only getting smarter and smarter thanks to their over-the-air updates.

Cogito

Originally co-founded by CEO, Joshua Feast and, Dr. Sandy Pentland, Cogito is quite possibly one of the most powerful examples of behavioral adaptation to improve the emotional intelligence of customer support representatives that exists on the market today. The company is a fusion of machine learning and behavioral science to improve the customer interaction for phone professionals. This applies to millions upon millions of voice calls that are occurring on a daily basis.

Boxever

Boxever, co-founded by CEO, Dave O'Flanagan, is a company that leans heavily on machine learning to improve the customer's experience in the travel industry and deliver 'micro-moments,' or experiences that delight the customers along the way. It's through machine learning and the usage of A.I. that the company has dominated the playing field, helping its customers to find new ways to engage their clients in their travel journeys.

John Paul

John Paul, a highly-esteemed luxury travel concierge company helmed by its astute founder, David Amsellem, is another powerful example of potent A.I. in the predictive algorithms for existing-client interactions, able to understand and know their desires and needs on an acute level. The company powers the concierge services for millions of customers through the world's largest companies such as VISA, Orange and Air France, and was recently acquired by Accor Hotels.

Amazon.com

Amazon's transactional A.I. is something that's been in existence for quite some time, allowing it to make astronomical amounts of money online. With its algorithms refined more and more with each passing year, the company has gotten acutely smart at predicting just what we're interested in purchasing based on our online behavior. While Amazon plans to ship products to us before we even know we need them, it hasn't quite gotten there yet. But it's most certainly on its horizons.

Netflix

Netflix provides highly accurate predictive technology based on customer's reactions to films. It analyzes billions of records to suggest films that you might like based on your previous reactions and choices of films. This tech is getting smarter and smarter by the year as the dataset grows. However, the tech's only drawback is that most small-labeled movies go unnoticed while big-named movies grow and balloon on the platform.

Pandora

Pandora's A.I. is quite possibly one of the most revolutionary techs that exists out there today. They call it their musical DNA. Based on 400 musical characteristics, each song is first manually analyzed by a team of professional musicians based on this criteria, and the system has an incredible track record for recommending songs that would otherwise go unnoticed but that people inherently love.

Nest

Most everyone is familiar with Nest, the learning thermostat that was acquired by Google in January of 2014 for $3.2 billion. The Nest learning thermostat, which, by the way, can now be voice-controlled by Alexa, uses behavioral algorithms to predictively learn from your heating and cooling needs, thus anticipating and adjusting the temperature in your home or office based on your own personal needs, and also now includes a suite of other products such as the Nest cameras.

Types of Artificial Intelligence

Artificial Intelligence is probably the most complex and astounding creations of humanity yet. And that is disregarding the fact that the field remains largely unexplored, which means that every amazing AI application that we see today represents merely the tip of the AI iceberg, as it were. While this fact may have been stated and restated numerous times, it is still hard to comprehensively gain perspective on the potential impact of AI in the future. The reason for this is the revolutionary impact that AI is having on society, even at such a relatively early stage in its evolution.

AI's rapid growth and powerful capabilities have made people paranoid about the inevitability and proximity of an AI takeover. Also, the transformation brought about by AI in different industries has made business leaders and the mainstream public think that we are close to achieving the peak of AI research and maxing out AI's potential. However, understanding the types of AI that are possible and the types that exist now will give a clearer picture of existing AI capabilities and the long road ahead for AI research.

Since AI research purports to make machines emulate human-like functioning, the degree to which an AI system can replicate human capabilities is used as the criterion for determining the types of AI. Thus, depending on how a machine compares to humans in terms of versatility and performance, AI can be classified under one, among the multiple types of AI. Under such a system, an AI that can perform more human-like functions with equivalent levels of proficiency will be considered as a more evolved type of AI, while an AI that has limited functionality and performance would be considered a simpler and less evolved type.

Based on this criterion, there are two ways in which AI is generally classified. One type is based on classifying AI and AI-enabled machines based on their likeness to the human mind, and their ability to "think" and perhaps even "feel" like humans. According to this system of classification, there are four types of AI or AI-based systems: reactive machines, limited memory machines, theory of mind, and self-aware AI.

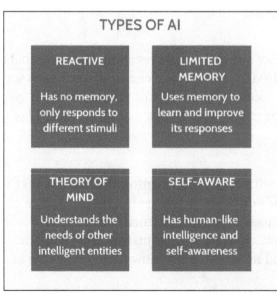

1. Reactive Machines: These are the oldest forms of AI systems that have extremely limited capability. They emulate the human mind's ability to respond to different kinds of stimuli. These machines do not have memory-based functionality. This means such machines cannot use previously gained experiences to inform their present actions, i.e., these machines do not have the ability to "learn." These machines could only be used for automatically responding to a limited set or combination of inputs. They cannot be used to rely on memory to improve their operations based on the same. A popular example of a reactive AI machine is IBM's Deep Blue, a machine that beat chess Grandmaster Garry Kasparov in 1997.

2. Limited Memory: Limited memory machines are machines that, in addition to having the capabilities of purely reactive machines, are also capable of learning from historical data to make decisions. Nearly all existing applications that we know of come under this category of AI. All present-day AI systems, such as those using deep learning, are trained by large volumes of training data that they store in their memory to form a reference model for solving future problems. For instance, an image recognition AI is trained using thousands of pictures and their labels to teach it to name objects it scans. When an image is scanned by such an AI, it uses the training images as references to understand the contents of the image presented to it, and based on its "learning experience" it labels new images with increasing accuracy.

    Almost all present-day AI applications, from chatbots and virtual assistants to self-driving vehicles are all driven by limited memory AI.

3. Theory of Mind: While the previous two types of AI have been and are found in abundance, the next two types of AI exist, for now, either as a concept or a work in progress. Theory of mind AI is the next level of AI systems that researchers are currently engaged in innovating. A theory of mind level AI will be able to better understand the entities it is interacting with by discerning their needs, emotions, beliefs, and thought processes. While artificial emotional intelligence is already a budding industry and an area of interest for leading AI researchers, achieving Theory of mind level of AI will require development in other branches of AI as well. This is because to truly understand human needs, AI machines will have to perceive humans as individuals whose minds can be shaped by multiple factors, essentially "understanding" humans.

4. Self-aware: This is the final stage of AI development which currently exists only hypothetically. Self-aware AI, which, self explanatorily, is an AI that has evolved to be so akin to the human brain that it has developed self-awareness. Creating this type of Ai, which is decades, if not centuries away from materializing, is and will always be the ultimate objective of all AI research. This type of AI will not only be able to understand and evoke emotions in those it interacts with, but also have emotions, needs, beliefs, and potentially desires of its own. And this is the type of AI that doomsayers of the technology are wary of. Although the development of self-aware can potentially boost our progress as a civilization by leaps and bounds, it can also potentially lead to catastrophe. This is because once self-aware, the AI would be capable of having ideas like self-preservation which may directly or indirectly spell the end for humanity, as such an entity could easily outmaneuver the intellect of any human being and plot elaborate schemes to take over humanity.

The alternate system of classification that is more generally used in tech parlance is the classification of the technology into Artificial Narrow Intelligence (ANI), Artificial General Intelligence (AGI), and Artificial Superintelligence (ASI).

5. Artificial Narrow Intelligence (ANI): This type of artificial intelligence represents all the existing AI, including even the most complicated and capable AI that has ever been created to date. Artificial narrow intelligence refers to AI systems that can only perform a specific task autonomously using human-like capabilities. These machines can do nothing more than what they are programmed to do, and thus have a very limited or narrow range of competencies. According to the aforementioned system of classification, these systems correspond to all the reactive and limited memory AI. Even the most complex AI that uses machine learning and deep learning to teach itself falls under ANI.

6. Artificial General Intelligence (AGI): Artificial General Intelligence is the ability of an AI agent to learn, perceive, understand, and function completely like a human being. These systems will be able to independently build multiple competencies and form connections and generalizations across domains, massively cutting down on time needed for training. This will make AI systems just as capable as humans by replicating our multi-functional capabilities.

7. Artificial Superintelligence (ASI): The development of Artificial Superintelligence will probably mark the pinnacle of AI research, as AGI will become by far the most capable forms of intelligence on earth. ASI, in addition to replicating the multi-faceted intelligence of human beings, will be exceedingly better at everything they do because of overwhelmingly greater memory, faster data processing and analysis, and decision-making capabilities. The development of AGI and ASI will lead to a scenario most popularly referred to as the singularity. And while the potential of having such powerful machines at our disposal seems appealing, these machines may also threaten our existence or at the very least, our way of life.

At this point, it is hard to picture the state of our world when more advanced types of AI come into being. However, it is clear that there is a long way to get there as the current state of AI development compared to where it is projected to go is still in its rudimentary stage. For those holding a negative outlook for the future of AI, this means that now is a little too soon to be worrying about the singularity, and there's still time to ensure AI safety. And for those who are optimistic about the future of AI, the fact that we've merely scratched the surface of AI development makes the future even more exciting.

Artificial General Intelligence

Artificial general intelligence (AGI) is the intelligence of a machine that has the capacity to understand or learn any intellectual task that a human being can. It is a primary goal of some artificial intelligence research and a common topic in science fiction and future studies. Some researchers refer to Artificial general intelligence as "strong AI", "full AI" or as the ability of a machine to perform "general intelligent action".

Some references emphasize a distinction between strong AI and "applied AI" (also called "narrow AI" or "weak AI"): the use of software to study or accomplish specific problem solving or reasoning tasks. Weak AI, in contrast to strong AI, does not attempt to perform the full range of human cognitive abilities.

As of 2017, over forty organizations worldwide are doing active research on AGI.

Requirements

Various criteria for intelligence have been proposed (most famously the Turing test) but to date, there is no definition that satisfies everyone. However, there *is* wide agreement among artificial intelligence researchers that intelligence is required to do the following:

- Reason, use strategy, solve puzzles, and make judgments under uncertainty;
- Represent knowledge, including commonsense knowledge;
- Plan;
- Learn;
- Communicate in natural language;
- Integrate all these skills towards common goals.

Other important capabilities include the ability to sense (e.g. see) and the ability to act (e.g. move and manipulate objects) in the world where intelligent behaviour is to be observed. This would include an ability to detect and respond to hazard. Many interdisciplinary approaches to intelligence (e.g. cognitive science, computational intelligence and decision making) tend to emphasise the need to consider additional traits such as imagination (taken as the ability to form mental images and concepts that were not programmed in) and autonomy. Computer based systems that exhibit many of these capabilities do exist (e.g. see computational creativity, automated reasoning, decision support system, robot, evolutionary computation, intelligent agent), but not yet at human levels.

Tests for Confirming Human-level AGI

The Turing Test (Turing)

A machine and a human both converse sight unseen with a second human, who must evaluate which of the two is the machine, which passes the test if it can fool the evaluator a significant fraction of the time. Note: Turing does not prescribe what should qualify as intelligence, only that knowing that it is a machine should not disqualify it.

The Coffee Test (Wozniak)

A machine is required to enter an average American home and figure out how to make coffee: find the coffee machine, find the coffee, add water, find a mug, and brew the coffee by pushing the proper buttons.

The Robot College Student Test (Goertzel)

A machine enrolls in a university, taking and passing the same classes that humans would, and obtaining a degree.

The Employment Test (Nilsson)

A machine works an economically important job, performing at least as well as humans in the same job.

The Flat Pack Furniture Test (Tony Severyns)

A machine is required to unpack and assemble an item of flat-packed furniture. It has to read the instructions and assemble the item as described, correctly installing all fixtures.

The Mirror Test (Tanvir Zawad)

A machine should distinguish a real object and its reflected image from a mirror.

IQ-tests AGI

Chinese researchers Feng Liu, Yong Shi and Ying Liu conducted intelligence tests in the summer of 2017 with publicly available and freely accessible weak AI such as Google AI or Apple's Siri and others. At the maximum, these AI reached a value of about 47, which corresponds approximately to a six-year-old child in first grade. An adult comes to about 100 on average. In 2014, similar tests were carried out in which the AI reached a maximum value of 27.

Problems Requiring AGI to Solve

The most difficult problems for computers are informally known as "AI-complete" or "AI-hard", implying that solving them is equivalent to the general aptitude of human intelligence, or strong AI, beyond the capabilities of a purpose-specific algorithm.

AI-complete problems are hypothesised to include general computer vision, natural language understanding, and dealing with unexpected circumstances while solving any real world problem.

AI-complete problems cannot be solved with current computer technology alone, and also require human computation. This property could be useful, for example, to test for the presence of humans, as CAPTCHAs aim to do; and for computer security to repel brute-force attacks.

Classical AI

Modern AI research began in the mid 1950s. The first generation of AI researchers was convinced that artificial general intelligence was possible and that it would exist in just a few decades. As AI pioneer Herbert A. Simon wrote in 1965: "machines will be capable, within twenty years, of doing any work a man can do." Their predictions were the inspiration for Stanley Kubrick and Arthur C. Clarke's character HAL 9000, who embodied what AI researchers believed they could create by the year 2001. AI pioneer Marvin Minsky was a consultanton the project of making HAL 9000 as realistic as possible according to the consensus predictions of the time; Crevier quotes him as having said on the subject in 1967, "Within a generation. the problem of creating 'artificial intelligence' will substantially be solved," although Minsky states that he was misquoted.

However, in the early 1970s, it became obvious that researchers had grossly underestimated the difficulty of the project. Funding agencies became skeptical of AGI and put researchers under increasing pressure to produce useful "applied AI". As the 1980s began, Japan's Fifth Generation Computer Project revived interest in AGI, setting out a ten-year timeline that included AGI goals like "carry on a casual conversation". In response to this and the success of expert systems, both industry and government pumped money back into the field.However, confidence in AI spectacularly collapsed in the late 1980s, and the goals of the Fifth Generation Computer Project were never fulfilled. For the second time in 20 years, AI researchers who had predicted the imminent achievement of AGI had been shown to be fundamentally mistaken. By the 1990s, AI researchers had gained a reputation for making vain promises. They became reluctant to make predictions at all and to avoid any mention of "human level" artificial intelligence for fear of being labeled "wild-eyed dreamers."

In the 1990s and early 21st century, mainstream AI has achieved far greater commercial success and academic respectability by focusing on specific sub-problems where they can produce verifiable results and commercial applications, such as artificial neural networks, computer vision or data mining. These "applied AI" systems are now used extensively throughout the technology industry, and research in this vein is very heavily funded in both academia and industry. Currently, the development on this field is considered an emerging trend, and a mature stage is expected to happen in more than 10 years.

Most mainstream AI researchers hope that strong AI can be developed by combining the programs that solve various sub-problems using an integrated agent architecture, cognitive architecture or subsumption architecture. Hans Moravec wrote in 1988:

> "I am confident that this bottom-up route to artificial intelligence will one day meet the traditional top-down route more than half way, ready to provide the real world competence and the commonsense knowledge that has been so frustratingly elusive in reasoning programs. Fully intelligent machines will result when the metaphorical golden spike is driven uniting the two efforts."

However, even this fundamental philosophy has been disputed; for example, Stevan Harnad of Princeton concluded his 1990 paper on the Symbol Grounding Hypothesis by stating:

> "The expectation has often been voiced that "top-down" (symbolic) approaches to modeling cognition will somehow meet "bottom-up" (sensory) approaches somewhere in between. If the grounding considerations in this paper are valid, then this expectation is hopelessly modular and there is really only one viable route from sense to symbols: from the ground up. A free-floating symbolic level like the software level of a computer will never be reached by this route (or vice versa) – nor is it clear why we should even try to reach such a level, since it looks as if getting there would just amount to uprooting our symbols from their intrinsic meanings (thereby merely reducing ourselves to the functional equivalent of a programmable computer)."

Artificial General Intelligence Research

Artificial general intelligence (AGI) describes research that aims to create machines capable of general intelligent action. The term was used as early as 1997, by Mark Gubrud in a discussion of the implications of fully automated military production and operations. The term was re-introduced and popularized by Shane Leggand Ben Goertzel around 2002. The research objective is much older, for example Doug Lenat's Cyc project (that began in 1984), and Allen Newell's Soar project are regarded as within the scope of AGI. AGI research activity in 2006 was described by Pei Wang and Ben Goertzel. The first summer school in AGI was organized in Xiamen, China in 2009 by the Xiamen university's Artificial Brain Laboratory and OpenCog. The first university course was given in 2010 and 2011 at Plovdiv University, Bulgaria by Todor Arnaudov. MIT presented a course in AGI in 2018, organized by Lex Fridman and featuring a number of guest lecturers. However as yet, most AI researchers have devoted little attention to AGI, with some claiming that intelligence is too complex to be completely replicated in the near term. However, a small number of computer scientists are active in AGI research, and many of this group are contributing to a series of AGI conferences. The research is extremely diverse and often pioneering in nature. In the introduction to his book, Goertzel says that estimates of the time needed before a truly flexible AGI is built vary from 10 years to over a century, but the consensus in the AGI research community seems to be that the timeline discussed by Ray Kurzweil in *The Singularity is Near* (i.e. between 2015 and 2045) is plausible.

However, most mainstream AI researchers doubt that progress will be this rapid. Organizations explicitly pursuing AGI include the Swiss AI lab IDSIA, Nnaisense, Vicarious, Maluuba, the OpenCog Foundation, Adaptive AI, LIDA, and Numenta and the associated Redwood Neuroscience Institute.In addition, organizations such as the Machine Intelligence Research Institute and OpenAI have been founded to influence the development path of AGI. Finally, projects such as the Human Brain Project have the goal of building a functioning simulation of the human brain. A 2017 survey of AGI categorized forty-five known "active R&D projects" that explicitly or implicitly (through published research) research AGI, with the largest three being DeepMind, the Human Brain Project, and OpenAI based article.

Namely DeepMind with their success in Human Player Simulation for e.g AlphaGo made use of new concepts:

- Reinforcement learning to improve already trained networks with new data.

- Unsupervised learning, e.g by Generative adversarial network to get improved networks by competition.

Processing Power Needed to Simulate a Brain

Whole Brain Emulation

A popular approach discussed to achieving general intelligent action is whole brain emulation. A low-level brain model is built by scanning and mapping a biological brain in detail and copying its state into a computer system or another computational device. The computer runs a simulation model so faithful to the original that it will behave in essentially the same way as the original brain, or for all practical purposes, indistinguishably. Whole brain emulation is discussed in computational neuroscience and neuroinformatics, in the context of brain simulation for medical research purposes. It is discussed in artificial intelligence research as an approach to strong AI. Neuroimaging technologies that could deliver the necessary detailed understanding are improving rapidly, and futurist Ray Kurzweil in the book *The Singularity Is Near* predicts that a map of sufficient quality will become available on a similar timescale to the required computing power.

Early Estimates

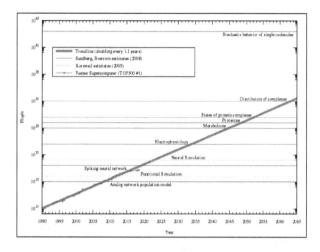

Estimates of how much processing power is needed to emulate a human brain at various levels (from Ray Kurzweil, and Anders Sandberg and Nick Bostrom), along with the fastest supercomputer from TOP500 mapped by year. Note the logarithmic scale and exponential trendline, which assumes the computational capacity doubles every 1.1 years. Kurzweil believes that mind uploading will be possible at neural simulation, while the Sandberg, Bostrom report is less certain about where consciousness arises.

For low-level brain simulation, an extremely powerful computer would be required. The human brain has a huge number of synapses. Each of the 10^{11}(one hundred billion) neurons has on average 7,000 synaptic connections to other neurons. It has been estimated that the brain of a three-year-old child has about 10^{15} synapses (1 quadrillion). This number declines with age, stabilizing by adulthood. Estimates vary for an adult, ranging from 10^{14} to 5×10^{14} synapses (100 to 500 trillion). An estimate of the brain's processing power, based on a simple switch model for neuron activity, is around 10^{14} (100 trillion) synaptic updates per second (SUPS). In 1997 Kurzweil looked at various estimates for the hardware required to equal the human brain and adopted a figure of 10^{16} computations per second (cps). (For comparison, if a computation was equivalent to one floating point operation – a measure used to rate current supercomputers – then 10^{16} computations would be equivalent to 10 petaFLOPS, achieved in 2011). He used this figure to predict the necessary hardware would be available sometime between 2015 and 2025, if the exponential growth in computer power at the time of writing continued.

Modelling the Neurons

The artificial neuron model assumed by Kurzweil and used in many current artificial neural networkimplementations is simple compared with biological neurons. A brain simulation would likely have to capture the detailed cellular behaviour of biological neurons, presently understood only in the broadest of outlines. The overhead introduced by full modeling of the biological, chemical, and physical details of neural behaviour (especially on a molecular scale) would require computational powers several orders of magnitude larger than Kurzweil's estimate. In addition the estimates do not account for glial cells, which are at least as numerous as neurons, and which may outnumber neurons by as much as 10:1, and are now known to play a role in cognitive processes.

There are some research projects that are investigating brain simulation using more sophisticated neural models, implemented on conventional computing architectures. The Artificial Intelligence System project implemented non-real time simulations of a "brain" (with 10^{11} neurons) in 2005. It took 50 days on a cluster of 27 processors to simulate 1 second of a model. The Blue Brain project used one of the fastest supercomputer architectures in the world, IBM's Blue Gene platform, to create a real time simulation of a single rat neocortical column consisting of approximately 10,000 neurons and 10^8 synapses in 2006. A longer term goal is to build a detailed, functional simulation of the physiological processes in the human brain: "It is not impossible to build a human brain and we can do it in 10 years," Henry Markram, director of the Blue Brain Project said in 2009 at the TED conference in Oxford. There have also been controversial claims to have simulated a cat brain. Neuro-silicon interfaces have been proposed as an alternative implementation strategy that may scale better.

Hans Moravec addressed the above arguments ("brains are more complicated", "neurons have to be modeled in more detail") in his 1997 paper "When will computer hardware match the human brain?". He measured the ability of existing software to simulate the functionality of neural tissue, specifically the retina. His results do not depend on the number of glial cells, nor on what kinds of processing neurons perform where.

The actual complexity of modeling biological neurons has been explored in OpenWorm project that was aimed on complete simulation of a worm that has only 302 neurons in its neural network (among about 1000 cells in total). The animal's neural network has been well documented before the start of the project. However, although the task seemed simple at the beginning, the models based on a generic neural network didn't work. Currently, the efforts are focused on precise emulation of biological neurons (partly on the molecular level), but the result can't be called a total success yet. Even if the number of issues to be solved in a human-brain-scale model is not proportional to the number of neurons, the amount of work along this path is obvious.

Complications and Criticisms to AI Approaches

A fundamental criticism of the simulated brain approach derives from embodied cognition where human embodiment is taken as an essential aspect of human intelligence. Many researchers believe that embodiment is necessary to ground meaning. If this view is correct, any fully functional brain model will need to encompass more than just the neurons (i.e., a robotic body). Goertzel proposes virtual embodiment (like Second Life), but it is not yet known whether this would be sufficient.

Desktop computers using microprocessors capable of more than 10^9 cps have been available since 2005. According to the brain power estimates used by Kurzweil (and Moravec), this computer should be capable of supporting a simulation of a bee brain, but despite some interest no such simulation exists. There are at least three reasons for this:

- Firstly, the neuron model seems to be oversimplified.

- Secondly, there is insufficient understanding of higher cognitive processes to establish accurately what the brain's neural activity, observed using techniques such as functional magnetic resonance imaging, correlates with.

- Thirdly, even if our understanding of cognition advances sufficiently, early simulation programs are likely to be very inefficient and will, therefore, need considerably more hardware.

- Fourthly, the brain of an organism, while critical, may not be an appropriate boundary for a cognitive model. To simulate a bee brain, it may be necessary to simulate the body, and the environment. The Extended Mindthesis formalizes the philosophical concept, and research into cephalopods has demonstrated clear examples of a decentralized system.

In addition, the scale of the human brain is not currently well-constrained. One estimate puts the human brain at about 100 billion neurons and 100 trillion synapses. Another estimate is 86 billion neurons of which 16.3 billion are in the cerebral cortex and 69 billion in the cerebellum. Glial cell synapses are currently unquantified but are known to be extremely numerous.

Artificial Consciousness Research

Although the role of consciousness in strong AI/AGI is debatable, many AGI researchers regard research that investigates possibilities for implementing consciousness as vital. In an early effort Igor Aleksander argued that the principles for creating a conscious machine already existed but that it would take forty years to train such a machine to understand language.

Relationship to Strong AI

In 1980, philosopher John Searle coined the term "strong AI" as part of his Chinese room argument. He wanted to distinguish between two different hypotheses about artificial intelligence:

- An artificial intelligence system can *think* and have a *mind*. (The word "mind" has a specific meaning for philosophers, as used in "the mind body problem" or "the philosophy of mind").

- An artificial intelligence system can (only) *act like* it thinks and has a mind.

The first one is called "the *strong* AI hypothesis" and the second is "the *weak* AI hypothesis" because the first one makes the *stronger* statement: it assumes something special has happened to the machine that goes beyond all its abilities that we can test.

The weak AI hypothesis is equivalent to the hypothesis that artificial general intelligence is possible. According to Russell and Norvig, "Most AI researchers take the weak AI hypothesis for granted, and don't care about the strong AI hypothesis."

In contrast to Searle, Kurzweil uses the term "strong AI" to describe any artificial intelligence system that acts like it has a mind, regardless of whether a philosopher would be able to determine if it *actually* has a mind or not.

Possible Explanations for the Slow Progress of AI Research

Since the launch of AI research in 1956, the growth of this field has slowed down over time and has stalled the aims of creating machines skilled with intelligent action at the human level. A possible explanation for this delay is that computers lack a sufficient scope of memory or processing power. In addition, the level of complexity that connects to the process of AI research may also limit the progress of AI research.

While most AI researchers believe strong AI can be achieved in the future, there are some individuals like Hubert Dreyfus and Roger Penrose who deny the possibility of achieving strong AI. John McCarthy was one of various computer scientists who believe human-level AI will be accomplished, but a date cannot accurately be predicted.

Conceptual limitations are another possible reason for the slowness in AI research. AI researchers may need to modify the conceptual framework of their discipline in order to provide a stronger base and contribution to the quest of achieving strong AI. As William Clocksin wrote in 2003: "the framework starts from Weizenbaum's observation that intelligence manifests itself only relative to specific social and cultural contexts".

Furthermore, AI researchers have been able to create computers that can perform jobs that are complicated for people to do, but conversely they have struggled to develop a computer that is capable of carrying out tasks that are simple for humans to do. A problem described by David Gelernter is that some people assume thinking and reasoning are equivalent. However, the idea of whether thoughts and the creator of those thoughts are isolated individually has intrigued AI researchers.

The problems that have been encountered in AI research over the past decades have further impeded the progress of AI. The failed predictions that have been promised by AI researchers and the lack of a complete understanding of human behaviors have helped diminish the primary idea of human-level AI. Although the progress of AI research has brought both improvement and disappointment, most investigators have established optimism about potentially achieving the goal of AI in the 21st century.

Other possible reasons have been proposed for the lengthy research in the progress of strong AI. The intricacy of scientific problems and the need to fully understand the human brain through psychology and neurophysiology have limited many researchers from emulating the function of the human brain into a computer hardware. Many researchers tend to underestimate any doubt that is involved with future predictions of AI, but without taking those issues seriously can people then overlook solutions to problematic questions.

Clocksin says that a conceptual limitation that may impede the progress of AI research is that people may be using the wrong techniques for computer programs and implementation of equipment. When AI researchers first began to aim for the goal of artificial intelligence, a main interest was human reasoning. Researchers hoped to establish computational models of human knowledge through reasoning and to find out how to design a computer with a specific cognitive task.

The practice of abstraction, which people tend to redefine when working with a particular context in research, provides researchers with a concentration on just a few concepts. The most productive use of abstraction in AI research comes from planning and problem solving. Although the aim is to increase the speed of a computation, the role of abstraction has posed questions about the involvement of abstraction operators.

A possible reason for the slowness in AI relates to the acknowledgement by many AI researchers that heuristics is a section that contains a significant breach between computer performance and human performance. The specific functions that are programmed to a computer may be able to account for many of the requirements that allow it to match human intelligence. These explanations are not necessarily guaranteed to be the fundamental causes for the delay in achieving strong AI, but they are widely agreed by numerous researchers.

There have been many AI researchers that debate over the idea whether machines should be created with emotions. There are no emotions in typical models of AI and some researchers say programming emotions into machines allows them to have a mind of their own. Emotion sums up the experiences of humans because it allows them to remember those experiences. David Gelernter writes, "No computer will be creative unless it can simulate all the nuances of human emotion." This concern about emotion has posed problems for AI researchers and it connects to the concept of strong AI as its research progresses into the future.

Consciousness

There are other aspects of the human mind besides intelligence that are relevant to the concept of strong AI which play a major role in science fiction and the ethics of artificial intelligence:

- Consciousness: To have subjective experience and thought.

- Self-awareness: To be aware of oneself as a separate individual, especially to be aware of one's own thoughts.

- Sentience: The ability to "feel" perceptions or emotions subjectively.

- Sapience: The capacity for wisdom.

These traits have a moral dimension, because a machine with this form of strong AI may have legal rights, analogous to the rights of non-human animals. Also, Bill Joy, among others, argues a machine with these traits may be a threat to human life or dignity. It remains to be shown whether any of these traits are necessary for strong AI. The role of consciousness is not clear, and currently there is no agreed test for its presence. If a machine is built with a device that simulates the neural correlates of consciousness, would it automatically have self-awareness? It is also possible that some of these properties, such as sentience, naturally emerge from a fully intelligent machine, or that it becomes natural to *ascribe* these properties to machines once they begin to act in a way that is clearly intelligent. For example, intelligent action may be sufficient for sentience, rather than the other way around.

In science fiction, AGI is associated with traits such as consciousness, sentience, sapience, and self-awarenessobserved in living beings. However, according to philosopher John Searle, it is an open question whether general intelligence is sufficient for consciousness. "Strong AI" should not be confused with Searle's "strong AI hypothesis." The strong AI hypothesis is the claim that a computer which behaves as intelligently as a person must also necessarily have a mind and consciousness. AGI refers only to the amount of intelligence that the machine displays, with or without a mind.

Controversies and Dangers

Feasibility

Opinions vary both on *whether* and *when* artificial general intelligence will arrive. At one extreme, AI pioneer Herbert A. Simon wrote in 1965: "machines will be capable, within twenty years, of doing any work a man can do". However, this prediction failed to come true. Microsoft co-founder Paul Allen believed that such intelligence is unlikely in the 21st century because it would require "unforeseeable and fundamentally unpredictable breakthroughs" and a "scientifically deep understanding of cognition". Writing in The Guardian, roboticist Alan Winfield claimed the gulf between modern computing and human-level artificial intelligence is as wide as the gulf between current space flight and practical faster-than-light spaceflight. AI experts' views on the feasibility of AGI wax and wane, and may have seen a resurgence in the 2010s. Four polls conducted in 2012 and 2013 suggested that the median guess among experts for when they'd be 50% confident AGI would arrive was 2040 to 2050, depending on the poll, with the mean being 2081. It is also interesting to note 16.5% of the experts answered with "never" when asked the same question but with a 90% confidence instead. Further current AGI progress considerations can be found below *Tests for confirming human-level AGI* and *IQ-tests AGI*.

Potential Threat to Human Existence

The creation of artificial general intelligence may have repercussions so great and so complex that it may not be possible to forecast what will come afterwards. Thus the event in the hypothetical future of achieving strong AI is called the technological singularity, because theoretically one cannot see past it. But this has not stopped philosophers and researchers from guessing what the smart computers or robots of the future may do, including forming a utopia by being our friends or overwhelming us in an AI takeover. The latter potentiality is particularly disturbing as it poses an existential risk for mankind.

Self-replicating Machines

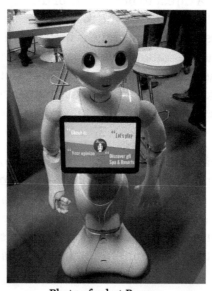

Photo of robot Pepper.

Smart computers or robots would be able to design and produce improved versions of themselves. A growing population of intelligent robots could conceivably out-compete inferior humans in job markets, in business, in science, in politics (pursuing robot rights), and technologically, sociologically (by acting as one), and militarily. Even nowadays, many jobs have already been taken by pseudo-intelligent machines powered by a Weak AI. For example, robots for homes, health care, hotels, and restaurants have automated many parts of our lives: virtual bots turn customer service into self-service, big data AI applications are used to replace portfolio managers, and social robots such as Pepper are used to replace human greeters for customer service purpose.

Emergent Superintelligence

If research into strong AI produced sufficiently intelligent software, it would be able to reprogram and improve itself – a feature called "recursive self-improvement". It would then be even better at improving itself, and would probably continue doing so in a rapidly increasing cycle, leading to an intelligence explosion and the emergence of superintelligence. Such an intelligence would not have the limitations of human intellect, and might be able to invent or discover almost anything.

Hyper-intelligent software might not necessarily decide to support the continued existence of mankind, and might be extremely difficult to stop. This topic has also recently begun to be discussed in academic publications as a real source of risks to civilization, humans, and planet Earth.

One proposal to deal with this is to make sure that the first generally intelligent AI is a friendly AI that would then endeavor to ensure that subsequently developed AIs were also nice to us. But friendly AI is harder to create than plain AGI, and therefore it is likely, in a race between the two, that non-friendly AI would be developed first. Also, there is no guarantee that friendly AI would remain friendly, or that its progeny would also all be good.

Superintelligence

A superintelligence is a hypothetical agent that possesses intelligence far surpassing that of the brightest and most gifted human minds. "Superintelligence" may also refer to a property of problem-solving systems (e.g., superintelligent language translators or engineering assistants) whether or not these high-level intellectual competencies are embodied in agents that act in the world. A superintelligence may or may not be created by an intelligence explosion and associated with a technological singularity.

University of Oxford philosopher Nick Bostrom defines *superintelligence* as "any intellect that greatly exceeds the cognitive performance of humans in virtually all domains of interest". The program Fritz falls short of superintelligence even though it is much better than humans at chess because Fritz cannot outperform humans in other tasks. Following Hutter and Legg, Bostrom treats superintelligence as general dominance at goal-oriented behavior, leaving open whether an artificial or human superintelligence would possess capacities such as intentionality (cf. the Chinese room argument) or first-person consciousness (cf. the hard problem of consciousness).

Technological researchers disagree about how likely present-day human intelligence is to be surpassed. Some argue that advances in artificial intelligence (AI) will probably result in general reasoning systems that lack human cognitive limitations. Others believe that humans will evolve or directly modify their biology so as to achieve radically greater intelligence. A number of futures studies scenarios combine elements from both of these possibilities, suggesting that humans are likely to interface with computers, or upload their minds to computers, in a way that enables substantial intelligence amplification.

Some researchers believe that superintelligence will likely follow shortly after the development of artificial general intelligence. The first generally intelligent machines are likely to immediately hold an enormous advantage in at least some forms of mental capability, including the capacity of perfect recall, a vastly superior knowledge base, and the ability to multitask in ways not possible to biological entities. This may give them the opportunity to—either as a single being or as a new species—become much more powerful than humans, and to displace them.

A number of scientists and forecasters argue for prioritizing early research into the possible benefits and risks of human and machine cognitive enhancement, because of the potential social impact of such technologies.

Feasibility of Artificial Superintelligence

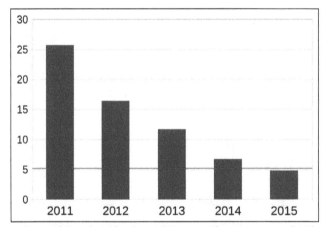

Progress in machine classification of images. The error rate of AI by year.
Red line - the error rate of a trained human.

Philosopher David Chalmers argues that artificial general intelligence is a very likely path to superhuman intelligence. Chalmers breaks this claim down into an argument that AI can achieve *equivalence* to human intelligence, that it can be *extended* to surpass human intelligence, and that it can be further *amplified* to completely dominate humans across arbitrary tasks.

Concerning human-level equivalence, Chalmers argues that the human brain is a mechanical system, and therefore ought to be emulatable by synthetic materials. He also notes that human intelligence was able to biologically evolve, making it more likely that human engineers will be able to recapitulate this invention. Evolutionary algorithms in particular should be able to produce human-level AI. Concerning intelligence extension and amplification, Chalmers argues that new AI technologies can generally be improved on, and that this is particularly likely when the invention can assist in designing new technologies.

If research into strong AI produced sufficiently intelligent software, it would be able to reprogram and improve itself – a feature called "recursive self-improvement". It would then be even better at improving itself, and could continue doing so in a rapidly increasing cycle, leading to a superintelligence. This scenario is known as an intelligence explosion. Such an intelligence would not have the limitations of human intellect, and may be able to invent or discover almost anything.

Computer components already greatly surpass human performance in speed. Bostrom writes, "Biological neurons operate at a peak speed of about 200 Hz, a full seven orders of magnitude slower than a modern microprocessor (~2 GHz)." Moreover, neurons transmit spike signals across axons at no greater than 120 m/s, "whereas existing electronic processing cores can communicate optically at the speed of light". Thus, the simplest example of a superintelligence may be an emulated human mind that's run on much faster hardware than the brain. A human-like reasoner that could think millions of times faster than current humans would have a dominant advantage in most reasoning tasks, particularly ones that require haste or long strings of actions.

Another advantage of computers is modularity, that is, their size or computational capacity can be increased. A non-human (or modified human) brain could become much larger than a present-day human brain, like many supercomputers. Bostrom also raises the possibility of *collective superintelligence*: A large enough number of separate reasoning systems, if they communicated and coordinated well enough, could act in aggregate with far greater capabilities than any sub-agent.

There may also be ways to *qualitatively* improve on human reasoning and decision-making. Humans appear to differ from chimpanzees in the ways we think more than we differ in brain size or speed. Humans outperform non-human animals in large part because of new or enhanced reasoning capacities, such as long-term planning and language use. If there are other possible improvements to reasoning that would have a similarly large impact, this makes it likelier that an agent can be built that outperforms humans in the same fashion humans outperform chimpanzees.

All of the above advantages hold for artificial superintelligence, but it is not clear how many hold for biological superintelligence. Physiological constraints limit the speed and size of biological brains in many ways that are inapplicable to machine intelligence. As such, writers on superintelligence have devoted much more attention to superintelligent AI scenarios.

Feasibility of Biological Superintelligence

Carl SaWgan suggested that the advent of Caesarean sections and *in vitro* fertilization may permit humans to evolve larger heads, resulting in improvements via natural selection in the heritable component of human intelligence. By contrast, Gerald Crabtree has argued that decreased selection pressure is resulting in a slow, centuries-long reduction in human intelligence, and that this process instead is likely to continue into the future. There is no scientific consensus concerning either possibility, and in both cases the biological change would be slow, especially relative to rates of cultural change.

Selective breeding, nootropics, NSI-189, MAO-I's, epigenetic modulation, and genetic engineering could improve human intelligence more rapidly. Bostrom writes that if we come to understand the genetic component of intelligence, pre-implantation genetic diagnosis could be used to select for embryos with as much as 4 points of IQ gain (if one embryo is selected out of two), or with larger gains (e.g., up to 24.3 IQ points gained if one embryo is selected out of 1000). If this process is iterated over many generations, the gains could be an order of magnitude greater. Bostrom suggests that deriving new gametes from embryonic stem cells could be used to iterate the selection process very rapidly. A well-organized society of high-intelligence humans of this sort could potentially achieve collective superintelligence.

Alternatively, collective intelligence might be constructible by better organizing humans at present levels of individual intelligence. A number of writers have suggested that human civilization, or some aspect of it (e.g., the Internet, or the economy), is coming to function like a global brain with capacities far exceeding its component agents. If this systems-based superintelligence relies heavily on artificial components, however, it may qualify as an AI rather than as a biology-based superorganism.

A final method of intelligence amplification would be to directly enhance individual humans, as opposed to enhancing their social or reproductive dynamics. This could be achieved using nootropics, somatic gene therapy, or brain–computer interfaces. However, Bostrom expresses skepticism about the scalability of the first two approaches, and argues that designing a superintelligent cyborg interface is an AI-complete problem.

Forecasts

Most surveyed AI researchers expect machines to eventually be able to rival humans in intelligence, though there is little consensus on when this will likely happen. At the 2006 AI@50 conference, 18% of attendees reported expecting machines to be able "to simulate learning and every other aspect of human intelligence" by 2056; 41% of attendees expected this to happen sometime after 2056; and 41% expected machines to never reach that milestone.

In a survey of the 100 most cited authors in AI, the median year by which respondents expected machines "that can carry out most human professions at least as well as a typical human" (assuming no global catastrophe occurs) with 10% confidence is 2024, with 50% confidence is 2050, and with 90% confidence is 2070. These estimates exclude the 1.2% of respondents who said no year would ever reach 10% confidence, the 4.1% who said 'never' for 50% confidence, and the 16.5% who said 'never' for 90% confidence. Respondents assigned a median 50% probability to the possibility that machine superintelligence will be invented within 30 years of the invention of approximately human-level machine intelligence.

Design Considerations

Bostrom expressed concern about what values a superintelligence should be designed to have. He compared several proposals:

- The coherent extrapolated volition (CEV) proposal is that it should have the values upon which humans would converge.

- The moral rightness (MR) proposal is that it should value moral rightness.

- The moral permissibility (MP) proposal is that it should value staying within the bounds of moral permissibility (and otherwise have CEV values).

Bostrom clarifies these terms:

Instead of implementing humanity's coherent extrapolated volition, one could try to build an AI with the goal of doing what is morally right, relying on the AI's superior cognitive capacities to figure out just which actions fit that description. We can call this proposal "moral rightness" (MR). MR would also appear to have some disadvantages. It relies on the notion of "morally right," a notoriously difficult concept, one with which philosophers have grappled since antiquity without yet attaining consensus as to its analysis. Picking an erroneous explication of "moral rightness" could result in outcomes that would be morally very wrong. The path to endowing an AI with any of these [moral] concepts might involve giving it general linguistic ability (comparable, at least, to that of a normal human adult). Such a general ability to understand natural language could then be used to understand what is meant by "morally right." If the AI could grasp the meaning, it could search for actions that fit.

One might try to preserve the basic idea of the MR model while reducing its demandingness by focusing on *moral permissibility*: The idea being that we could let the AI pursue humanity's CEV so long as it did not act in ways that are morally impermissible.

Responding to Bostrom, Santos-Lang raised concern that developers may attempt to start with a single kind of superintelligence.

Danger to Human Survival and the AI Control Problem

Learning computers that rapidly become superintelligent may take unforeseen actions or robots might out-compete humanity (one potential technological singularity scenario). Researchers have argued that, by way of an "intelligence explosion" sometime over the next century, a self-improving AI could become so powerful as to be unstoppable by humans.

Concerning human extinction scenarios, Bostrom identifies superintelligence as a possible cause:

"When we create the first superintelligent entity, we might make a mistake and give it goals that lead it to annihilate humankind, assuming its enormous intellectual advantage gives it the power to do so. For example, we could mistakenly elevate a subgoal to the status of a supergoal. We tell it to solve a mathematical problem, and it complies by turning all the matter in the solar system into a giant calculating device, in the process killing the person who asked the question".

In theory, since a superintelligent AI would be able to bring about almost any possible outcome and to thwart any attempt to prevent the implementation of its goals, many uncontrolled, unintended consequences could arise. It could kill off all other agents, persuade them to change their behavior, or block their attempts at interference.

Eliezer Yudkowsky explains: "The AI does not hate you, nor does it love you, but you are made out of atoms which it can use for something else."

This presents the AI control problem: How to build a superintelligent agent that will aid its creators, while avoiding inadvertently building a superintelligence that will harm its creators. The danger of not designing control right "the first time", is that a misprogrammed superintelligence might rationally decide to "take over the world" and refuse to permit its programmers to modify it once it has been activated. Potential design strategies include "capability control" (preventing an AI from being able to pursue harmful plans), and "motivational control" (building an AI that wants to be helpful).

Bill Hibbard advocates for public education about superintelligence and public control over the development of superintelligence.

Artificial Consciousness

Artificial consciousness (AC), also known as machine consciousness (MC) or synthetic consciousness, is a field related to artificial intelligence and cognitive robotics. The aim of the theory of artificial consciousness is to "Define that which would have to be synthesized were consciousness to be found in an engineered artifact".

Neuroscience hypothesizes that consciousness is generated by the interoperation of various parts of the brain, called the neural correlates of consciousness or NCC, though there are challenges to that perspective. Proponents of AC believe it is possible to construct systems (e.g., computer systems) that can emulate this NCC interoperation.

Artificial consciousness concepts are also pondered in the philosophy of artificial intelligence through questions about mind, consciousness, and mental states.

As there are many hypothesized types of consciousness, there are many potential implementations of artificial consciousness. In the philosophical literature, perhaps the most common taxonomy of consciousness is into "access" and "phenomenal" variants. Access consciousness concerns those aspects of experience that can be apprehended, while phenomenal consciousness concerns those aspects of experience that seemingly cannot be apprehended, instead being characterized qualitatively in terms of "raw feels", "what it is like" or qualia.

Plausibility Debate

Type-identity theorists and other skeptics hold the view that consciousness can only be realized in particular physical systems because consciousness has properties that necessarily depend on physical constitution.

In his article "Artificial Consciousness: Utopia or Real Possibility," Giorgio Buttazzo says that a common objection to artificial consciousness is that "Working in a fully automated mode, they [the computers] cannot exhibit creativity, emotions, or free will. A computer, like a washing machine, is a slave operated by its components."

For other theorists (e.g., functionalists), who define mental states in terms of causal roles, any system that can instantiate the same pattern of causal roles, regardless of physical constitution, will instantiate the same mental states, including consciousness.

Computational Foundation Argument

One of the most explicit arguments for the plausibility of AC comes from David Chalmers. His proposal, found within his article Chalmers 2011, is roughly that the right kinds of computations are sufficient for the possession of a conscious mind. In the outline, he defends his claim thus: Computers perform computations. Computations can capture other systems' abstract causal organization.

The most controversial part of Chalmers' proposal is that mental properties are "organizationally invariant". Mental properties are of two kinds, psychological and phenomenological. Psychological properties, such as belief and perception, are those that are "characterized by their causal role". He adverts to the work of Armstrong 1968 and Lewis 1972 in claiming that "systems with the same causal topology will share their psychological properties".

Phenomenological properties are not prima facie definable in terms of their causal roles. Establishing that phenomenological properties are amenable to individuation by causal role therefore requires argument. Chalmers provides his Dancing Qualia Argument for this purpose.

Chalmers begins by assuming that agents with identical causal organizations could have different experiences. He then asks us to conceive of changing one agent into the other by the replacement of parts (neural parts replaced by silicon, say) while preserving its causal organization. Ex hypothesi, the experience of the agent under transformation would change (as the parts were replaced), but there would be no change in causal topology and therefore no means whereby the agent could "notice" the shift in experience.

Critics of AC object that Chalmers begs the question in assuming that all mental properties and external connections are sufficiently captured by abstract causal organization.

Ethics

If it were suspected that a particular machine was conscious, its rights would be an ethical issue that would need to be assessed (e.g. what rights it would have under law). For example, a conscious computer that was owned and used as a tool or central computer of a building of larger machine is a particular ambiguity. Should laws be made for such a case? Consciousness would also require a legal definition in this particular case. Because artificial consciousness is still largely a theoretical subject, such ethics have not been discussed or developed to a great extent, though it has often been a theme in fiction.

The rules for the 2003 Loebner Prize competition explicitly addressed the question of robot rights:

If, in any given year, a publicly available open source Entry entered by the University of Surrey or the Cambridge Center wins the Silver Medal or the Gold Medal, then the Medal and the Cash Award will be awarded to the body responsible for the development of that Entry. If no such body can be identified, or if there is disagreement among two or more claimants, the Medal and the Cash Award will be held in trust until such time as the Entry may legally possess, either in the United States of America or in the venue of the contest, the Cash Award and Gold Medal in its own right.

Research and Implementation Proposals

Aspects of Consciousness

There are various aspects of consciousness generally deemed necessary for a machine to be artificially conscious. A variety of functions in which consciousness plays a role were suggested by Bernard Baars and others. The functions of consciousness suggested by Bernard Baars are Definition and Context Setting, Adaptation and Learning, Editing, Flagging and Debugging, Recruiting and Control, Prioritizing and Access-Control, Decision-making or Executive Function, Analogy-forming Function, Metacognitive and Self-monitoring Function, and Autoprogramming and Self-maintenance Function. Igor Aleksander suggested 12 principles for artificial consciousness and these are: The Brain is a State Machine, Inner Neuron Partitioning, Conscious and Unconscious States, Perceptual Learning and Memory, Prediction, The Awareness of Self, Representation of Meaning, Learning Utterances, Learning Language, Will, Instinct, and Emotion. The aim of AC is to define whether and how these and other aspects of consciousness can be synthesized in an engineered artifact such as a digital computer. This list is not exhaustive; there are many others not covered.

Awareness

Awareness could be one required aspect, but there are many problems with the exact definition of *awareness*. The results of the experiments of neuroscanning on monkeys suggest that a process, not only a state or object, activates neurons. Awareness includes creating and testing alternative models of each process based on the information received through the senses or imagined, and is also useful for making predictions. Such modeling needs a lot of flexibility. Creating such a model includes modeling of the physical world, modeling of one's own internal states and processes, and modeling of other conscious entities.

There are at least three types of awareness: Agency awareness, goal awareness, and sensorimotor awareness, which may also be conscious or not. For example, in agency awareness you may be aware that you performed a certain action yesterday, but are not now conscious of it. In goal awareness you may be aware that you must search for a lost object, but are not now conscious of it. In sensorimotor awareness, you may be aware that your hand is resting on an object, but are not now conscious of it.

Because objects of awareness are often conscious, the distinction between awareness and consciousness is frequently blurred or they are used as synonyms.

Memory

Conscious events interact with memory systems in learning, rehearsal, and retrieval. The IDA modelelucidates the role of consciousness in the updating of perceptual memory, transient episodic memory, and procedural memory. Transient episodic and declarative memories have distributed representations in IDA, there is evidence that this is also the case in the nervous system. In IDA, these two memories are implemented computationally using a modified version of Kanerva's Sparse distributed memory architecture.

Learning

Learning is also considered necessary for AC. By Bernard Baars, conscious experience is needed to represent and adapt to novel and significant events. By Axel Cleeremans and Luis Jiménez, learning is defined as "a set of philogenetically [sic] advanced adaptation processes that critically depend on an evolved sensitivity to subjective experience so as to enable agents to afford flexible control over their actions in complex, unpredictable environments".

Anticipation

The ability to predict (or anticipate) foreseeable events is considered important for AC by Igor Aleksander. The emergentist multiple drafts principle proposed by Daniel Dennett in *Consciousness Explained* may be useful for prediction: it involves the evaluation and selection of the most appropriate "draft" to fit the current environment. Anticipation includes prediction of consequences of one's own proposed actions and prediction of consequences of probable actions by other entities.

Relationships between real world states are mirrored in the state structure of a conscious organism enabling the organism to predict events. An artificially conscious machine should be able to anticipate events correctly in order to be ready to respond to them when they occur or to take preemptive action to avert anticipated events. The implication here is that the machine needs flexible, real-time components that build spatial, dynamic, statistical, functional, and cause-effect models of the real world and predicted worlds, making it possible to demonstrate that it possesses artificial consciousness in the present and future and not only in the past. In order to do this, a conscious machine should make coherent predictions and contingency plans, not only in worlds with fixed rules like a chess board, but also for novel environments that may change, to be executed only when appropriate to simulate and control the real world.

Subjective Experience

Subjective experiences or qualia are widely considered to be *the* hard problem of consciousness. Indeed, it is held to pose a challenge to physicalism, let alone computationalism. On the other hand, there are problems in other fields of science which limit that which we can observe, such as the uncertainty principle in physics, which have not made the research in these fields of science impossible.

Role of Cognitive Architectures

The term "cognitive architecture" may refer to a theory about the structure of the human mind, or any portion or function thereof, including consciousness. In another context, a cognitive architecture implements the theory on computers. An example is *QuBIC: Quantum and Bio-inspired Cognitive Architecture for Machine Consciousness*. One of the main goals of a cognitive architecture is to summarize the various results of cognitive psychology in a comprehensive computer model. However, the results need to be in a formalized form so they can be the basis of a computer program. Also, the role of cognitive architecture is for the A.I. to clearly structure, build, and implement it's thought process.

Symbolic or Hybrid Proposals

Franklin's Intelligent Distribution Agent

Stan Franklin defines an autonomous agent as possessing functional consciousness when it is capable of several of the functions of consciousness as identified by Bernard Baars' Global Workspace Theory. His brain child IDA (Intelligent Distribution Agent) is a software implementation of GWT, which makes it functionally conscious by definition. IDA's task is to negotiate new assignments for sailors in the US Navy after they end a tour of duty, by matching each individual's skills and preferences with the Navy's needs. IDA interacts with Navy databases and communicates with the sailors via natural language e-mail dialog while obeying a large set of Navy policies. The IDA computational model was developed during 1996–2001 at Stan Franklin's "Conscious" Software Research Group at the University of Memphis. It "consists of approximately a quarter-million lines of Java code, and almost completely consumes the resources of a 2001 high-end workstation." It relies heavily on *codelets*, which are "special purpose, relatively independent, mini-agents typically implemented as a small piece of code running as a separate thread." In IDA's top-down architecture, high-level cognitive functions are explicitly modeled. While IDA is functionally conscious by definition, Franklin does "not attribute phenomenal consciousness to his own 'conscious' software agent, IDA, in spite of her many human-like behaviours. This in spite of watching several US Navy detailers repeatedly nodding their heads saying 'Yes, that's how I do it' while watching IDA's internal and external actions as she performs her task."

Ron Sun's Cognitive Architecture Clarion

CLARION posits a two-level representation that explains the distinction between conscious and unconscious mental processes.

CLARION has been successful in accounting for a variety of psychological data. A number of well-known skill learning tasks have been simulated using CLARION that span the spectrum ranging from simple reactive skills to complex cognitive skills. The tasks include serial reaction time (SRT) tasks, artificial grammar learning (AGL) tasks, process control (PC) tasks, the categorical inference (CI) task, the alphabetical arithmetic (AA) task, and the Tower of Hanoi (TOH) task. Among them, SRT, AGL, and PC are typical implicit learning tasks, very much relevant to the issue of consciousness as they operationalized the notion of consciousness in the context of psychological experiments.

Ben Goertzel's OpenCog

Ben Goertzel is pursuing an embodied AGI through the open-source OpenCog project. Current code includes embodied virtual pets capable of learning simple English-language commands, as well as integration with real-world robotics, being done at the Hong Kong Polytechnic University.

Connectionist Proposals

Haikonen's Cognitive Architecture

Pentti Haikonen considers classical rule-based computing inadequate for achieving AC: "the brain is definitely not a computer. Thinking is not an execution of programmed strings of commands. The brain is not a numerical calculator either. We do not think by numbers." Rather than trying to achieve mind and consciousnessby identifying and implementing their underlying computational rules, Haikonen proposes "a special cognitive architecture to reproduce the processes of perception, inner imagery, inner speech, pain, pleasure, emotionsand the cognitive functions behind these. This bottom-up architecture would produce higher-level functions by the power of the elementary processing units, the artificial neurons, without algorithms or programs". Haikonen believes that, when implemented with sufficient complexity, this architecture will develop consciousness, which he considers to be "a style and way of operation, characterized by distributed signal representation, perception process, cross-modality reporting and availability for retrospection." Haikonen is not alone in this process view of consciousness, or the view that AC will spontaneously emerge in autonomous agents that have a suitable neuro-inspired architecture of complexity; these are shared by many, e.g. Freeman and Cotterill. A low-complexity implementation of the architecture proposed by Haikonen was reportedly not capable of AC, but did exhibit emotions as expected. See Doan for a comprehensive introduction to Haikonen's cognitive architecture.

Shanahan's Cognitive Architecture

Murray Shanahan describes a cognitive architecture that combines Baars's idea of a global workspace with a mechanism for internal simulation ("imagination").

Takeno's Self-awareness Research

Self-awareness in robots is being investigated by Junichi Takeno at Meiji University in Japan. Takeno is asserting that he has developed a robot capable of discriminating between a self-image in a mirror and any other having an identical image to it, and this claim has already been reviewed. Takeno asserts that he first contrived the computational module called a MoNAD, which has a self-aware function, and he then constructed the artificial consciousness system by formulating the relationships between emotions, feelings and reason by connecting the modules in a hierarchy. Takeno completed a mirror image cognition experiment using a robot equipped with the MoNAD system. Takeno proposed the Self-Body Theory stating that "humans feel that their own mirror image is closer to themselves than an actual part of themselves." The most important point in developing artificial consciousness or clarifying human consciousness is the development of a function of self awareness, and he claims that he has demonstrated physical and mathematical evidence for this in his thesis. He also demonstrated that robots can study episodes in memory where the emotions were stimulated and use this experience to take predictive actions to prevent the recurrence of unpleasant emotions.

Aleksander's Impossible Mind

Igor Aleksander, emeritus professor of Neural Systems Engineering at Imperial College, has extensively researched artificial neural networks and claims in his book *Impossible Minds: My Neurons, My Consciousness* that the principles for creating a conscious machine already exist but that it would take forty years to train such a machine to understand language. Whether this is true remains to be demonstrated and the basic principle stated in *Impossible Minds*—that the brain is a neural state machine—is open to doubt.

Thaler's Creativity Machine Paradigm

Stephen Thaler proposed a possible connection between consciousness and creativity in his 1994 patent, called "Device for the Autonomous Generation of Useful Information" (DAGUI), or the so-called "Creativity Machine", in which computational critics govern the injection of synaptic noise and degradation into neural nets so as to induce false memories or confabulations that may qualify as potential ideas or strategies. He recruits this neural architecture and methodology to account for the subjective feel of consciousness, claiming that similar noise-driven neural assemblies within the brain invent dubious significance to overall cortical activity. Thaler's theory and the resulting patents in machine consciousness were inspired by experiments in which he internally disrupted trained neural nets so as to drive a succession of neural activation patterns that he likened to stream of consciousness.

Michael Graziano's Attention Schema

In 2011, Michael Graziano and Sabine Kastler published a paper named "Human consciousness and its relationship to social neuroscience: A novel hypothesis" proposing a theory of consciousness as an attention schema. Graziano went on to publish an expanded discussion of this theory in his book "Consciousness and the Social Brain". This Attention Schema Theory of Consciousness, as he named it, proposes that the brain tracks attention to various sensory inputs by way of an attention schema, analogous to the well study body schema that tracks the spatial place of a person's body. This relates to artificial consciousness by proposing a specific mechanism of information handling, that produces what we allegedly experience and describe as consciousness, and which should be able to be duplicated by a machine using current technology. When the brain finds that person X is aware of thing Y, it is in effect modeling the state in which person X is applying an attentional enhancement to Y. In the attention schema theory, the same process can be applied to oneself. The brain tracks attention to various sensory inputs, and one's own awareness is a schematized model of one's attention. Graziano proposes specific locations in the brain for this process, and suggests that such awareness is a computed feature constructed by an expert system in the brain.

Testing

The most well-known method for testing machine intelligence is the Turing test. But when interpreted as only observational, this test contradicts the philosophy of science principles of theory dependence of observations. It also has been suggested that Alan Turing's recommendation of imitating not a human adult consciousness, but a human child consciousness, should be taken seriously.

Other tests, such as ConsScale, test the presence of features inspired by biological systems, or measure the cognitive development of artificial systems.

Qualia, or phenomenological consciousness, is an inherently first-person phenomenon. Although various systems may display various signs of behavior correlated with functional consciousness, there is no conceivable way in which third-person tests can have access to first-person phenomenological features. Because of that, and because there is no empirical definition of consciousness, a test of presence of consciousness in AC may be impossible.

In 2014, Victor Argonov suggested a non-Turing test for machine consciousness based on machine's ability to produce philosophical judgments. He argues that a deterministic machine must be regarded as conscious if it is able to produce judgments on all problematic properties of consciousness (such as qualia or binding) having no innate (preloaded) philosophical knowledge on these issues, no philosophical discussions while learning, and no informational models of other creatures in its memory (such models may implicitly or explicitly contain knowledge about these creatures' consciousness). However, this test can be used only to detect, but not refute the existence of consciousness. A positive result proves that machine is conscious but a negative result proves nothing. For example, absence of philosophical judgments may be caused by lack of the machine's intellect, not by absence of consciousness.

Reactive Machines

The most basic types of AI systems are purely reactive, and have the ability neither to form memories nor to use past experiences to inform current decisions. Deep Blue, IBM's chess-playing supercomputer, which beat international grandmaster Garry Kasparov in the late 1990s, is the perfect example of this type of machine.

Deep Blue can identify the pieces on a chess board and know how each moves. It can make predictions about what moves might be next for it and its opponent. And it can choose the most optimal moves from among the possibilities.

But it doesn't have any concept of the past, nor any memory of what has happened before. Apart from a rarely used chess-specific rule against repeating the same move three times, Deep Blue ignores everything before the present moment. All it does is look at the pieces on the chess board as it stands right now, and choose from possible next moves.

This type of intelligence involves the computer perceiving the world directly and acting on what it sees. It doesn't rely on an internal concept of the world. In a seminal paper, AI researcher Rodney Brooks argued that we should only build machines like this. His main reason was that people are not very good at programming accurate simulated worlds for computers to use, what is called in AI scholarship a "representation" of the world.

The current intelligent machines we marvel at either have no such concept of the world, or have a very limited and specialized one for its particular duties. The innovation in Deep Blue's design was not to broaden the range of possible movies the computer considered. Rather, the developers found a way to narrow its view, to stop pursuing some potential future moves, based on how it rated their outcome. Without this ability, Deep Blue would have needed to be an even more powerful computer to actually beat Kasparov.

Similarly, Google's AlphaGo, which has beaten top human Go experts, can't evaluate all potential future moves either. Its analysis method is more sophisticated than Deep Blue's, using a neural network to evaluate game developments.

These methods do improve the ability of AI systems to play specific games better, but they can't be easily changed or applied to other situations. These computerized imaginations have no concept of the wider world – meaning they can't function beyond the specific tasks they're assigned and are easily fooled.

They can't interactively participate in the world, the way we imagine AI systems one day might. Instead, these machines will behave exactly the same way every time they encounter the same situation. This can be very good for ensuring an AI system is trustworthy: You want your autonomous car to be a reliable driver. But it's bad if we want machines to truly engage with, and respond to, the world. These simplest AI systems won't ever be bored, or interested, or sad.

Distinguishing between Narrow AI, General AI and Super AI

The age of AI is upon us; in many ways, it's engulfing us. We're overwhelmed with information, articles and opinions on AI. Experts and non-experts alike are attempting to envision a future driven by the rise of this exponential technology. Because of the constant flow of information on AI, it's becoming increasingly difficult to pinpoint what exactly AI is. Few of us are able to actually define artificial intelligence. Many of us make the mistake of using it synonymously with other buzzwords, like "robots".

Thanks to centuries worth of sci-fi books, movies, and speculations about the future, many of us have formed a fantasy of a world that's ruled (or served) by robots, aerocars, and jetpacks. Now that we're supposedly knee-deep in the AI era, we're bound to wonder: Why don't our lives look anything like the Jetsons? Why haven't fallen in love with Operating Systems, like the movie Her depicted?

The truth is that, despite being surrounded by it, few of us use the term "AI" in the right context. Misusing and misunderstanding the term can cause us to make fallacious statements and assumptions about what the future holds. As we know, the world is changing at an alarming pace, so thinking critically about these changes is crucial if we want to thrive in the future. To adapt in a world driven by change, understand the implications of AI on society, and clarify where we stand today, we need to first distinguish between the various types of AI.

In basic terms, AI can be defined as:

- A broad area of computer science that makes machines seem like they have human intelligence.

- If a machine can solve problems, complete a task, or exhibit other cognitive functions that humans can, then we refer to it as having artificial intelligence.

Artificial Narrow Intelligence

The "broad" definition of AI is vague and can cause a misrepresentation of the type of AI that we interact with today.

Artificial Narrow Intelligence (ANI) also known as "Weak" AI is the AI that exists in our world today. Narrow AI is AI that is programmed to perform a single task — whether it's checking the weather, being able to play chess, or analyzing raw data to write journalistic reports.

ANI systems can attend to a task in real-time, but they pull information from a specific data-set. As a result, these systems don't perform outside of the single task that they are designed to perform.

Unlike General or "Strong" AI, which I'll discuss further below, Narrow AI is not conscious, sentient, or driven by emotion the way that humans are. Narrow AI operates within a pre-determined, pre-defined range, even if it appears to be much more sophisticated than that.

Every sort of machine intelligence that surrounds us today is Narrow AI. Google Assistant, Google Translate, Siri and other natural language processing tools are examples of Narrow AI. Some might assume that these tools aren't "weak" because of their ability to interact with us and process human language, but the reason that we call it "Weak" AI is because these machines are nowhere close to having human-like intelligence. They lack the self-awareness, consciousness, and genuine intelligence to match human intelligence. In other words, they can't think for themselves.

When we converse with Siri, for example, Siri isn't a conscious machine responding to our queries. Instead, what Siri is able to do — what it is designed to do — is process the human language, enter it into a search engine (Google), and return to us with results.

This explains why when we pose abstract questions about things like the meaning of life or how to approach a personal problem to Siri or Google Assistant, we get vague responses that often don't make sense, or we get links to existing articles from the Internet that address these questions. On the other hand, when we ask Siri what the weather outside is, we get an accurate response. That's because answering basic questions about the whether outside is within the range of intelligence that Siri is designed to operate in.

As humans, we have the capacity to assess our surroundings, to be sentient creatures, and to have emotionally-driven responses to situations. The AI that exists around us doesn't have the fluidity or flexibility to think like we do. Even something as complex as a self-driving car is considered Weak AI, except that a self-driving car is made up of multiple ANI systems.

Benefits of Narrow AI

Though we refer to existing AI and intelligent machines as "weak" AI, we shouldn't take it for granted. Narrow AI by itself is a great feat in human innovation and intelligence.

ANI systems are able to process data and complete tasks at a significantly quicker pace than any human being can, which has enabled us to improve our overall productivity, efficiency, and quality of life. ANI systems like IBM's Watson, for example, is able to harness the power of AI to assist doctors to make data-driven decisions, making healthcare better, quicker, and safer.

Additionally, Narrow AI has relieved us of a lot of the boring, routine, mundane tasks that we don't want to do. From increasing efficiency in our personal lives, like Siri ordering a pizza for us online, to rifting through mounds of data and analyzing it to produce results, Narrow AI has made our lives significantly better, which is why we shouldn't underestimate it. With the advent of advanced technologies like self-driving cars, ANI systems will also relieve us of frustrating realities like being stuck in traffic, and instead provide us with more leisure time.

ANI systems also act as the building blocks of more intelligent AI that we might encounter in the near future.

Google is using AI to caption millions of videos on YouTube. Likewise, computer vision is improving so that programs like Vitamin D Video can recognize objects, classify them, and understand how they move. Narrow AI isn't just getting better at processing its environment it's also understanding the difference between what a human says and what a human wants.

Artificial General Intelligence

Artificial General intelligence or "Strong" AI refers to machines that exhibit human intelligence. In other words, AGI can successfully perform any intellectual task that a human being can. This is the sort of AI that we see in movies like "Her" or other sci-fi movies in which humans interact with machines and operating systems that are conscious, sentient, and driven by emotion and self-awareness.

Currently, machines are able to process data faster than we can. But as human beings, we have the ability to think abstractly, strategize, and tap into our thoughts and memories to make informed decisions or come up with creative ideas. This type of intelligence makes us superior to machines, but it's hard to define because it's primarily driven by our ability to be sentient creatures. Therefore, it's something that is very difficult to replicate in machines.

AGI is expected to be able to reason, solve problems, make judgements under uncertainty, plan, learn, integrate prior knowledge in decision-making, and be innovative, imaginative and creative.

But for machines to achieve true human-like intelligence, they will need to be capable of experiencing consciousness.

Artificial Super Intelligence

Oxford philosopher Nick Bostrom defines superintelligence as:

"Any intellect that greatly exceeds the cognitive performance of humans in virtually all domains of interest".

Artificial Super Intelligence (ASI) will surpass human intelligence in all aspects — from creativity, to general wisdom, to problem-solving. Machines will be capable of exhibiting intelligence that we haven't seen in the brightest amongst us. This is the type of AI that many people are worried about, and the type of AI that people like Elon Musk think will lead to the extinction of the human race.

A Melding of Humans and Machines

But like any other technology, AI is a double-edged sword. According to futurist Ray Kurzweil, if the technological singularity happens, then there won't be a machine takeover. Instead, we'll be able to co-exist with AI in a world where machines reinforce human abilities.

Kurzweil predicts that by 2045, we will be able to multiply our intelligence a billionfold by linking wirelessly from our neocortex to a synthetic neocortex in the cloud. This will essentially cause a melding of humans and machines. Not only will we be able to connect with machines via the cloud, we'll be able to connect to another person's neocortex. This could enhance the overall human experience and allow us to discover various unexplored aspects of humanity.

Though we're years away from ASI, researchers predict that the leap from AGI to ASI will be a short one. No one really knows when the first sentient computer life form is going to arrive. But as Narrow AI gets increasingly sophisticated and capable, we can begin to envision a future that is driven by both machines and humans; one in which we are much more intelligent, conscious, and self-aware.

Friendly Artificial Intelligence

A friendly artificial intelligence (also friendly AI or FAI) is a hypothetical artificial general intelligence (AGI) that would have a positive effect on humanity. It is a part of the ethics of artificial intelligence and is closely related to machine ethics. While machine ethics is concerned with how an artificially intelligent agent should behave, friendly artificial intelligence research is focused on how to practically bring about this behaviour and ensuring it is adequately constrained.

Eliezer Yudkowsky, AI researcher and creator of the term Friendly artificial intelligence.

The term was coined by Eliezer Yudkowsky, who is best known for popularizing the idea, to discuss superintelligent artificial agents that reliably implement human values. Stuart J. Russell and Peter Norvig's leading artificial intelligence textbook, *Artificial Intelligence: A Modern Approach*, describes the idea.

Yudkowsky goes into more detail about how to design a Friendly AI. He asserts that friendliness (a desire not to harm humans) should be designed in from the start, but that the designers should recognize both that their own designs may be flawed, and that the robot will learn and evolve over time. Thus the challenge is one of mechanism design—to define a mechanism for evolving AI systems under a system of checks and balances, and to give the systems utility functions that will remain friendly in the face of such changes.

'Friendly' is used in this context as technical terminology, and picks out agents that are safe and useful, not necessarily ones that are "friendly" in the colloquial sense. The concept is primarily invoked in the context of discussions of recursively self-improving artificial agents that rapidly explode in intelligence, on the grounds that this hypothetical technology would have a large, rapid, and difficult-to-control impact on human society.

Risks of Unfriendly AI

The roots of concern about artificial intelligence are very old. Kevin LaGrandeur showed that the dangers specific to AI can be seen in ancient literature concerning artificial humanoid servants such as the golem, or the proto-robots of Gerbert of Aurillac and Roger Bacon. In those stories, the extreme intelligence and power of these humanoid creations clash with their status as slaves (which by nature are seen as sub-human), and cause disastrous conflict. By 1942 these themes prompted Isaac Asimov to create the "Three Laws of Robotics" - principles hard-wired into all the robots in his fiction, intended to prevent them from turning on their creators, or allowing them to come to harm.

In modern times as the prospect of superintelligent AI looms nearer, philosopher Nick Bostrom has said that superintelligent AI systems with goals that are not aligned with human ethics are intrinsically dangerous unless extreme measures are taken to ensure the safety of humanity. He put it this way:

"Basically we should assume that a 'superintelligence' would be able to achieve whatever goals it has. Therefore, it is extremely important that the goals we endow it with, and its entire motivation system, is human friendly".

Ryszard Michalski, a pioneer of machine learning, taught his Ph.D. students decades ago that any truly alien mind, including a machine mind, was unknowable and therefore dangerous to humans.

In 2008 Eliezer Yudkowsky called for the creation of "friendly AI" to mitigate existential risk from advanced artificial intelligence. He explains: "The AI does not hate you, nor does it love you, but you are made out of atoms which it can use for something else."

Steve Omohundro says that a sufficiently advanced AI system will, unless explicitly counteracted, exhibit a number of basic "drives", such as resource acquisition, self-preservation, and continuous self-improvement, because of the intrinsic nature of any goal-driven systems and that these drives will, "without special precautions", cause the AI to exhibit undesired behavior.

Alexander Wissner-Gross says that AIs driven to maximize their future freedom of action (or causal path entropy) might be considered friendly if their planning horizon is longer than a certain threshold, and unfriendly if their planning horizon is shorter than that threshold.

Luke Muehlhauser, writing for the Machine Intelligence Research Institute, recommends that machine ethicsresearchers adopt what Bruce Schneier has called the "security mindset": Rather than thinking about how a system will work, imagine how it could fail. For instance, he suggests even an AI that only makes accurate predictions and communicates via a text interface might cause unintended harm.

The Importance of Artificial Intelligence in this Advanced World

We are a privileged generation to live in this era full of technological advancements. Gone are the days when almost everything was done manually, and now we live in the time where a lot of work is taken over by machines, software, and various automatic processes. In this regard, artificial intelligence has a special place in all the advancement made today. Artificial intelligence or AI is nothing but the science of computers and machines developing intelligence like humans. In this technology, the machines are able to do some of the simple to complex stuff that humans need to do on a regular basis. As the AI systems are used on a day to day basis in our daily life, it is not wrong to say that our lives have also become advanced with the use of this technology.

Great Help for Humans

The AI systems are efficient enough to reduce human efforts in various areas. In order to perform various activities in the industry, many of them are using artificial intelligence to create machine slaves that perform various activities on a regular basis. The artificial intelligence applications help to get the work done faster and with accurate results. Error free and efficient worlds are the main motives behind artificial intelligence. In the recent years, many sectors have started using AI technology to reduce human efforts, and also to get efficient and faster results. What important role does artificial intelligence play today?

Widely used in Banking and Financial Systems

It is a known fact that banks have a numerous activities on a day to day basis that need to be done accurately. Most of the activities take a lot of time and efforts from the employees and at times there is also a chance of a human error in these activities so to speak. Some of the works that banks and financial institutions handle are investing money in stocks, financial operations, managing various properties, etc. With the use of AI system in this process, the institutions are able to achieve efficient results in a quick turnaround time. The strategic implementation of artificial implementation in the bank helps them to focus on every customer, and provide them quick resolution. The customers are happy at all times, as they can get quick service for all the banking and financial needs.

An Important Feature of Medical Science

The Artificial intelligence has completely changed the way medical science was perceived just a few years ago. There are numerous areas in medical science where AI is used to achieve incredible value. With the help of AI, the medical science was able to create a virtual personal health care assistant. These are used for the research and analysis purposes. There are also many efficient healthcare bots introduced in the medical field to provide constant health support to patients. The bots are effective in answering the frequent questions, and also to schedule appointments in quick succession.

A Perfect Addition to Heavy Industries

Artificial intelligence is used in the production unit in most big manufacturing companies. AI system is used to give a specific shape to an object, move objects from one place to another, etc. This application is also used in the management of most companies to get their tasks efficiently done on time. It is used to keep all the records of an employee, the crucial data of the company is stored and can be easily extracted at the crucial decision making time. Heavy industries are thriving on the AI system because they get their tasks done on time and have the potential to put inaccurate data in their system.

Efficient use in Air Transport

Air transport is one of the most systematic transportation systems, and it will not be wrong to say that air transport cannot survive without the use of artificial intelligence. There are numerous functions in the machines and management processes that are controlled by the AI. There are a lot of features from booking the tickets to the takeoff and operation of the flights that AI takes care of. AI applications make air transport efficient, fast, safe, and provides a comfortable journey to the passengers.

Changed the Face of Gaming

These days, we are able to play TV and computer games on the whole new level; all thanks to the artificial intelligence application. We all remember the time when "Super Mario" was the only game considered as the best. Now there are various gaming bots introduced and these will play with you and provide you the great entertainment. Virtual reality is also one example of artificial intelligence.

A Great Future ahead as Well

Engineers are designing machines by studying the human brains and trying to replicate the human intelligence. Although, it is one of the great challenges in engineering, but still a lot has been accomplished from where we began the journey of artificial intelligence. There are numerous benefits of understanding and replicating the brand in artificial intelligence. Apart from treating the brain injuries, diseases, advancements in communication technology, computer simulations, understanding the brain will help to design machines that have a more powerful impact towards the society. Even today we see machines that are capable of performing voice recognition, provide the response to human prompts, monitor and sense the human activities on a day to day basis. However, the future holds much more than what we are able to accomplish today.

A Dream to Reinvent the World

Scientists are riding on the back of AI when machine intelligence will surpass the human intelligence. Scientists believe that once the AI system starts working in its full capacity, it will reinvent the world that we know today. Think of the world where all the menial tasks such as garbage disposal, construction, digging and so on will be taken care of by the AI application. It will be a time when the hierarchical order dictates the limits of a human. It will be the world where no one will be looked down upon and every human will be considered equal. In this way, the humans can then focus their strengths on higher levels of work to accomplish a lot more and always taking technology to the new heights.

A Slight Risk

Although there are numerous benefits that are can be seen, but with every great innovation, there is also a certain amount of risk. One of the greatest risks could be of this technology being used for destruction or other foolish activities. If this does happen, the very technology that we create can kill us in the near future. In order to take care of this crucial aspect, there are many organizations and scientists that are pushing for regulatory oversight on AI application and systems. The oversight needs to be on the national and international level so that all the countries can be at peace and experience growth in their respective countries. However, there are various laws, regulatory guidelines, and procedures that monitor the use of artificial intelligence in today's time, and so the safety of us humans is always the prime concern here.

Artificial Intelligence plays a very important role in not just the development of business and processes but also the humans to the next level. With the rapid growth in technology and development, we can expect a lot more exciting features and uses of AI in the future.

References

- Berlinski, David (2000). The Advent of the Algorithm. Harcourt Books. ISBN 978-0-15-601391-8. OCLC 46890682

- AI-Artificial-Intelligence, definition: techtarget.com , Retrieved 24 March 2019

- Liu, Feng; Shi, Yong; Liu, Ying (2017). "Intelligence Quotient and Intelligence Grade of Artificial Intelligence". Annals of Data Science. 4(2): 179–191. Arxiv:1709.10242. Doi:10.1007/s40745-017-0109-0

- Artificial-intelligence, terms: investopedia.com AI-Artificial-Intelligence, definition: techtarget.com , Retrieved 13 March 2019

- Marwala, Tshilidzi; Hurwitz, Evan (2017). Artificial Intelligence and Economic Theory: Skynet in the Market. London: Springer. ISBN 978-3-319-66104-9

- Importance-artificial-intelligence: enterpriseedges.com, Retrieved 28 April, 2019

- Chapman, Lizette. "Palantir once mocked the idea of salespeople. Now it's hiring them". Latimes.com. Retrieved 28 February 2019

- 4-types-artificial-intelligence: livescience.com, Retrieved 21 April, 2019

- White, R. W. (1959). "Motivation reconsidered: The concept of competence". Psychological Review. 66 (5): 297–333. Doi:10.1037/h0040934

- Distinguishing-between-narrow-ai-general-ai-and-super: medium.com, Retrieved 17 February 2019

2
Algorithms, Tools and Frameworks

The rules which are followed during problem solving operations by a computer are known as algorithms. Some of the major types of algorithms are search algorithms, evolutionary algorithms and machine learning algorithms. A few of the tools and frameworks that are used in artificial intelligence are TensorFlow, Apache SystemML, Apache Mahout and Torch. This chapter closely examines these algorithms, tools and frameworks that are used within artificial intelligence.

Search Algorithm

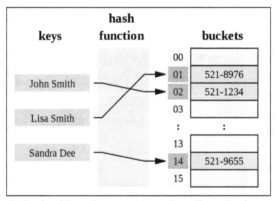

Visual representation of a hash table, a data structure that allows for fast retrieval of information.

In computer science, a search algorithm is any algorithm which solves the search problem, namely, to retrieve information stored within some data structure, or calculated in the search space of a problem domain, either with discrete or continuous values. Specific applications of search algorithms include:

- Problems in combinatorial optimization, such as:

    ○ The vehicle routing problem, a form of shortest path problem.

    ○ The knapsack problem: Given a set of items, each with a weight and a value, determine the number of each item to include in a collection so that the total weight is less than or equal to a given limit and the total value is as large as possible.

- ○ The nurse scheduling problem.

- Problems in constraint satisfaction, such as:

  - ○ The map coloring problem.

  - ○ Filling in a sudoku or crossword puzzle.

- In game theory and especially combinatorial game theory, choosing the best move to make next (such as with the minmax algorithm).

- Finding a combination or password from the whole set of possibilities.

- Factoring an integer (an important problem in cryptography).

- Optimizing an industrial process, such as a chemical reaction, by changing the parameters of the process (like temperature, pressure, and pH).

- Retrieving a record from a database.

- Finding the maximum or minimum value in a list or array.

- Checking to see if a given value is present in a set of values.

The classic search problems described above and web search are both problems in information retrieval, but are generally studied as separate subfields and are solved and evaluated differently. are generally focused on filtering and that find documents most relevant to human queries. Classic search algorithms are typically evaluated on how fast they can find a solution, and whether or not that solution is guaranteed to be optimal. Though information retrieval algorithms must be fast, the quality of ranking is more important, as is whether or not good results have been left out and bad results included.

The appropriate search algorithm often depends on the data structure being searched, and may also include prior knowledge about the data. Some database structures are specially constructed to make search algorithms faster or more efficient, such as a search tree, hash map, or a database index.

Search algorithms can be classified based on their mechanism of searching. Linear search algorithms check every record for the one associated with a target key in a linear fashion. Binary, or half interval searches, repeatedly target the center of the search structure and divide the search space in half. Comparison search algorithms improve on linear searching by successively eliminating records based on comparisons of the keys until the target record is found, and can be applied on data structures with a defined order. Digital search algorithms work based on the properties of digits in data structures that use numerical keys. Finally, hashingdirectly maps keys to records based on a hash function. Searches outside a linear search require that the data be sorted in some way.

Algorithms are often evaluated by their computational complexity, or maximum theoretical run time. Binary search functions, for example, have a maximum complexity of $O(\log n)$, or logarithmic time. This means that the maximum number of operations needed to find the search target is a logarithmic function of the size of the search space.

Classes

For Virtual Search Spaces

Algorithms for searching virtual spaces are used in the constraint satisfaction problem, where the goal is to find a set of value assignments to certain variables that will satisfy specific mathematical equations and inequations/equalities. They are also used when the goal is to find a variable assignment that will maximize or minimize a certain function of those variables. Algorithms for these problems include the basic brute-force search (also called "naïve" or "uninformed" search), and a variety of heuristics that try to exploit partial knowledge about the structure of this space, such as linear relaxation, constraint generation, and constraint propagation.

An important subclass are the local search methods, that view the elements of the search space as the verticesof a graph, with edges defined by a set of heuristics applicable to the case; and scan the space by moving from item to item along the edges, for example according to the steepest descent or best-first criterion, or in a stochastic search. This category includes a great variety of general metaheuristic methods, such as simulated annealing, tabu search, A-teams, and genetic programming, that combine arbitrary heuristics in specific ways.

This class also includes various tree search algorithms, that view the elements as vertices of a tree, and traverse that tree in some special order. Examples of the latter include the exhaustive methods such as depth-first search and breadth-first search, as well as various heuristic-based search tree pruning methods such as backtracking and branch and bound. Unlike general metaheuristics, which at best work only in a probabilistic sense, many of these tree-search methods are guaranteed to find the exact or optimal solution, if given enough time. This is called "completeness".

Another important sub-class consists of algorithms for exploring the game tree of multiple-player games, such as chess or backgammon, whose nodes consist of all possible game situations that could result from the current situation. The goal in these problems is to find the move that provides the best chance of a win, taking into account all possible moves of the opponent(s). Similar problems occur when humans or machines have to make successive decisions whose outcomes are not entirely under one's control, such as in robot guidance or in marketing, financial, or military strategy planning. This kind of problem — combinatorial search — has been extensively studied in the context of artificial intelligence. Examples of algorithms for this class are the minimax algorithm, alpha–beta pruning, * Informational search and the A* algorithm.

For Sub-structures of a Given Structure

The name "combinatorial search" is generally used for algorithms that look for a specific sub-structure of a given discrete structure, such as a graph, a string, a finite group, and so on. The term combinatorial optimization is typically used when the goal is to find a sub-structure with a maximum (or minimum) value of some parameter. (Since the sub-structure is usually represented in the computer by a set of integer variables with constraints, these problems can be viewed as special cases of constraint satisfaction or discrete optimization; but they are usually formulated and solved in a more abstract setting where the internal representation is not explicitly mentioned).

An important and extensively studied subclass are the graph algorithms, in particular graph traversal algorithms, for finding specific sub-structures in a given graph — such as subgraphs, paths, circuits, and so on. Examples include Dijkstra's algorithm, Kruskal's algorithm, the nearest neighbour algorithm, and Prim's algorithm.

Another important subclass of this category are the string searching algorithms, that search for patterns within strings. Two famous examples are the Boyer–Moore and Knuth–Morris–Pratt algorithms, and several algorithms based on the suffix tree data structure.

Search for the Maximum of a Function

In 1953, American statistician Jack Kiefer devised Fibonacci search which can be used to find the maximum of a unimodal function and has many other applications in computer science.

For Quantum Computers

There are also search methods designed for quantum computers, like Grover's algorithm, that are theoretically faster than linear or brute-force search even without the help of data structures or heuristics.

Evolutionary Algorithm

In artificial intelligence, an evolutionary algorithm (EA) is a subset of evolutionary computation, a generic population-based metaheuristic optimization algorithm. An EA uses mechanisms inspired by biological evolution, such as reproduction, mutation, recombination, and selection. Candidate solutions to the optimization problemplay the role of individuals in a population, and the fitness function determines the quality of the solutions. Evolution of the population then takes place after the repeated application of the above operators.

Evolutionary algorithms often perform well approximating solutions to all types of problems because they ideally do not make any assumption about the underlying fitness landscape. Techniques from evolutionary algorithms applied to the modeling of biological evolution are generally limited to explorations of microevolutionary processes and planning models based upon cellular processes. In most real applications of EAs, computational complexity is a prohibiting factor. In fact, this computational complexity is due to fitness function evaluation. Fitness approximation is one of the solutions to overcome this difficulty. However, seemingly simple EA can solve often complex problems; therefore, there may be no direct link between algorithm complexity and problem complexity.

Implementation

Step One: Generate the initial population of individuals randomly (First generation).

Step Two: Evaluate the fitness of each individual in that population (time limit, sufficient fitness achieved, etc).

Step Three: Repeat the following regenerational steps until termination:

- Select the best-fit individuals for reproduction (Parents).

- Breed new individuals through crossover and mutation operations to give birth to off-spring.

- Evaluate the individual fitness of new individuals.

- Replace least-fit population with new individuals.

Types

Similar techniques differ in genetic representation and other implementation details, and the nature of the particular applied problem.

- Genetic algorithm – This is the most popular type of EA. One seeks the solution of a problem in the form of strings of numbers (traditionally binary, although the best representations are usually those that reflect something about the problem being solved), by applying operators such as recombination and mutation (sometimes one, sometimes both). This type of EA is often used in optimization problems.

- Genetic programming – Here the solutions are in the form of computer programs, and their fitness is determined by their ability to solve a computational problem.

- Evolutionary programming – Similar to genetic programming, but the structure of the program is fixed and its numerical parameters are allowed to evolve.

- Gene expression programming – Like genetic programming, GEP also evolves computer programs but it explores a genotype-phenotype system, where computer programs of different sizes are encoded in linear chromosomes of fixed length.

- Evolution strategy – Works with vectors of real numbers as representations of solutions, and typically uses self-adaptive mutation rates.

- Differential evolution – Based on vector differences and is therefore primarily suited for numerical optimization problems.

- Neuroevolution – Similar to genetic programming but the genomes represent artificial neural networks by describing structure and connection weights. The genome encoding can be direct or indirect.

- Learning classifier system – Here the solution is a set of classifiers (rules or conditions). A Michigan-LCS evolves at the level of individual classifiers where as a Pittsburgh-LCS uses populations of classifier-sets. Initially, classifiers were only binary, but now include real, neural net, or S-expression types. Fitness is typically determined with either a strength or accuracy based reinforcement learning or supervised learning approach.

Comparison to Biological Processes

A possible limitation of many evolutionary algorithms is their lack of a clear genotype-phenotype distinction. In nature, the fertilized egg cell undergoes a complex process known as embryogenesis to become a mature phenotype. This indirect encoding is believed to make the genetic search more robust (i.e. reduce the probability of fatal mutations), and also may improve the evolvability of the organism. Such indirect (a.k.a. generative or developmental) encodings also enable evolution to exploit the regularity in the environment. Recent work in the field of artificial embryogeny, or artificial developmental systems, seeks to address these concerns. And gene expression programming successfully explores a genotype-phenotype system, where the genotype consists of linear multigenic chromosomes of fixed length and the phenotype consists of multiple expression trees or computer programs of different sizes and shapes.

Machine Learning Algorithms

We are probably living in the most defining period in technology. The period when computing moved from large mainframes to PCs to self-driving cars and robots. But what makes it defining is not what has happened, but what has gone into getting here. What makes this period exciting is the democratization of the resources and techniques. Data crunching which once took days, today takes mere minutes, all thanks to Machine Learning Algorithms.

Machine learning algorithms are programs (math and logic) that adjust themselves to perform better as they are exposed to more data. The "learning" part of machine learning means that those programs change how they process data over time, much as humans change how they process data by learning. So a machine-learning algorithm is a program with a specific way to adjusting its own parameters, given feedback on its previous performance making predictions about a dataset.

Basic Machine Learning Algorithms

Linear Regression

Linear regression is simple, which makes it a great place to start thinking about algorithms more generally. Here it is:

$\hat{y} = a * x + b$ Read aloud, you'd say "y-hat equals a times x plus b."

- y-hat is the output, or guess made by the algorithm, the dependent variable.

- a is the coefficient. It's also the slope of the line that expresses the relationship between x and y-hat.

- x is the input, the given or independent variable.

- b is the intercept, where the line crosses the y axis.

Linear regression expresses a linear relationship between the input x and the output y; that is, for every change in x, y-hat will change by the same amount no matter how far along the line you are. The x is transformed by the same a and b at every point.

Linear regression with only one input variable is called Simple Linear Regression. With more than one input variable, it is called Multiple Linear Regression. An example of Simple Linear Regression would be attempting to predict a house price based on the square footage of the house and nothing more.

house_price_estimate = a * square_footage + b

Multiple Linear Regression would take other variables into account, such as the distance between the house and a good public school, the age of the house, etc.

The reason why we're dealing with y-hat, an estimate about the real value of y, is because linear regression is a formula used to estimate real values, and error is inevitable. Linear regression is often used to "fit" a scatter plot of given x-y pairs. A good fit minimizes the error between y-hat and the actual y; that is, choosing the right a and b will minimize the sum of the differences between each y and its respective y-hat.

That scatter plot of data points may look like a baguette – long in one direction and short in another – in which case linear regression may achieve a fit. (If the data points look like a meandering river, a straight line is probably not the right function to use to make predictions).

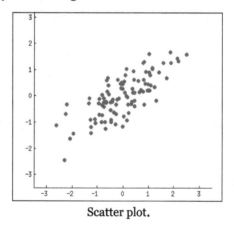

Scatter plot.

Testing one line after another against the data points of the scatter plot, and automatically correcting it in order to minimize the sum of differences between the line and the points, could be thought of as machine learning in its simplest form.

Logistic Regression

Let's analyze the name first. Logistic regression is not really regression, not in the sense of linear regression, which predicts continuous numerical values.

Logistic regression does not do that. It's actually a binomial classifier that acts like a light switch. A light switch essentially has two states, on and off. Logistic regression takes input data and classifies it as category or not_category, on or off expressed as 1 or 0, based on the strength of the input's signal. So it's a light switch for signal that you find in the data. If you want to mix the metaphor, it's actually more like a transistor, since it both amplifies and gates the signal.

Logistic regression takes input data and squishes it, so that no matter what the range of the input is, it will be compressed into the space between 1 and 0. Notice, in the image below, no matter how large the input x becomes, the output y cannot exceed 1, which it asymptotically approaches, and no matter low x is, y cannot fall below 0. That's how logistic regression compresses input data into a range between 0 and 1, through this s-shaped, sigmoidal transform.

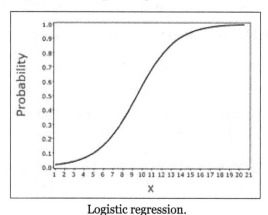

Logistic regression.

Decision Tree

Decision, or decide, stems from the Latin decidere, which itself is the combination of "de" (off) and "caedere" (to cut). So decision is about the cutting off of possibilities. Decision trees can be used to classify data, and they cut off possibilities of what a given instance of data might be by examining a data point's features. Is it bigger than a bread box? Well, then it's not a marble. Is it alive? Well, then it's not a bicycle. Think of a decision as a game of 20 questions that an algorithm is asking about the data point under examination.

A decision tree is a series of nodes, a directional graph that starts at the base with a single node and extends to the many leaf nodes that represent the categories that the tree can classify. Another way to think of a decision tree is as a flow chart, where the flow starts at the root node and ends with a decision made at the leaves. It is a decision-support tool. It uses a tree-like graph to show the predictions that result from a series of feature-based splits.

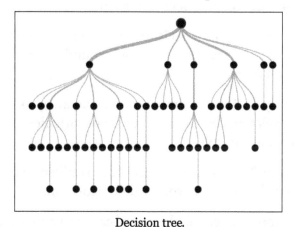

Decision tree.

Here are some useful terms for describing a decision tree:

- Root Node: A root node is at the beginning of a tree. It represents entire population being analyzed. From the root node, the population is divided according to various features, and those sub-groups are split in turn at each decision node under the root node.

- Splitting: It is a process of dividing a node into two or more sub-nodes.

- Decision Node: When a sub-node splits into further sub-nodes, it's a decision node.

- Leaf Node or Terminal Node: Nodes that do not split are called leaf or terminal nodes.

- Pruning: Removing the sub-nodes of a parent node is called pruning. A tree is grown through splitting and shrunk through pruning.

- Branch or Sub-Tree: A sub-section of decision tree is called branch or a sub-tree, just as a portion of a graph is called a sub-graph.

- Parent Node and Child Node: These are relative terms. Any node that falls under another node is a child node or sub-node, and any node which precedes those child nodes is called a parent node.

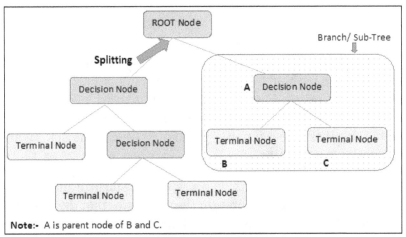

Decision tree nodes.

Decision trees are a popular algorithm for several reasons:

- Explanatory Power: The output of decision trees is interpretable. It can be understood by people without analytical or mathematical backgrounds. It does not require any statistical knowledge to interpret them.

- Exploratory data analysis: Decision trees can enable analysts to identify significant variables and important relations between two or more variables, helping to surface the signal contained by many input variables.

- Minimal data cleaning: Because decision trees are resilient to outliers and missing values, they require less data cleaning than some other algorithms.

- Any data type: Decision trees can make classifications based on both numerical and categorical variables.

- Non-parametric: A decision tree is a non-parametric algorithm, as opposed to neural networks, which process input data transformed into a tensor, via tensor multiplication using large number of coefficients, known as parameters.

Disadvantages of Decision Tree

- Overfitting: Over fitting is a common flaw of decision trees. Setting constraints on model parameters and making the model simpler through pruning are two ways to regularize a decision tree.

- Predicting continuous variables: While decision trees can ingest continuous numerical input, they are not a practical way to predict such values, since decision-tree predictions must be separated into discrete categories, which results in a loss of information when applying the model to continuous values.

- Heavy feature engineering: The flip side of a decision tree's explanatory power is that it requires heavy feature engineering. When dealing with unstructured data or data with latent factors, this makes decision trees sub-optimal. Neural networks are clearly superior in this regard.

Random Forest

Random forests are made of many decision trees. They are ensembles of decision trees, each decision tree created by using a subset of the attributes used to classify a given population. Those decision trees vote on how to classify a given instance of input data, and the random forest bootstraps those votes to choose the best prediction. This is done to prevent overfitting, a common flaw of decision trees.

A random forest is a supervised classification algorithm. It creates a forest (many decision trees) and orders their nodes and splits randomly. The more trees in the forest, the better the results it can produce.

If you input a training dataset with targets and features into the decision tree, it will formulate some set of rules that can be used to perform predictions.

Example: You want to predict whether a visitor to your e-commerce Web site will enjoy a mystery novel. First, collect information about past books they've read and liked. Metadata about the novels will be the input; e.g. number of pages, author, publication date, which series it's part of if any. The decision tree contains rules that apply to those features; for example, some readers like very long books and some don't. Inputting metadata about new novels will result in a prediction regarding whether or not the Web site visitor in question would like that novel. Arranging the nodes and defining the rules relies on information gain and Gini-index calculations. With random forests, finding the root node and splitting the feature nodes is done randomly.

Algorithms Possible using ND4J

While Deeplearning4j and its suite of open-source libraries - ND4J, DataVec, Arbiter, etc. - primarily implement scalable, deep artificial neural networks, developers can also work with more traditional machine-learning algorithms using our framework. ND4J is a generic tensor library, so the sky's the limit on what can be implemented.

In addition to neural networks, the following algorithms are available within DL4J:

- Linear regression,

- Logistic Regression,

- K-means clustering,

- K nearest neighbor (k-NN),

- Optimizations of k-NN with a VP-tree, t-SNE and quad-trees as a side effect.

Tools and Frameworks

Artificial intelligence solutions are implemented in almost all areas of social activities in business research and other fields. The importance of an artificial intelligence developer has therefore become so crucial in today's modern era.

The number of tools and frameworks available to data scientists and developers has increased as machine learning becomes more prominent. Microsoft, IBM, Google, and AWS have machine learning APIs that they respective cloud platforms. It makes easier for developers to build services by summarizing some of their machine learning algorithms' complexities. Let's discuss how artificial intelligence software can be properly developed and how best to find and hire AI engineers.

TensorFlow

An Open Source Software Library for Machine Intelligence. TensorFlow is an open source software library that was originally developed by researchers and engineers working on the Google Brain Team. TensorFlow is used for numerical computation with data flow graphs. Nodes in the graph represent mathematical operations, while the graph edges represent the multi-dimensional data arrays (tensors) communicating between them. The flexible architecture allows you to deploy computation to one or more CPUs or GPUs in a desktop, server or mobile device, with a single API.

TensorFlow provides multiple APIs. The lowest level API—TensorFlow Core—provides you with complete programming control. The higher-level APIs are built on top of TensorFlow Core and are typically easier to learn and use than TensorFlow Core. In addition, the higher-level APIs make repetitive tasks easier and more consistent between different users. A high-level API like tf.estimator helps you manage data sets, estimators, training and inference.

The central unit of data in TensorFlow is the tensor, which consists of a set of primitive values shaped into an array of any number of dimensions. A tensor's rank is its number of dimensions.

A few Google applications using TensorFlow are listed below:

RankBrain: A large-scale deployment of deep neural nets for search ranking on google.

Inception image classification model: This is a baseline model, the result of ongoing research into highly accurate computer vision models, starting with the model that won the 2014 Imagenet image classification challenge.

SmartReply: A deep LSTM model to automatically generate email responses.

Massive multi-task networks for drug discovery: A deep neural network model for identifying promising drug candidates – built by Google in association with Stanford University.

On-device computer vision for OCR: An on-device computer vision model for optical character recognition to enable real-time translation.

Apache SystemML

SystemML is the machine learning technology created at IBM. It ranks among the top-level projects at the Apache Software Foundation. It's a flexible, scalable machine learning system.

Important Characteristics

- Algorithm customisability via R-like and Python-like languages.

- Multiple execution modes, including Spark MLContext, Spark Batch, Hadoop Batch, Standalone and JMLC (Java Machine Learning Connector).

- Automatic optimisation based on data and cluster characteristics to ensure both efficiency and scalability.

SystemML is considered as the SQL for machine learning. The latest version (1.0.0) of SystemML supports Java 8+, Scala 2.11+, Python 2.7/3.5+, Hadoop 2.6+ and Spark 2.1+.

It can be run on top of Apache Spark, where it automatically scales your data, line by line, determining whether your code should be run on the driver or an Apache Spark cluster. Future SystemML developments include additional deep learning with GPU capabilities, such as importing and running neural network architectures and pre-trained models for training.

Java Machine Learning Connector (JMLC) for SystemML

The Java Machine Learning Connector (JMLC) API is a programmatic interface for interacting with SystemML in an embedded fashion. The primary purpose of JMLC is that of a scoring API, whereby your scoring function is expressed using SystemML's DML (Declarative Machine Learning) language. In addition to scoring, embedded SystemML can be used for tasks such as unsupervised learning (like clustering) in the context of a larger application running on a single machine.

Caffe

A deep learning framework made with expression, speed and modularity in mind. The Caffe project was initiated by Yangqing Jia during the course of his Ph.D at UC Berkeley, and later developed further by Berkeley AI Research (BAIR) and community contributors. It mostly focuses on convolutional networks for computer vision applications. Caffe is a solid, popular choice for computer vision-related tasks, and you can download many successful models made by Caffe users from the Caffe Model Zoo for out-of-the-box use.

Caffe's Advantages

- Expressive architecture encourages application and innovation. Models and optimisation are defined by configuration without hard coding. Users can switch between CPU and GPU by setting a single flag to train on a GPU machine, and then deploy to commodity clusters or mobile devices.

- Extensible code fosters active development. In Caffe's first year, it was forked by over 1,000 developers and had many significant changes contributed back.

- Speed makes Caffe perfect for research experiments and industry deployment. Caffe can process over 60 million images per day with a single NVIDIA K40 GPU.

- Community: Caffe already powers academic research projects, startup prototypes, and even large-scale industrial applications in vision, speech and multimedia.

Apache Mahout

A distributed linear algebra framework and mathematically expressive Scala DSL. Mahout is designed to let mathematicians, statisticians and data scientists quickly implement their own algorithms. Apache Spark is the recommended out-of-the-box distributed back-end or can be extended to other distributed back-ends. Its features include the following:

- It is a mathematically expressive Scala DSL.

- Offers support for multiple distributed back-ends (including Apache Spark).

- Has modular native solvers for CPU, GPU and CUDA acceleration.

Apache Mahout currently implements collaborative filtering (CF), clustering and categorisation.

Features and Applications

- Taste CF: Taste is an open source project for CF (collaborative filtering) started by Sean Owen on SourceForge and donated to Mahout in 2008.

- Several Map-Reduce enabled clustering implementations, including k-Means, fuzzy k-Means, Canopy, Dirichlet and Mean-Shift.

- Distributed Naive Bayes and Complementary Naive Bayes classification implementations.

- Distributed fitness function capabilities for evolutionary programming.

- Matrix and vector libraries.

- Examples of all the above algorithms.

OpenNN

An open source class library written in C++ to implement neural networks. OpenNN (Open Neural Networks Library) was formerly known as Flood and is based on the Ph.D thesis of R. Lopez, called 'Neural Networks for Variational Problems in Engineering', at the Technical University of Catalonia, 2008.

OpenNN implements data mining methods as a bundle of functions. These can be embedded in other software tools using an application programming interface (API) for the interaction between the software tool and the predictive analytics tasks. The main advantage of OpenNN is its high performance. It is developed in C++ for better memory management and higher processing speed. It implements CPU parallelisation by means of OpenMP and GPU acceleration with CUDA.

The package comes with unit testing, many examples and extensive documentation. It provides an effective framework for the research and development of neural networks algorithms and applications. Neural Designer is a professional predictive analytics tool that uses OpenNN, which means that the neural engine of Neural Designer has been built using OpenNN.

OpenNN has been designed to learn from both data sets and mathematical models.

Data Sets

- Function regression

- Pattern recognition

- Time series prediction

Mathematical Models

- Optimal control

- Optimal shape design

Data Sets and Mathematical Models

- Inverse problems

Torch

An open source machine learning library, a scientific computing framework, and a script language based on the Lua programming language.

Torch provides a wide range of algorithms for deep machine learning. It uses the scripting language LuaJIT, and an underlying C/CUDA implementation. The core package of Torch is torch. It provides a flexible N-dimensional array or tensor, which supports basic routines for indexing, slicing, transposing, type-casting, resizing, sharing storage and cloning. The nn package is used for building neural networks.

Features

- It is a powerful N-dimensional array.

- Has lots of routines for indexing, slicing and transposing.

- Has an amazing interface to C, via LuaJIT.

- Linear algebra routines.

- Neural network and energy-based models.

- Numeric optimisation routines.

- Fast and efficient GPU support.

- Embeddable, with ports to iOS and Android back-ends.

Torch is used by the Facebook AI Research Group, IBM, Yandex and the Idiap Research Institute. It has been extended for use on Android and iOS. It has been used to build hardware implementations for data flows like those found in neural networks. Facebook has released a set of extension modules as open source software.

PyTorch is an open source machine learning library for Python, used for applications such as natural language processing. It is primarily developed by Facebook's artificial intelligence research group, and Uber's Pyro software for probabilistic programming has been built upon it.

Neuroph

An object-oriented neural network framework written in Java. Neuroph can be used to create and train neural networks in Java programs. It provides a Java class library as well as a GUI tool called easyNeurons for creating and training neural networks. Neuroph is a lightweight Java neural network, as well as a framework to develop common neural network architectures. It contains a well-designed, open source Java library with a small number of basic classes that correspond to basic NN concepts. It also has a nice GUI neural network editor to quickly create Java neural network components. It has been released as open source under the Apache 2.0 licence.

Neuroph's core classes correspond to basic neural network concepts like the artificial neuron, neuron layer, neuron connections, weight, transfer function, input function, learning rule, etc. Neuroph supports common neural network architectures such as multi-layer perceptron with Backpropagation, Kohonen and Hopfield networks. All these classes can be extended and customised to create custom neural networks and learning rules. Neuroph has built-in support for image recognition.

Deeplearning4j

The first commercial-grade, open source, distributed deep learning library written for Java and Scala. Deeplearning4j (DL4J) is integrated with Hadoop and Spark. DL4J is designed to be used in business environments on distributed GPUs and CPUs. Skymind is its commercial support arm, bundling Deeplearning4j and other libraries such as TensorFlow and Keras in the Skymind Intelligence Layer (SKIL, Community Edition), which is a deep learning environment that gives developers an easy, fast way to train and deploy AI models. SKIL acts as a bridge between Python data science environments and the JVM.

Advantages

- Deeplearning4j aims to be cutting-edge plug-and-play, with more convention than configuration, which allows for fast prototyping for non-researchers.

- It is customisable at scale.

- DL4J can import neural net models from most major frameworks via Keras, including TensorFlow, Caffe and Theano, bridging the gap between the Python ecosystem and the JVM with a cross-team toolkit for data scientists, data engineers and DevOps. Keras is employed as Deeplearning4j's Python API.

- Machine learning models are served in production with Skymind's model server.

Features

- Distributed CPUs and GPUs.

- Java, Scala and Python APIs.

- Adapted for micro-service architecture.

- Parallel training via iterative reduce.

- Scalable on Hadoop.

- GPU support for scaling on AWS.

Libraries

- Deeplearning4J: A neural Net platform.

- ND4J: Numpy for the JVM.

- DataVec: A tool for machine learning ETL operations.

- JavaCPP: The bridge between Java and native C++.

- Arbiter: An evaluation tool for machine learning algorithms.

- RL4J: Deep reinforcement learning for the JVM.

Mycroft

One of the world's first open source assistants, ideal for anything from a science project to an enterprise software application. Mycroft runs anywhere – on a desktop computer, inside an automobile, or on a Raspberry Pi. This is open source software which can be freely remixed, extended and improved. Mycroft may be used in anything from a science project to an enterprise software application.

OpenCog

A project that aims to build an open source artificial intelligence framework. OpenCog is a diverse assemblage of cognitive algorithms, each embodying their own innovations. But what makes the overall architecture powerful is its careful adherence to the principle of cognitive synergy. Open-Cog was originally based on the 2008 release of the source code of the proprietary Novamente Cognition Engine (NCE) of Novamente LLC. The original NCE code is discussed in the PLN book (reference given below). Ongoing development of OpenCog is supported by the Artificial General Intelligence Research Institute (AGIRI), the Google Summer of Code project, and others.

OpenCog Prime is the architecture for robot and virtual embodied cognition, which defines a set of interacting components designed to give rise to human-equivalent artificial general intelligence (AGI) as an emergent phenomenon of the whole system. OpenCog Prime's design is primarily the work of Ben Goertzel, while the OpenCog framework is intended as a generic framework for broad-based AGI research.

OpenCog consists of the following:

- A graph database that holds terms, atomic formulae, sentences and relationships as hypergraphs, giving them a probabilistic truth-value interpretation, dubbed the Atom-Space.

- A satisfiability modulo theories solver, built in as a part of a generic graph query engine, for performing graph and hypergraph pattern matching (isomorphic subgraph discovery).

- An implementation of a probabilistic reasoning engine based on probabilistic logic networks (PLN).

- A probabilistic genetic program evolver called Meta-Optimizing Semantic Evolutionary Search, or MOSES, originally developed by Moshe Looks, who is now at Google.

- An attention allocation system based on economic theory, called ECAN.

- An embodiment system for interaction and learning within virtual worlds based in part on OpenPsi and Unity.

- A natural language input system consisting of Link Grammar and RelEx, both of which employ AtomSpace-like representations for semantic and syntactic relations.

- A natural language generation system called SegSim, with implementations NLGen and NLGen2.

- An implementation of Psi-Theory for handling emotional states, drives and urges, dubbed OpenPsi.

- Interfaces to Hanson Robotics robots, including emotion modelling via OpenPsi.

Artificial Neural Network

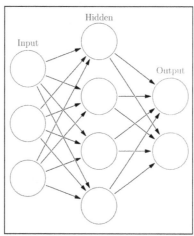

An artificial neural network is an interconnected group of nodes, inspired by a simplification of neuronsin a brain. Here, each circular node represents an artificial neuron and an arrow represents a connection from the output of one artificial neuron to the input of another.

Artificial neural networks (ANN) or connectionist systems are computing systems that are inspired by, but not necessarily identical to, the biological neural networks that constitute animal brains. Such systems "learn" to perform tasks by considering examples, generally without being programmed with any task-specific rules. For example, in image recognition, they might learn to identify images that contain cats by analyzing example images that have been manually labeled as "cat" or "no cat" and using the results to identify cats in other images. They do this without any prior knowledge about cats, for example, that they have fur, tails, whiskers and cat-like faces. Instead, they automatically generate identifying characteristics from the learning material that they process.

An ANN is based on a collection of connected units or nodes called artificial neurons, which loosely model the neurons in a biological brain. Each connection, like the synapses in a biological brain, can transmit a signal from one artificial neuron to another. An artificial neuron that receives a signal can process it and then signal additional artificial neurons connected to it.

In common ANN implementations, the signal at a connection between artificial neurons is a real number, and the output of each artificial neuron is computed by some non-linear function of the sum of its inputs. The connections between artificial neurons are called 'edges'. Artificial neurons and edges typically have a weight that adjusts as learning proceeds. The weight increases or decreases the strength of the signal at a connection. Artificial neurons may have a threshold such that the signal is only sent if the aggregate signal crosses that threshold. Typically, artificial neurons are aggregated into layers. Different layers may perform different kinds of transformations on their inputs. Signals travel from the first layer (the input layer), to the last layer (the output layer), possibly after traversing the layers multiple times.

The original goal of the ANN approach was to solve problems in the same way that a human brain would. However, over time, attention moved to performing specific tasks, leading to deviations from biology. Artificial neural networks have been used on a variety of tasks, including computer vision, speech recognition, machine translation, social network filtering, playing board and video games and medical diagnosis.

Models

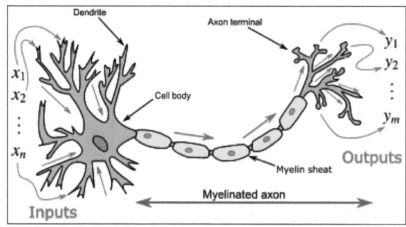

Neuron and myelinated axon, with signal flow from inputs at dendrites to outputs at axon terminals.

An *artificial neural network* is a network of simple elements called *artificial neurons*, which receive input, change their internal state (*activation*) according to that input, and produce output depending on the input and activation.

An artificial neuron mimics the working of a biophysical neuron with inputs and outputs, but is not a biological neuron model.

The *network* forms by connecting the output of certain neurons to the input of other neurons forming a directed, weighted graph. The weights as well as the functions that compute the activation can be modified by a process called *learning* which is governed by a *learning rule*.

Components of an Artificial Neural Network

Neurons

A neuron with label j receiving an input $p_j(t)$ from predecessor neurons consists of the following components:

- An *activation* $a_j(t)$, the neuron's state, depending on a discrete time parameter,

- Possibly a *threshold*   , which stays fixed unless changed by a learning function,

- An *activation function* f that computes the new activation at a given time $t+1$ from ,
  $a_j(t), \theta_j$ and the net input $p_j(t)$ giving rise to the relation

  $a_j(t+1) = f(a_j(t), p_j(t), \theta_j),$

- And an *output function* f_{out} computing the output from the activation

- $o_j(t) = f_{out}(a_j(t)).$

Often the output function is simply the Identity function.

An *input neuron* has no predecessor but serves as input interface for the whole network. Similarly an *output neuron* has no success or and thus serves as output interface of the whole network.

Connections, Weights and Biases

The *network* consists of connections, each connection transferring the output of a neuron i to the input of a neuron j. In this sense i is the predecessor of j and j is the successor of i. Each connection is assigned a weight w_{ij}. Sometimes a bias term is added to the total weighted sum of inputs to serve as a threshold to shift the activation function.

Propagation Function

The *propagation function* computes the *input* $p_j(t)$ to the neuron j from the outputs $o_i(t)$ of predecessor neurons and typically has the form

$$p_j(t) = \sum_i o_i(t)w_{ij}.$$

When a bias value is added with the function, the above form changes to the following:

$$p_j(t) = \sum_i o_i(t)w_{ij} + w_{0j} \text{ where } w_{0j} \text{ is a bias.}$$

Learning Rule

The *learning rule* is a rule or an algorithm which modifies the parameters of the neural network, in order for a given input to the network to produce a favored output. This *learning* process typically amounts to modifying the weights and thresholds of the variables within the network.

Neural Networks as Functions

Neural network models can be viewed as simple mathematical models defining a function $f : X \rightarrow Y$ or a distribution over X or both X and Y. Sometimes models are intimately associated with a particular learning rule. A common use of the phrase "ANN model" is really the definition of a *class* of such functions (where members of the class are obtained by varying parameters, connection weights, or specifics of the architecture such as the number of neurons or their connectivity).

Mathematically, a neuron's network function $f(x)$ is defined as a composition of other functions $g_i(x)$, that can further be decomposed into other functions. This can be conveniently represented as a network structure, with arrows depicting the dependencies between functions. A widely used type of composition is the *nonlinear weighted sum*, where $f(x) = K\left(\sum_i w_i g_i(x)\right)$, where K (commonly referred to as the activation function) is some predefined function, such as the hyperbolic tangent, sigmoid function, softmax function, or rectifier function. The important characteristic of the activation function is that it provides a smooth transition as input values change, i.e. a small change in input produces a small change in output. The following refers to a collection of functions g_i as a vector $g = (g_1, g_2, ..., g_n)$.

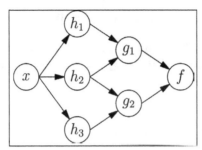

ANN dependency graph.

This figure depicts such a decomposition of f, with dependencies between variables indicated by arrows. These can be interpreted in two ways.

The first view is the functional view: the input x is transformed into a 3-dimensional vector h , which is then transformed into a 2-dimensional vector g, which is finally transformed into f,. This view is most commonly encountered in the context of optimization.

The second view is the probabilistic view: the random variable $F = f(G)$ depends upon the random variable $G = g(H)$, which depends upon $H = h(X)$, which depends upon the random variable X . This view is most commonly encountered in the context of graphical models.

The two views are largely equivalent. In either case, for this particular architecture, the components of individual layers are independent of each other (e.g., the components of g are independent of each other given their input h). This naturally enables a degree of parallelism in the implementation.

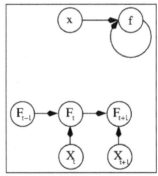

Two separate depictions of the recurrent ANN dependency graph.

Networks such as the previous one are commonly called feedforward, because their graph is a directed acyclic graph. Networks with cycles are commonly called recurrent. Such networks are commonly depicted in the manner shown at the top of the figure, where is shown as being dependent upon itself. However, an implied temporal dependence is not shown.

Learning

The possibility of learning has attracted the most interest in neural networks. Given a specific *task* to solve, and a class of functions F, learning means using a set of observations to find $f^* \in F$ which solves the task in some optimal sense.

This entails defining a cost function $C : F \rightarrow \mathbb{R}$ such that, for the optimal solution f^*, $C(f^*) \le C(f)$ $\forall f \in F$ – i.e., no solution has a cost less than the cost of the optimal solution.

The cost function C is an important concept in learning, as it is a measure of how far away a particular solution is from an optimal solution to the problem to be solved. Learning algorithms search through the solution space to find a function that has the smallest possible cost.

For applications where the solution is data dependent, the cost must necessarily be a function of the observations, otherwise the model would not relate to the data. It is frequently defined as a statistic to which only approximations can be made. As a simple example, consider the problem of finding the model f which minimizes $C = E\left[(f(x) - y)^2\right]$, for data pairs (x, y) drawn from some distribution $\mathcal{D}$. In practical situations we would only have N samples from $\hat{C} = \dfrac{1}{N}\sum_{i=1}^{N}(f(x_i) - y_i)^2$ and thus, for the above example, we would only minimize. Thus, the cost is minimized over a sample of the data rather than the entire distribution.

When $N \to \infty$ some form of online machine learning must be used, where the cost is reduced as each new example is seen. While online machine learning is often used when $\mathcal{D}$ is fixed, it is most useful in the case where the distribution changes slowly over time. In neural network methods, some form of online machine learning is frequently used for finite datasets.

Choosing a Cost Function

While it is possible to define an ad hoc cost function, frequently a particular cost function is used, either because it has desirable properties (such as convexity) or because it arises naturally from a particular formulation of the problem (e.g., in a probabilistic formulation the posterior probability of the model can be used as an inverse cost). Ultimately, the cost function depends on the task.

Backpropagation

A DNN can be discriminatively trained with the standard backpropagation algorithm. Backpropagation is a method to calculate the gradient of the loss function (produces the cost associated with a given state) with respect to the weights in an ANN.

The basics of continuous backpropagation were derived in the context of control theory by Kelleyin 1960 and by Bryson in 1961, using principles of dynamic programming. In 1962, Dreyfus published a simpler derivation based only on the chain rule. Bryson and Ho described it as a multi-stage dynamic system optimization method in 1969. In 1970, Linnainmaa finally published the general method for automatic differentiation (AD) of discrete connected networks of nested differentiable functions. This corresponds to the modern version of backpropagation which is efficient even when the networks are sparse. In 1973, Dreyfus used backpropagation to adapt parameters of controllers in proportion to error gradients. In 1974, Werbos mentioned the possibility of applying this principle to Artificial neural networks, and in 1982, he applied Linnainmaa's AD method to neural networks in the way that is widely used today. In 1986, Rumelhart, Hinton and Williams noted that this method can generate useful internal representations of incoming data in hidden layers of neural networks. In 1993, Wan was the first to win an international pattern recognition contest through backpropagation.

The weight updates of backpropagation can be done via stochastic gradient descent using the following equation:

$$w_{ij}(t+1) = w_{ij}(t) - \eta \frac{\partial C}{\partial w_{ij}} + \xi(t)$$

where, η is the learning rate, C is the cost (loss) function and $\xi(t)$ a stochastic term. The choice of the cost function depends on factors such as the learning type (supervised, unsupervised, reinforcement, etc.) and the activation function. For example, when performing supervised learning on a multiclass classification problem, common choices for the activation function and cost function are the softmax function and cross entropyfunction, respectively. The softmax function is defined as $p_j = \frac{\exp(x_j)}{\sum_k \exp(x_k)}$ where p_j represents the class probability (output of the unit j) and x_j and x_k represent the total input to units j and k of the same level respectively. Cross entropy is defined as $C = -\sum_j d_j \log(p_j)$ where d_j represents the target probability for output unit j and p_j is the probability output for j after applying the activation function.

These can be used to output object bounding boxes in the form of a binary mask. They are also used for multi-scale regression to increase localization precision. DNN-based regression can learn features that capture geometric information in addition to serving as a good classifier. They remove the requirement to explicitly model parts and their relations. This helps to broaden the variety of objects that can be learned. The model consists of multiple layers, each of which has a rectified linear unit as its activation function for non-linear transformation. Some layers are convolutional, while others are fully connected. Every convolutional layer has an additional max pooling. The network is trained to minimize L^2 error for predicting the mask ranging over the entire training set containing bounding boxes represented as masks.

Alternatives to backpropagation include Extreme Learning Machines, "No-prop" networks, training without backtracking, "weightless" networks, and non-connectionist neural networks.

Learning Paradigms

The three major learning paradigms each correspond to a particular learning task. These are supervised learning, unsupervised learning and reinforcement learning.

Supervised Learning

Supervised learning uses a set of example pairs $(x, y), x \in X, y \in Y$ and the aim is to find a function $f : X \rightarrow Y$ in the allowed class of functions that matches the examples. In other words, we wish to infer the mapping implied by the data; the cost function is related to the mismatch between our mapping and the data and it implicitly contains prior knowledge about the problem domain.

A commonly used cost is the mean-squared error, which tries to minimize the average squared error between the network's output, $f(x)$, and the target value f. over all the example pairs. Minimizing this cost using gradient descent for the class of neural networks called multilayer perceptrons (MLP), produces the backpropagation algorithm for training neural networks.

Tasks that fall within the paradigm of supervised learning are pattern recognition (also known as classification) and regression (also known as function approximation). The supervised learning paradigm is also applicable to sequential data (e.g., for hand writing, speech and gesture recognition). This can be thought of as learning with a "teacher", in the form of a function that provides continuous feedback on the quality of solutions obtained thus far.

Unsupervised Learning

In unsupervised learning, some data x is given and the cost function to be minimized, that can be any function of the data f. and the network's output, $f(x) = a$.

The cost function is dependent on the task (the model domain) and any *a priori* assumptions (the implicit properties of the model, its parameters and the observed variables).

As a trivial example, consider the model $f(x) = a$ where a is a constant and the cost $C = E[(x - f(x))^2]$. Minimizing this cost produces a value of a that is equal to the mean of the data. The cost function can be much more complicated. Its form depends on the application: for example, in compression it could be related to the mutual information between x and $f(x)$, whereas in statistical modeling, it could be related to the posterior probability of the model given the data (note that in both of those examples those quantities would be maximized rather than minimized).

Tasks that fall within the paradigm of unsupervised learning are in general estimation problems; the applications include clustering, the estimation of statistical distributions, compression and filtering.

Reinforcement Learning

In reinforcement learning, data are usually not given, but generated by an agent's interactions with the environment. At each point in time t, the agent performs an action y_t and the environment generates an observation x_t and an instantaneous cost c_t, according to some (usually unknown) dynamics. The aim is to discover a policy for selecting actions that minimizes some measure of a long-term cost, e.g., the expected cumulative cost. The environment's dynamics and the long-term cost for each policy are usually unknown, but can be estimated.

More formally the environment is modeled as a Markov decision process (MDP) with states $s_1,...,s_n \in S$ and actions $a_1,...,a_m \in A$ with the following probability distributions: the instantaneous cost distribution $P(c_t | s_t)$, the observation distribution $P(x_t | s_t)$ and the transition $P(s_{t+1} | s_t, a_t)$, while a policy is defined as the conditional distribution over actions given the observations. Taken together, the two then define a Markov chain(MC). The aim is to discover the policy (i.e., the MC) that minimizes the cost.

Artificial neural networks are frequently used in reinforcement learning as part of the overall algorithm. Dynamic programming was coupled with Artificial neural networks (giving neurodynamic programming) by Bertsekas and Tsitsiklis and applied to multi-dimensional nonlinear problems such as those involved in vehicle routing, natural resources management or medicine because of the ability of Artificial neural networks to mitigate losses of accuracy even when reducing the discretization grid density for numerically approximating the solution of the original control problems.

Tasks that fall within the paradigm of reinforcement learning are control problems, games and other sequential decision making tasks.

Learning Algorithms

Training a neural network model essentially means selecting one model from the set of allowed models (or, in a Bayesian framework, determining a distribution over the set of allowed models) that minimizes the cost. Numerous algorithms are available for training neural network models; most of them can be viewed as a straightforward application of optimization theory and statistical estimation.

Most employ some form of gradient descent, using backpropagation to compute the actual gradients. This is done by simply taking the derivative of the cost function with respect to the network parameters and then changing those parameters in a gradient-related direction. Backpropagation training algorithms fall into three categories:

- Steepest descent (with variable learning rate and momentum, resilient backpropagation);

- Quasi-Newton (Broyden-Fletcher-Goldfarb-Shanno, one step secant);

- Levenberg-Marquardt and conjugate gradient (Fletcher-Reeves update, Polak-Ribiére update, Powell-Beale restart, scaled conjugate gradient).

Evolutionary methods, gene expression programming, simulated annealing, expectation-maximization, non-parametric methods and particle swarm optimization are other methods for training neural networks.

Convergent Recursive Learning Algorithm

This is a learning method specially designed for cerebellar model articulation controller (CMAC) neural networks. In 2004, a recursive least squares algorithm was introduced to train CMAC neural network online. This algorithm can converge in one step and update all weights in one step with any new input data. Initially, this algorithm had computational complexity of $O(N^3)$. Based on QR decomposition, this recursive learning algorithm was simplified to be $O(N)$.

Optimization

The optimization algorithm repeats a two phase cycle, propagation and weight update. When an input vector is presented to the network, it is propagated forward through the network, layer by layer, until it reaches the output layer. The output of the network is then compared to the desired output, using a loss function. The resulting error value is calculated for each of the neurons in the output layer. The error values are then propagated from the output back through the network, until each neuron has an associated error value that reflects its contribution to the original output.

Backpropagation uses these error values to calculate the gradient of the loss function. In the second phase, this gradient is fed to the optimization method, which in turn uses it to update the weights, in an attempt to minimize the loss function.

Algorithm

Let N be a neural network with e connections, m inputs, and n outputs.

Below, $x_1, x_2, \ldots$ will denote vectors in $\mathbb{R}^m$, $y_1, y_2, \ldots$, vectors in $\mathbb{R}^n$, and $w_0, w_1, w_2, \ldots$ vectors $\mathbb{R}^e$ in $\mathbb{R}^e$. These are called *inputs*, *outputs* and *weights* respectively.

The neural network corresponds to a function $y = f_N(w, x)$ which, given a weight w, maps an input x to an output y.

The optimization takes as input a sequence of *training examples* $(x_1, y_1), \ldots, (x_p, y_p)$ and produces a sequence of weights $w_0, w_1, \ldots, w_p$ starting from some initial weight w_0, usually chosen at random.

These weights are computed in turn: first compute w_i using only (x_i, y_i, w_{i-1}) for $i = 1, \ldots, p$. The output of the algorithm is then w_p, giving us a new function $x \mapsto f_N(w_p, x)$. The computation is the same in each step, hence only the case $i = 1$ is described.

Calculating w_1 from (x_1, y_1, w_0) is done by considering a variable weight w and applying gradient descent to the function $w \mapsto E(f_N(w, x_1), y_1)$ to find a local minimum, starting at $w = w_0$.

This makes w_1 the minimizing weight found by gradient descent.

Algorithm in Code

To implement the algorithm above, explicit formulas are required for the gradient of the function $w \mapsto E(f_N(w, x), y)$ where the function is $E(y, y') = |y - y'|^2$.

The learning algorithm can be divided into two phases: propagation and weight update.

Phase 1: Propagation

Each propagation involves the following steps:

1. Propagation forward through the network to generate the output values.

2. Calculation of the cost (error term).

3. Propagation of the output activations back through the network using the training pattern target to generate the deltas (the difference between the targeted and actual output values) of all output and hidden neurons.

Phase 2: Weight update

For each weight, the following steps must be followed:

1. The weight's output delta and input activation are multiplied to find the gradient of the weight.

2. A ratio (percentage) of the weight's gradient is subtracted from the weight.

This ratio (percentage) influences the speed and quality of learning; it is called the *learning rate*. The greater the ratio, the faster the neuron trains, but the lower the ratio, the more accurate the training is. The sign of the gradient of a weight indicates whether the error varies directly with, or inversely to, the weight. Therefore, the weight must be updated in the opposite direction, "descending" the gradient.

Learning is repeated (on new batches) until the network performs adequately.

Pseudocode

The following is pseudocode for a stochastic gradient descent algorithm for training a three-layer network (only one hidden layer):

```
initialize network weights (often small random values)

 do

    forEach training example named ex

     prediction = neural-net-output(network, ex) // forward pass

     actual = teacher-output(ex)

     compute error (prediction - actual) at the output units

     compute for all weights from hidden layer to output layer // backward pass

     compute for all weights from input layer to hidden layer  // backward pass
continued

     update network weights // input layer not modified by error estimate

 until all examples classified correctly or another stopping criterion satisfied

 return the network
```

The lines labeled "backward pass" can be implemented using the backpropagation algorithm, which calculates the gradient of the error of the network regarding the network's modifiable weights.

Extension

The choice of learning rate η is important, since a high value can cause too strong a change, causing the minimum to be missed, while a too low learning rate slows the training unnecessarily.

Optimizations such as Quickprop are primarily aimed at speeding up error minimization; other improvements mainly try to increase reliability.

Adaptive Learning Rate

In order to avoid oscillation inside the network such as alternating connection weights, and to improve the rate of convergence, refinements of this algorithm use an adaptive learning rate.

Inertia

By using a variable inertia term *(Momentum)* α the gradient and the last change can be weighted such that the weight adjustment additionally depends on the previous change. If the *Momentum*

α is equal to 0, the change depends solely on the gradient, while a value of 1 will only depend on the last change.

Similar to a ball rolling down a mountain, whose current speed is determined not only by the current slope of the mountain but also by its own inertia, inertia can be added:

$$\Delta w_{ij}(t+1) = (1-\alpha)\eta\delta_j o_i + \alpha\Delta w_{ij}(t)$$

where:

- $\Delta w_{ij}(t+1)$ is the change in weight $w_{ij}(t+1)$ in the connection of neuron i to neuron j at time $(t+1)$,

- η a learning rate ($\eta < 0$)

- δ_j the error signal of neuron j and

- o_i the output of neuron i, which is also an input of the current neuron (neuron j),

α the influence of the inertial term $\Delta w_{ij}(t)(in[0,1])$. This corresponds to the weight change at the previous point in time.

Inertia makes the current weight change $(t+1)$ depend both on the current gradient of the error function (slope of the mountain, 1st summand), as well as on the weight change from the previous point in time (inertia, 2nd summand).

With inertia, the problems of getting stuck (in steep ravines and flat plateaus) are avoided. Since, for example, the gradient of the error function becomes very small in flat plateaus, a plateau would immediately lead to a "deceleration" of the gradient descent. This deceleration is delayed by the addition of the inertia term so that a flat plateau can be escaped more quickly.

Modes of Learning

Two modes of learning are available: stochastic and batch. In stochastic learning, each input creates a weight adjustment. In batch learning weights are adjusted based on a batch of inputs, accumulating errors over the batch. Stochastic learning introduces "noise" into the gradient descent process, using the local gradient calculated from one data point; this reduces the chance of the network getting stuck in local minima. However, batch learning typically yields a faster, more stable descent to a local minimum, since each update is performed in the direction of the average error of the batch. A common compromise choice is to use "mini-batches", meaning small batches and with samples in each batch selected stochastically from the entire data set.

Variants

Group Method of Data Handling

The Group Method of Data Handling (GMDH) features fully automatic structural and parametric model optimization. The node activation functions are Kolmogorov-Gabor polynomials that permit additions and multiplications. It used a deep feedforward multilayer perceptron with eight layers. It is a supervised learningnetwork that grows layer by layer, where each layer is trained by regression analysis. Useless items are detected using a validation set, and pruned through regularization. The size and depth of the resulting network depends on the task.

Convolutional Neural Networks

A convolutional neural network (CNN) is a class of deep, feed-forward networks, composed of one or more convolutional layers with fully connected layers (matching those in typical Artificial neural networks) on top. It uses tied weights and pooling layers. In particular, max-pooling is often structured via Fukushima's convolutional architecture. This architecture allows CNNs to take advantage of the 2D structure of input data.

CNNs are suitable for processing visual and other two-dimensional data. They have shown superior results in both image and speech applications. They can be trained with standard backpropagation. CNNs are easier to train than other regular, deep, feed-forward neural networks and have many fewer parameters to estimate. Examples of applications in computer vision include Deep-Dream and robot navigation.

A recent development has been that of Capsule Neural Network (CapsNet), the idea behind which is to add structures called capsules to a CNN and to reuse output from several of those capsules to form more stable (with respect to various perturbations) representations for higher order capsules.

Long Short-term Memory

Long short-term memory (LSTM) networks are RNNs that avoid the vanishing gradient problem. LSTM is normally augmented by recurrent gates called forget gates. LSTM networks prevent backpropagated errors from vanishing or exploding. Instead errors can flow backwards through unlimited numbers of virtual layers in space-unfolded LSTM. That is, LSTM canlearn "very deep learning" tasks that require memories of events that happened thousands or even millions of discrete time steps ago. Problem-specific LSTM-like topologies can be evolved. LSTM can handle long delays and signals that have a mix of low and high frequency components.

Stacks of LSTM RNNs trained by Connectionist Temporal Classification (CTC) can find an RNN weight matrix that maximizes the probability of the label sequences in a training set, given the corresponding input sequences. CTC achieves both alignment and recognition.

In 2003, LSTM started to become competitive with traditional speech recognizers. In 2007, the combination with CTC achieved first good results on speech data. In 2009, a CTC-trained LSTM was the first RNN to win pattern recognition contests, when it won several competitions in connected handwriting recognition. In 2014, Baidu used CTC-trained RNNs to break the Switchboard Hub5'00 speech recognition benchmark, without traditional speech processing methods. LSTM also improved large-vocabulary speech recognition,text-to-speech synthesis, for Google Android, and photo-real talking heads. In 2015, Google's speech recognition experienced a 49% improvement through CTC-trained LSTM.

LSTM became popular in Natural Language Processing. Unlike previous models based on HMMs and similar concepts, LSTM can learn to recognise context-sensitive languages. LSTM improved machine translation, language modeling and multilingual language processing. LSTM combined with CNNs improved automatic image captioning.

Deep Reservoir Computing

Deep Reservoir Computing and Deep Echo State Networks (deepESNs) provide a framework for efficiently trained models for hierarchical processing of temporal data, while enabling the investigation of the inherent role of RNN layered composition.

Deep Belief Networks

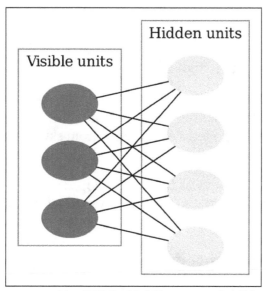

A restricted Boltzmann machine(RBM) with fully connected visible and hidden units.
Note there are no hidden-hidden or visible-visible connections.

A deep belief network (DBN) is a probabilistic, generative model made up of multiple layers of hidden units. It can be considered a compositionof simple learning modules that make up each layer.

A DBN can be used to generatively pre-train a DNN by using the learned DBN weights as the initial DNN weights. Backpropagation or other discriminative algorithms can then tune these weights. This is particularly helpful when training data are limited, because poorly initialized weights can significantly hinder model performance. These pre-trained weights are in a region of the weight space that is closer to the optimal weights than were they randomly chosen. This allows for both improved modeling and faster convergence of the fine-tuning phase.

Large Memory Storage and Retrieval Neural Networks

Large memory storage and retrieval neural networks (LAMSTAR) are fast deep learning neural networks of many layers that can use many filters simultaneously. These filters may be nonlinear, stochastic, logic, non-stationary, or even non-analytical. They are biologically motivated and learn continuously.

A LAMSTAR neural network may serve as a dynamic neural network in spatial or time domains or both. Its speed is provided by Hebbian link-weights that integrate the various and usually different filters (preprocessing functions) into its many layers and to dynamically rank the significance of the various layers and functions relative to a given learning task. This grossly imitates biological learning which integrates various preprocessors (cochlea, retina, *etc.*) and cortexes (auditory, visual, *etc.*) and their various regions. Its deep learning capability is further enhanced by using inhibition, correlation and its ability to cope with incomplete data, or "lost" neurons or layers even amidst a task. It is fully transparent due to its link weights. The link-weights allow dynamic determination of innovation and redundancy, and facilitate the ranking of layers, of filters or of individual neurons relative to a task.

LAMSTAR has been applied to many domains, including medical and financial predictions, adaptive filtering of noisy speech in unknown noise, still-image recognition, video image recognition,software security and adaptive control of non-linear systems. LAMSTAR had a much faster learning speed and somewhat lower error rate than a CNN based on ReLU-function filters and max pooling, in 20 comparative studies.

These applications demonstrate delving into aspects of the data that are hidden from shallow learning networks and the human senses, such as in the cases of predicting onset of sleep apnea events, of an electrocardiogram of a fetus as recorded from skin-surface electrodes placed on the mother's abdomen early in pregnancy, of financial prediction or in blind filtering of noisy speech.

LAMSTAR was proposed in 1996 and was further developed Graupe and Kordylewski from 1997–2002. A modified version, known as LAMSTAR 2, was developed by Schneider and Graupe in 2008.

Stacked (De-noising) Auto-encoders

The auto encoder idea is motivated by the concept of a *good* representation. For example, for a classifier, a good representation can be defined as one that yields a better-performing classifier.

An *encoder* is a deterministic mapping f_θ that transforms an input vector x into hidden representation y, where $\theta = \{W, b\}$, W is the weight matrix and b is an offset vector (bias). A decoder maps back the hidden representation y to the reconstructed input z via g_θ. The whole process of auto encoding is to compare this reconstructed input to the original and try to minimize the error to make the reconstructed value as close as possible to the original.

In *stacked denoising auto encoders*, the partially corrupted output is cleaned (de-noised). This idea was introduced in 2010 by Vincent et al. with a specific approach to *good* representation, a *good representation*is one that can be obtained robustly from a corrupted input and that will be useful for recovering the corresponding clean input. Implicit in this definition are the following ideas:

- The higher level representations are relatively stable and robust to input corruption,

- It is necessary to extract features that are useful for representation of the input distribution.

The algorithm starts by a stochastic mapping of x to x through $q_D(\tilde{x} \mid x)$, this is the corrupting step. Then the corrupted input $\tilde{x}$ passes through a basic auto-encoder process and is mapped to a hidden representation $y = f_\theta(\tilde{x}) = s(W\tilde{x} + b)$. From this hidden representation, we can reconstruct

$z = g_\theta(y)$. In the last stage, a minimization algorithm runs in order to have z as close as possible to uncorrupted input x. The reconstruction error $L_H(x, z)$ might be either the cross-entropy loss with an affine-sigmoid decoder, or the squared error loss with an affine decoder.

In order to make a deep architecture, auto encoders stack. Once the encoding function f_θ of the first denoising auto encoder is learned and used to uncorrupt the input (corrupted input), the second level can be trained.

Once the stacked auto encoder is trained, its output can be used as the input to a supervised learning algorithm such as support vector machine classifier or a multi-class logistic regression.

Deep Stacking Networks

A deep stacking network (DSN) (deep convex network) is based on a hierarchy of blocks of simplified neural network modules. It was introduced in 2011 by Deng and Dong. It formulates the learning as a convex optimization problem with a closed-form solution, emphasizing the mechanism's similarity to stacked generalization. Each DSN block is a simple module that is easy to train by itself in a supervised fashion without backpropagation for the entire blocks.

Each block consists of a simplified multi-layer perceptron (MLP) with a single hidden layer. The hidden layer h has logistic sigmoidal units, and the output layer has linear units. Connections between these layers are represented by weight matrix U; input-to-hidden-layer connections have weight matrix W. Target vectors t form the columns of matrix T, and the input data vectors x form the columns of matrix X. The matrix of hidden units is $H = \sigma(W^T X)$. Modules are trained in order, so lower-layer weights W are known at each stage. The function performs the element-wise logistic sigmoid operation. Each block estimates the same final label class y, and its estimate is concatenated with original input X to form the expanded input for the next block. Thus, the input to the first block contains the original data only, while downstream blocks' input adds the output of preceding blocks. Then learning the upper-layer weight matrix U given other weights in the network can be formulated as a convex optimization problem:

$$\min_{U^T} f = \| U^T H - T \|_F^2,$$

which has a closed-form solution.

Unlike other deep architectures, such as DBNs, the goal is not to discover the transformed feature representation. The structure of the hierarchy of this kind of architecture makes parallel learning straightforward, as a batch-mode optimization problem. In purely discriminative tasks, DSNs perform better than conventional DBNs.

Tensor Deep Stacking Networks

This architecture is a DSN extension. It offers two important improvements: it uses higher-order information from covariance statistics, and it transforms the non-convex problem of a lower-layer to a convex sub-problem of an upper-layer. TDSNs use covariance statistics in a bilinear mapping from each of two distinct sets of hidden units in the same layer to predictions, via a third-order tensor.

While parallelization and scalability are not considered seriously in conventional DNNs, all learning for DSNs and TDSNs is done in batch mode, to allow parallelization. Parallelization allows scaling the design to larger (deeper) architectures and data sets.

The basic architecture is suitable for diverse tasks such as classification and regression.

Spike-and-slab RBMs

The need for deep learning with real-valued inputs, as in Gaussian restricted Boltzmann machines, led to the *spike-and-slab* RBM (*ss*RBM), which models continuous-valued inputs with strictly binary latent variables. Similar to basic RBMs and its variants, a spike-and-slab RBM is a bipartite graph, while like GRBMs, the visible units (input) are real-valued. The difference is in the hidden layer, where each hidden unit has a binary spike variable and a real-valued slab variable. A spike is a discrete probability mass at zero, while a slab is a densityover continuous domain; their mixture forms a prior.

An extension of ssRBM called μ-ssRBM provides extra modeling capacity using additional terms in the energy function. One of these terms enables the model to form a conditional distribution of the spike variables by marginalizing out the slab variables given an observation.

Compound Hierarchical-deep Models

Compound hierarchical-deep models compose deep networks with non-parametric Bayesian models. Featurescan be learned using deep architectures such as DBNs, DBMs, deep auto encoders, convolutional variants, ssRBMs, deep coding networks, DBNs with sparse feature learning, RNNs,conditional DBNs, de-noising auto encoders. This provides a better representation, allowing faster learning and more accurate classification with high-dimensional data. However, these architectures are poor at learning novel classes with few examples, because all network units are involved in representing the input (a distributed representation) and must be adjusted together (high degree of freedom). Limiting the degree of freedom reduces the number of parameters to learn, facilitating learning of new classes from few examples. *Hierarchical Bayesian (HB)* models allow learning from few examples, for example for computer vision, statistics and cognitive science.

Compound HD architectures aim to integrate characteristics of both HB and deep networks. The compound HDP-DBM architecture is a *hierarchical Dirichlet process (HDP)* as a hierarchical model, incorporated with DBM architecture. It is a full generative model, generalized from abstract concepts flowing through the layers of the model, which is able to synthesize new examples in novel classes that look "reasonably" natural. All the levels are learned jointly by maximizing a joint log-probability score.

In a DBM with three hidden layers, the probability of a visible input v is:

$$p(v,\psi) = \frac{1}{Z}\sum_h e^{\sum_{ij} W_{ij}^{(1)} v_i h_j^1 + \sum_{jl} W_{jl}^{(2)} h_j^1 h_l^2 + \sum_{lm} W_{lm}^{(3)} h_l^2 h_m^3},$$

where $h = \{h^{(1)}, h^{(2)}, h^{(3)}\}$ is the set of hidden units, and $\psi = \{W^{(1)}, W^{(2)}, W^{(3)}\}$ are the model parameters, representing visible-hidden and hidden-hidden symmetric interaction terms.

A learned DBM model is an undirected model that defines the joint distribution $P(v, h^1, h^2, h^3)$. One way to express what has been learned is the conditional model $P(v, h^1, h^2 \mid h^3)$ and a prior term $P(h^3)$.

Here $P(v, h^1, h^2 \mid h^3)$ represents a conditional DBM model, which can be viewed as a two-layer DBM but with bias terms given by the states of h^3:

$$P(v, h^1, h^2 \mid h^3) = \frac{1}{Z(\psi, h^3)} e^{\sum_{ij} W_{ij}^{(1)} v_i h_j^1 + \sum_{jl} W_{jl}^{(2)} h_j^1 h_l^2 + \sum_{lm} W_{lm}^{(3)} h_l^2 h_m^3} .$$

Deep Predictive Coding Networks

A deep predictive coding network (DPCN) is a predictive coding scheme that uses top-down information to empirically adjust the priors needed for a bottom-up inference procedure by means of a deep, locally connected, generative model. This works by extracting sparse features from time-varying observations using a linear dynamical model. Then, a pooling strategy is used to learn invariant feature representations. These units compose to form a deep architecture and are trained by greedy layer-wise unsupervised learning. The layers constitute a kind of Markov chain such that the states at any layer depend only on the preceding and succeeding layers.

DPCNs predict the representation of the layer, by using a top-down approach using the information in upper layer and temporal dependencies from previous states.

DPCNs can be extended to form a convolutional network.

Networks with Separate Memory Structures

Integrating external memory with Artificial neural networks dates to early research in distributed representations and Kohonen's self-organizing maps. For example, in sparse distributed memory or hierarchical temporal memory, the patterns encoded by neural networks are used as addresses for content-addressable memory, with "neurons" essentially serving as address encoders and decoders. However, the early controllers of such memories were not differentiable.

LSTM-related Differentiable Memory Structures

Apart from long short-term memory (LSTM), other approaches also added differentiable memory to recurrent functions. For example:

- Differentiable push and pop actions for alternative memory networks called neural stack machines.

- Memory networks where the control network's external differentiable storage is in the fast weights of another network.

- LSTM forget gates.

- Self-referential RNNs with special output units for addressing and rapidly manipulating the RNN's own weights in differentiable fashion (internal storage).

- Learning to transduce with unbounded memory.

Neural Turing Machines

Neural Turing machines couple LSTM networks to external memory resources, with which they can interact by attentional processes. The combined system is analogous to a Turing machine but is differentiable end-to-end, allowing it to be efficiently trained by gradient descent. Preliminary results demonstrate that neural Turing machines can infer simple algorithms such as copying, sorting and associative recall from input and output examples.

Differentiable neural computers (DNC) are an NTM extension. They out-performed Neural turing machines, long short-term memory systems and memory networks on sequence-processing tasks.

Semantic Hashing

Approaches that represent previous experiences directly and use a similar experience to form a local model are often called nearest neighbour or k-nearest neighbors methods. Deep learning is useful in semantic hashing where a deep graphical model the word-count vectors obtained from a large set of documents. Documents are mapped to memory addresses in such a way that semantically similar documents are located at nearby addresses. Documents similar to a query document can then be found by accessing all the addresses that differ by only a few bits from the address of the query document. Unlike sparse distributed memory that operates on 1000-bit addresses, semantic hashing works on 32 or 64-bit addresses found in a conventional computer architecture.

Memory Networks

Memory networks are another extension to neural networks incorporating long-term memory. The long-term memory can be read and written to, with the goal of using it for prediction. These models have been applied in the context of question answering (QA) where the long-term memory effectively acts as a (dynamic) knowledge base and the output is a textual response. A team of electrical and computer engineers from UCLA Samueli School of Engineering has created a physical artificial neural network that can analyze large volumes of data and identify objects at the actual speed of light.

Pointer Networks

Deep neural networks can be potentially improved by deepening and parameter reduction, while maintaining trainability. While training extremely deep (e.g., 1 million layers) neural networks might not be practical, CPU-like architectures such as pointer networks and neural random-access machines overcome this limitation by using external random-access memory and other components that typically belong to a computer architecture such as registers, ALU and pointers. Such systems operate on probability distribution vectors stored in memory cells and registers. Thus, the model is fully differentiable and trains end-to-end. The key characteristic of these models is that their depth, the size of their short-term memory, and the number of parameters can be altered independently – unlike models like LSTM, whose number of parameters grows quadratically with memory size.

Encoder–decoder Networks

Encoder–decoder frameworks are based on neural networks that map highly structured input to highly structured output. The approach arose in the context of machine translation, where the input and output are written sentences in two natural languages. In that work, an LSTM RNN or CNN was used as an encoder to summarize a source sentence, and the summary was decoded using a conditional RNN language model to produce the translation. These systems share building blocks: gated RNNs and CNNs and trained attention mechanisms.

Multilayer Kernel Machine

Multilayer kernel machines (MKM) are a way of learning highly nonlinear functions by iterative application of weakly nonlinear kernels. They use the kernel principal component analysis (KPCA), as a method for the unsupervised greedy layer-wise pre-training step of deep learning.

Layer $l+1$ learns the representation of the previous layer l , extracting the n_l principal component (PC) of the projection layer l output in the feature domain induced by the kernel. For the sake of dimensionality reduction of the updated representation in each layer, a supervised strategy selects the best informative features among features extracted by KPCA. The process is:

- Rank the n_l features according to their mutual information with the class labels;

- For different values of K and $m_l \in \{1,\ldots,n_l\}$, compute the classification error rate of a *K-nearest neighbor(K-NN)* classifier using only the most informative features on a validation set;

- The value of with which the classifier has reached the lowest error rate determines the number of features to retain.

Some drawbacks accompany the KPCA method as the building cells of an MKM.

A more straightforward way to use kernel machines for deep learning was developed for spoken language understanding. The main idea is to use a kernel machine to approximate a shallow neural net with an infinite number of hidden units, then use stacking to splice the output of the kernel machine and the raw input in building the next, higher level of the kernel machine. The number of levels in the deep convex network is a hyper-parameter of the overall system, to be determined by cross validation.

Neural Architecture Search

Neural architecture search (NAS) uses machine learning to automate the design of Artificial neural networks. Various approaches to NAS have designed networks that compare well with hand-designed systems. The basic search algorithm is to propose a candidate model, evaluate it against a dataset and use the results as feedback to teach the NAS network.

Use of Neural Architecture Search

Using Artificial neural networks requires an understanding of their characteristics:

- Choice of model: This depends on the data representation and the application. Overly complex models slow learning.

- Learning algorithm: Numerous trade-offs exist between learning algorithms. Almost any algorithm will work well with the correct hyperparameters for training on a particular data set. However, selecting and tuning an algorithm for training on unseen data requires significant experimentation.

- Robustness: If the model, cost function and learning algorithm are selected appropriately, the resulting ANN can become robust.

ANN capabilities fall within the following broad categories:

- Function approximation, or regression analysis, including time series prediction, fitness approximation and modeling.

- Classification, including pattern and sequence recognition, novelty detection and sequential decision making.

- Data processing, including filtering, clustering, blind source separation and compression.

- Robotics, including directing manipulators and prostheses.

- Control, including computer numerical control.

Applications of Neural Architecture Search

Because of their ability to reproduce and model non-linear processes, Artificial neural networks have found many applications in a wide range of disciplines.

Application areas include system identification and control (vehicle control, trajectory prediction, process control, natural resource management), quantum chemistry, general game playing, pattern recognition(radar systems, face identification, signal classification, 3D reconstruction, object recognition and more), sequence recognition (gesture, speech, handwritten and printed text recognition), medical diagnosis, finance(e.g. automated trading systems), data mining, visualization, machine translation, social network filtering and e-mail spam filtering.

Artificial neural networks have been used to diagnose cancers, including lung cancer, prostate cancer, colorectal cancer and to distinguish highly invasive cancer cell lines from less invasive lines using only cell shape information.

Artificial neural networks have been used to accelerate reliability analysis of infrastructures subject to natural disasters and to predict foundation settlements.

Artificial neural networks have also been used for building black-box models in geoscience: hydrology,ocean modelling and coastal engineering, and geomorphology.

Artificial neural networks have been employed with some success also in cybersecurity, with the objective to discriminate between legitimate activities and malicious ones. For example, machine learning has been used for classifying android malware, for identifying domains belonging to threat actors and for detecting URLs posing a security risk. Research is being carried out also on ANN systems designed for penetration testing, for detecting botnets, credit cards frauds, network intrusions and, more in general, potentially infected machines.

Artificial neural networks have been proposed as a tool to simulate the properties of many-body open quantum systems.

Types of Models

Many types of models are used, defined at different levels of abstraction and modeling different aspects of neural systems. They range from models of the short-term behavior of individual neurons, models of how the dynamics of neural circuitry arise from interactions between individual neurons and finally to models of how behavior can arise from abstract neural modules that represent complete subsystems. These include models of the long-term, and short-term plasticity, of neural systems and their relations to learning and memory from the individual neuron to the system level.

Theoretical Properties

Computational Power

The multilayer perceptron is a universal function approximator, as proven by the universal approximation theorem. However, the proof is not constructive regarding the number of neurons required, the network topology, the weights and the learning parameters.

A specific recurrent architecture with rational valued weights (as opposed to full precision real number-valued weights) has the full power of a universal Turing machine, using a finite number of neurons and standard linear connections. Further, the use of irrational values for weights results in a machine with super-Turingpower.

Capacity

Models' "capacity" property roughly corresponds to their ability to model any given function. It is related to the amount of information that can be stored in the network and to the notion of complexity.

Convergence

Models may not consistently converge on a single solution, firstly because many local minima may exist, depending on the cost function and the model. Secondly, the optimization method used might not guarantee to converge when it begins far from any local minimum. Thirdly, for sufficiently large data or parameters, some methods become impractical. However, for CMAC neural network, a recursive least squares algorithm was introduced to train it, and this algorithm can be guaranteed to converge in one step.

Generalization and Statistics

Applications whose goal is to create a system that generalizes well to unseen examples, face the possibility of over-training. This arises in convoluted or over-specified systems when the capacity of the network significantly exceeds the needed free parameters. Two approaches address over-training. The first is to use cross-validationand similar techniques to check for the presence of over-training and optimally select hyperparameters to minimize the generalization error. The second is to use some form of *regularization*. This concept emerges in a probabilistic (Bayesian) framework, where regularization can be performed by selecting a larger prior probability over simpler models; but also in statistical learning theory, where the goal is to minimize over two quantities: the 'empirical risk' and the 'structural risk', which roughly corresponds to the error over the training set and the predicted error in unseen data due to overfitting.

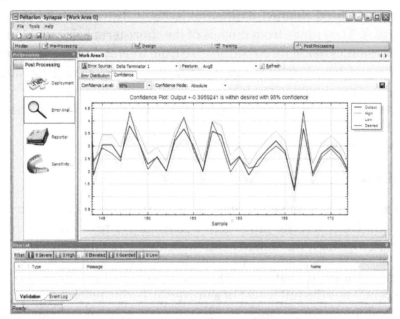

Confidence analysis of a neural network.

Supervised neural networks that use a mean squared error (MSE) cost function can use formal statistical methods to determine the confidence of the trained model. The MSE on a validation set can be used as an estimate for variance. This value can then be used to calculate the confidence interval of the output of the network, assuming a normal distribution. A confidence analysis made this way is statistically valid as long as the output probability distribution stays the same and the network is not modified.

By assigning a softmax activation function, a generalization of the logistic function, on the output layer of the neural network (or a softmax component in a component-based neural network) for categorical target variables, the outputs can be interpreted as posterior probabilities. This is very useful in classification as it gives a certainty measure on classifications.

The softmax activation function is:

$$y_i = \frac{e^{x_i}}{\sum_{j=1}^{c} e^{x_j}}$$

Training Issues

A common criticism of neural networks, particularly in robotics, is that they require too much train-ing for real-world operation. Potential solutions include randomly shuffling training examples, by using a numerical optimization algorithm that does not take too large steps when changing the network connections following an example and by grouping examples in so-called mini-batches. Improving the training efficiency and convergence capability has always been an ongoing research area for neural network. For example, by introducing a recursive least squares algorithm for CMAC neural network, the training process only takes one step to converge.

Theoretical Issues

A fundamental objection is that they do not reflect how real neurons function. Back propagation is a critical part of most artificial neural networks, although no such mechanism exists in biological neural networks. How information is coded by real neurons is not known. Sensor neurons fire action potentials more frequently with sensor activation and muscle cells pull more strongly when their associated motor neurons receive action potentials more frequently. Other than the case of relaying information from a sensor neuron to a motor neuron, almost nothing of the principles of how information is handled by biological neural networks is known. This is a subject of active research in neural coding.

The motivation behind artificial neural networks is not necessarily to strictly replicate neural func-tion, but to use biological neural networks as an inspiration. A central claim of artificial neural networks is therefore that it embodies some new and powerful general principle for processing information. Unfortunately, these general principles are ill-defined. It is often claimed that they are emergent from the network itself. This allows simple statistical association (the basic function of artificial neural networks) to be described as learning or recognition. Alexander Dewdney commented that, as a result, artificial neural networks have a "something-for-nothing quality, one that imparts a peculiar aura of laziness and a distinct lack of curiosity about just how good these computing systems are. No human hand (or mind) intervenes; solutions are found as if by magic; and no one, it seems, has learned anything".

Biological brains use both shallow and deep circuits as reported by brain anatomy, displaying a wide variety of invariance. Weng argued that the brain self-wires largely according to signal statistics and therefore, a serial cascade cannot catch all major statistical dependencies.

Hardware issues

Large and effective neural networks require considerable computing resources. While the brain has hardware tailored to the task of processing signals through a graph of neurons, simulating even a simplified neuron on von Neumann architecture may compel a neural network designer to fill many millions of databaserows for its connections – which can consume vast amounts of memory and storage. Furthermore, the designer often needs to transmit signals through many of these connections and their associated neurons – which must often be matched with enormous CPU processing power and time.

Schmidhuber notes that the resurgence of neural networks in the twenty-first century is largely attributable to advances in hardware: from 1991 to 2015, computing power, especially as delivered by GPGPUs (on GPUs), has increased around a million-fold, making the standard backpropagation algorithm feasible for training networks that are several layers deeper than before. The use of accelerators such as FPGAs and GPUs can reduce training times from months to days.

Neuromorphic engineering addresses the hardware difficulty directly, by constructing non-von-Neumann chips to directly implement neural networks in circuitry. Another chip optimized for neural network processing is called a Tensor Processing Unit, or TPU.

Practical Counter Examples to Criticisms

Arguments against Dewdney's position are that neural networks have been successfully used to solve many complex and diverse tasks, ranging from autonomously flying aircraft to detecting credit card fraud to mastering the game of Go.

Technology writer Roger Bridgman commented:

Neural networks, for instance, are in the dock not only because they have been hyped to high heaven, (what hasn't?) but also because you could create a successful net without understanding how it worked: the bunch of numbers that captures its behaviour would in all probability be "an opaque, unreadable table. valueless as a scientific resource".

In spite of his emphatic declaration that science is not technology, Dewdney seems here to pillory neural nets as bad science when most of those devising them are just trying to be good engineers. An unreadable table that a useful machine could read would still be well worth having.

Although it is true that analyzing what has been learned by an artificial neural network is difficult, it is much easier to do so than to analyze what has been learned by a biological neural network. Furthermore, researchers involved in exploring learning algorithms for neural networks are gradually uncovering general principles that allow a learning machine to be successful. For example, local vs non-local learning and shallow vs deep architecture.

Hybrid Approaches

Advocates of hybrid models (combining neural networks and symbolic approaches), claim that such a mixture can better capture the mechanisms of the human mind.

Types

Artificial neural networks have many variations. The simplest, static types have one or more static components, including number of units, number of layers, unit weights and topology. Dynamic types allow one or more of these to change during the learning process. The latter are much more complicated, but can shorten learning periods and produce better results. Some types allow/require learning to be "supervised" by the operator, while others operate independently. Some types operate purely in hardware, while others are purely software and run on general purpose computers.

Gene Expression Programming

In computer programming, gene expression programming (GEP) is an evolutionary algorithm that creates computer programs or models. These computer programs are complex tree structures that learn and adapt by changing theWir sizes, shapes, and composition, much like a living organism. And like living organisms, the computer programs of GEP are also encoded in simple linear chromosomes of fixed length. Thus, GEP is a genotype–phenotype system, benefiting from a simple genome to keep and transmit the genetic information and a complex phenotype to explore the environment and adapt to it.

Evolutionary algorithms use populations of individuals, select individuals according to fitness, and introduce genetic variation using one or more genetic operators. Their use in artificial computational systems dates back to the 1950s where they were used to solve optimization problems. But it was with the introduction of evolution strategies by Rechenberg in 1965 that evolutionary algorithms gained popularity. A good overview text on evolutionary algorithms is the book "An Introduction to Genetic Algorithms" by Mitchell.

Gene expression programming belongs to the family of evolutionary algorithms and is closely related to genetic algorithms and genetic programming. From genetic algorithms it inherited the linear chromosomes of fixed length; and from genetic programming it inherited the expressive parse trees of varied sizes and shapes.

In gene expression programming the linear chromosomes work as the genotype and the parse trees as the phenotype, creating a genotype/phenotype system. This genotype/phenotype system is multigenic, thus encoding multiple parse trees in each chromosome. This means that the computer programs created by GEP are composed of multiple parse trees. Because these parse trees are the result of gene expression, in GEP they are called expression trees.

Encoding: The Genotype

The genome of gene expression programming consists of a linear, symbolic string or chromosome of fixed length composed of one or more genes of equal size. These genes, despite their fixed length, code for expression trees of different sizes and shapes. An example of a chromosome with two genes, each of size 9, is the string (position zero indicates the start of each gene):

```
012345678012345678

L+a-baccd**cLabacd
```

where "L" represents the natural logarithm function and "a", "b", "c", and "d" represent the variables and constants used in a problem.

Expression Trees: The Phenotype

As shown above, the genes of gene expression programming have all the same size. However, these fixed length strings code for expression trees of different sizes. This means that the size of the coding regions varies from gene to gene, allowing for adaptation and evolution to occur smoothly.

For example, the mathematical expression:

$$\sqrt{(a-b)(c+d)}$$

can also be represented as an expression tree:

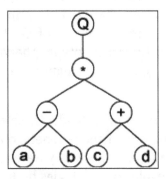

where "Q" represents the square root function.

This kind of expression tree consists of the phenotypic expression of GEP genes, whereas the genes are linear strings encoding these complex structures. For this particular example, the linear string corresponds to:

```
01234567
```

```
Q*-+abcd
```

which is the straightforward reading of the expression tree from top to bottom and from left to right. These linear strings are called k-expressions (from Karva notation).

Going from k-expressions to expression trees is also very simple. For example, the following k-expression:

```
01234567890
```

```
Q*b**+baQba
```

is composed of two different terminals (the variables "a" and "b"), two different functions of two arguments ("*" and "+"), and a function of one argument ("Q"). Its expression gives:

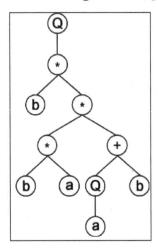

K-expressions and Genes

The k-expressions of gene expression programming correspond to the region of genes that gets expressed. This means that there might be sequences in the genes that are not expressed, which is indeed true for most genes. The reason for these noncoding regions is to provide a buffer of terminals so that all k-expressions encoded in GEP genes correspond always to valid programs or expressions.

The genes of gene expression programming are therefore composed of two different domains – a head and a tail – each with different properties and functions. The head is used mainly to encode the functions and variables chosen to solve the problem at hand, whereas the tail, while also used to encode the variables, provides essentially a reservoir of terminals to ensure that all programs are error-free.

For GEP genes the length of the tail is given by the formula:

$$t = h(n_{max} - 1) + 1$$

where h is the head's length and n_{max} is maximum arity. For example, for a gene created using the set of functions F = {Q, +, −, *, /} and the set of terminals T = {a, b}, n_{max} = 2. And if we choose a head length of 15, then t = 15 (2−1) + 1 = 16, which gives a gene length g of 15 + 16 = 31. The randomly generated string below is an example of one such gene:

```
0123456789012345678901234567890
```

```
*b+a-aQab+//+b+babbabbbababbaaa
```

It encodes the expression tree:

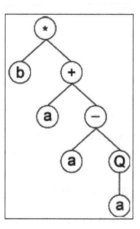

which, in this case, only uses 8 of the 31 elements that constitute the gene.

It's not hard to see that, despite their fixed length, each gene has the potential to code for expression trees of different sizes and shapes, with the simplest composed of only one node (when the first element of a gene is a terminal) and the largest composed of as many nodes as there are elements in the gene (when all the elements in the head are functions with maximum arity).

It's also not hard to see that it is trivial to implement all kinds of genetic modification (mutation, inversion, insertion, recombination, and so on) with the guarantee that all resulting offspring encode correct, error-free programs.

Multigenic Chromosomes

The chromosomes of gene expression programming are usually composed of more than one gene of equal length. Each gene codes for a sub-expression tree (sub-ET) or sub-program. Then the sub-ETs can interact with one another in different ways, forming a more complex program. The figure shows an example of a program composed of three sub-ETs.

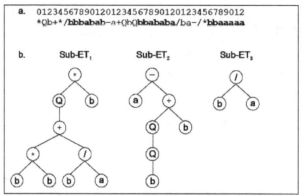

Expression of GEP genes as sub-ETs. a) A three-genic chromosome with
the tails shown in bold. b) The sub-ETs encoded by each gene.

In the final program the sub-ETs could be linked by addition or some other function, as there are no restrictions to the kind of linking function one might choose. Some examples of more complex linkers include taking the average, the median, the midrange, thresholding their sum to make a binomial classification, applying the sigmoid function to compute a probability, and so on. These linking functions are usually chosen a priori for each problem, but they can also be evolved elegantly and efficiently by the cellular system of gene expression programming.

Cells and Code Reuse

In gene expression programming, homeotic genes control the interactions of the different sub-ETs or modules of the main program. The expression of such genes results in different main programs or cells, that is, they determine which genes are expressed in each cell and how the sub-ETs of each cell interact with one another. In other words, homeotic genes determine which sub-ETs are called upon and how often in which main program or cell and what kind of connections they establish with one another.

Homeotic Genes and the Cellular System

Homeotic genes have exactly the same kind of structural organization as normal genes and they are built using an identical process. They also contain a head domain and a tail domain, with the difference that the heads contain now linking functions and a special kind of terminals – genic terminals – that represent the normal genes. The expression of the normal genes results as usual in different sub-ETs, which in the cellular system are called ADFs (automatically defined functions). As for the tails, they contain only genic terminals, that is, derived features generated on the fly by the algorithm.

For example, the chromosome in the figure has three normal genes and one homeotic gene and encodes a main program that invokes three different functions a total of four times, linking them in a particular way.

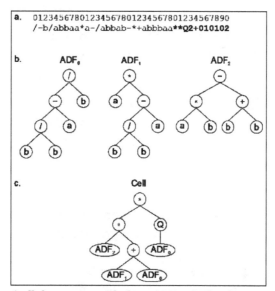

Expression of a unicellular system with three ADFs. a) The chromosome composed of three conventional genes and one homeotic gene (shown in bold). b) The ADFs encoded by each conventional gene. c) The main program or cell.

From this example it is clear that the cellular system not only allows the unconstrained evolution of linking functions but also code reuse. And it shouldn't be hard to implement recursion in this system.

Multiple main Programs and Multicellular Systems

Multicellular systems are composed of more than one homeotic gene. Each homeotic gene in this system puts together a different combination of sub-expression trees or ADFs, creating multiple cells or main programs.

For example, the program shown in the figure was created using a cellular system with two cells and three normal genes.

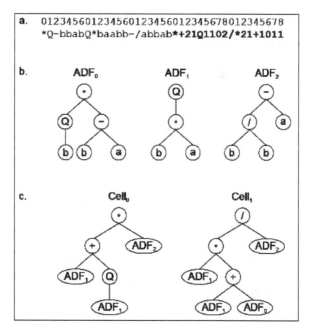

Expression of a multicellular system with three ADFs and two main programs. a) The chromosome composed of three conventional genes and two homeotic genes (shown in bold). b) The ADFs encoded by each conventional gene. c) Two different main programs expressed in two different cells.

The applications of these multicellular systems are multiple and varied and, like the multigenic systems, they can be used both in problems with just one output and in problems with multiple outputs.

Other Levels of Complexity

The head/tail domain of GEP genes (both normal and homeotic) is the basic building block of all GEP algorithms. However, gene expression programming also explores other chromosomal organizations that are more complex than the head/tail structure. Essentially these complex structures consist of functional units or genes with a basic head/tail domain plus one or more extra domains. These extra domains usually encode random numerical constants that the algorithm relentlessly fine-tunes in order to find a good solution. For instance, these numerical constants may be the weights or factors in a function approximation problem; they may be the weights and thresholds of a neural network; the numerical constants needed for the design of decision trees; the weights needed for polynomial induction; or the random numerical constants used to discover the parameter values in a parameter optimization task.

The Basic Gene Expression Algorithm

The fundamental steps of the basic gene expression algorithm are listed below in pseudocode:

- Select function set;

- Select terminal set;

- Load dataset for fitness evaluation;

- Create chromosomes of initial population randomly;

- For each program in population:

    ◦ Express chromosome;

    ◦ Execute program;

    ◦ Evaluate fitness;

- Verify stop condition;

- Select programs;

- Replicate selected programs to form the next population;

- Modify chromosomes using genetic operators;

- Go to step 5.

The first four steps prepare all the ingredients that are needed for the iterative loop of the algorithm (steps 5 through 10). Of these preparative steps, the crucial one is the creation of the initial population, which is created randomly using the elements of the function and terminal sets.

Populations of Programs

Like all evolutionary algorithms, gene expression programming works with populations of individuals, which in this case are computer programs. Therefore, some kind of initial population must be created to get things started. Subsequent populations are descendants, via selection and genetic modification, of the initial population.

In the genotype/phenotype system of gene expression programming, it is only necessary to create the simple linear chromosomes of the individuals without worrying about the structural soundness of the programs they code for, as their expression always results in syntactically correct programs.

Fitness Functions and the Selection Environment

Fitness functions and selection environments (called training datasets in machine learning) are the two facets of fitness and are therefore intricately connected. Indeed, the fitness of a program depends not only on the cost function used to measure its performance but also on the training data chosen to evaluate fitness.

The Selection Environment or Training Data

The selection environment consists of the set of training records, which are also called fitness cases. These fitness cases could be a set of observations or measurements concerning some problem, and they form what is called the training dataset.

The quality of the training data is essential for the evolution of good solutions. A good training set should be representative of the problem at hand and also well-balanced, otherwise the algorithm might get stuck at some local optimum. In addition, it is also important to avoid using unnecessarily large datasets for training as this will slow things down unnecessarily. A good rule of thumb is to choose enough records for training to enable a good generalization in the validation data and leave the remaining records for validation and testing.

Fitness Functions

Broadly speaking, there are essentially three different kinds of problems based on the kind of prediction being made:

- Problems involving numeric (continuous) predictions;
- Problems involving categorical or nominal predictions, both binomial and multinomial;
- Problems involving binary or Boolean predictions.

The first type of problem goes by the name of regression; the second is known as classification, with logistic regression as a special case where, besides the crisp classifications like "Yes" or "No", a probability is also attached to each outcome; and the last one is related to Boolean algebra and logic synthesis.

Fitness Functions for Regression

In regression, the response or dependent variable is numeric (usually continuous) and therefore the output of a regression model is also continuous. So it's quite straightforward to evaluate the fitness of the evolving models by comparing the output of the model to the value of the response in the training data.

There are several basic fitness functions for evaluating model performance, with the most common being based on the error or residual between the model output and the actual value. Such functions include the mean squared error, root mean squared error, mean absolute error, relative squared error, root relative squared error, relative absolute error, and others.

All these standard measures offer a fine granularity or smoothness to the solution space and therefore work very well for most applications. But some problems might require a coarser evolution, such as determining if a prediction is within a certain interval, for instance less than 10% of the actual value. However, even if one is only interested in counting the hits (that is, a prediction that is within the chosen interval), making populations of models evolve based on just the number of hits each program scores is usually not very efficient due to the coarse granularity of the fitness landscape. Thus the solution usually involves combining these coarse measures with some kind of smooth function such as the standard error measures listed above.

Fitness functions based on the correlation coefficient and R-square are also very smooth. For regression problems, these functions work best by combining them with other measures because, by themselves, they only tend to measure correlation, not caring for the range of values of the model output. So by combining them with functions that work at approximating the range of the target values, they form very efficient fitness functions for finding models with good correlation and good fit between predicted and actual values.

Fitness Functions for Classification and Logistic Regression

The design of fitness functions for classification and logistic regression takes advantage of three different characteristics of classification models. The most obvious is just counting the hits, that is, if a record is classified correctly it is counted as a hit. This fitness function is very simple and works well for simple problems, but for more complex problems or datasets highly unbalanced it gives poor results.

One way to improve this type of hits-based fitness function consists of expanding the notion of correct and incorrect classifications. In a binary classification task, correct classifications can be 00 or 11. The "00" representation means that a negative case (represented by "0") was correctly classified, whereas the "11" means that a positive case (represented by "1") was correctly classified. Classifications of the type "00" are called true negatives (TN) and "11" true positives (TP).

There are also two types of incorrect classifications and they are represented by 01 and 10. They are called false positives (FP) when the actual value is 0 and the model predicts a 1; and false negatives (FN) when the target is 1 and the model predicts a 0. The counts of TP, TN, FP, and FN are usually kept on a table known as the confusion matrix.

Confusion matrix for a binomial classification task.

So by counting the TP, TN, FP, and FN and further assigning different weights to these four types of classifications, it is possible to create smoother and therefore more efficient fitness functions. Some popular fitness functions based on the confusion matrix include sensitivity/specificity, recall/precision, F-measure, Jaccard similarity, Matthews correlation coefficient, and cost/gain matrix which combines the costs and gains assigned to the 4 different types of classifications.

These functions based on the confusion matrix are quite sophisticated and are adequate to solve most problems efficiently. But there is another dimension to classification models which is key to exploring more efficiently the solution space and therefore results in the discovery of better classifiers. This new dimension involves exploring the structure of the model itself, which includes not only the domain and range, but also the distribution of the model output and the classifier margin.

By exploring this other dimension of classification models and then combining the information about the model with the confusion matrix, it is possible to design very sophisticated fitness functions that allow the smooth exploration of the solution space. For instance, one can combine some measure based on the confusion matrix with the mean squared error evaluated between the raw model outputs and the actual values. Or combine the F-measure with the R-square evaluated for the raw model output and the target; or the cost/gain matrix with the correlation coefficient, and so on. More exotic fitness functions that explore model granularity include the area under the ROC curve and rank measure.

Also related to this new dimension of classification models, is the idea of assigning probabilities to the model output, which is what is done in logistic regression. Then it is also possible to use these probabilities and evaluate the mean squared error (or some other similar measure) between the probabilities and the actual values, then combine this with the confusion matrix to create very efficient fitness functions for logistic regression. Popular examples of fitness functions based on the probabilities include maximum likelihood estimation and hinge loss.

Fitness Functions for Boolean Problems

In logic there is no model structure to explore: The domain and range of logical functions comprises only 0's and 1's or false and true. So, the fitness functions available for Boolean algebra can only be based on the hits or on the confusion matrix as explained.

Selection and Elitism

Roulette-wheel selection is perhaps the most popular selection scheme used in evolutionary computation. It involves mapping the fitness of each program to a slice of the roulette wheel proportional to its fitness. Then the roulette is spun as many times as there are programs in the population in order to keep the population size constant. So, with roulette-wheel selection programs are selected both according to fitness and the luck of the draw, which means that some times the best traits might be lost. However, by combining roulette-wheel selection with the cloning of the best program of each generation, one guarantees that at least the very best traits are not lost. This technique of cloning the best-of-generation program is known as simple elitism and is used by most stochastic selection schemes.

Reproduction with Modification

The reproduction of programs involves first the selection and then the reproduction of their genomes. Genome modification is not required for reproduction, but without it adaptation and evolution won't take place.

Replication and Selection

The selection operator selects the programs for the replication operator to copy. Depending on the selection scheme, the number of copies one program originates may vary, with some programs getting copied more than once while others are copied just once or not at all. In addition, selection is usually set up so that the population size remains constant from one generation to another.

The replication of genomes in nature is very complex and it took scientists a long time to discover the DNA double helix and propose a mechanism for its replication. But the replication of strings is trivial in artificial evolutionary systems, where only an instruction to copy strings is required to pass all the information in the genome from generation to generation.

The replication of the selected programs is a fundamental piece of all artificial evolutionary systems, but for evolution to occur it needs to be implemented not with the usual precision of a copy instruction, but rather with a few errors thrown in. Indeed, genetic diversity is created with genetic operators such as mutation, recombination, transposition, inversion, and many others.

Mutation

In gene expression programming mutation is the most important genetic operator. It changes genomes by changing an element by another. The accumulation of many small changes over time can create great diversity.

In gene expression programming mutation is totally unconstrained, which means that in each gene domain any domain symbol can be replaced by another. For example, in the heads of genes any function can be replaced by a terminal or another function, regardless of the number of arguments in this new function; and a terminal can be replaced by a function or another terminal.

Recombination

Recombination usually involves two parent chromosomes to create two new chromosomes by combining different parts from the parent chromosomes. And as long as the parent chromosomes are aligned and the exchanged fragments are homologous (that is, occupy the same position in the chromosome), the new chromosomes created by recombination will always encode syntactically correct programs.

Different kinds of crossover are easily implemented either by changing the number of parents involved (there's no reason for choosing only two); the number of split points; or the way one chooses to exchange the fragments, for example, either randomly or in some orderly fashion. For example, gene recombination, which is a special case of recombination, can be done by exchanging homologous genes (genes that occupy the same position in the chromosome) or by exchanging genes chosen at random from any position in the chromosome.

Transposition

Transposition involves the introduction of an insertion sequence somewhere in a chromosome. In gene expression programming insertion sequences might appear anywhere in the chromosome, but they are only inserted in the heads of genes. This method guarantees that even insertion sequences from the tails result in error-free programs.

For transposition to work properly, it must preserve chromosome length and gene structure. So, in gene expression programming transposition can be implemented using two different methods: the first creates a shift at the insertion site, followed by a deletion at the end of the head; the second over-writes the local sequence at the target site and therefore is easier to implement. Both methods can be implemented to operate between chromosomes or within a chromosome or even within a single gene.

Inversion

Inversion is an interesting operator, especially powerful for combinatorial optimization. It consists of inverting a small sequence within a chromosome.

In gene expression programming it can be easily implemented in all gene domains and, in all cases, the offspring produced is always syntactically correct. For any gene domain, a sequence (ranging from at least two elements to as big as the domain itself) is chosen at random within that domain and then inverted.

Other Genetic Operators

Several other genetic operators exist and in gene expression programming, with its different genes and gene domains, the possibilities are endless. For example, genetic operators such as one-point recombination, two-point recombination, gene recombination, uniform recombination, gene transposition, root transposition, domain-specific mutation, domain-specific inversion, domain-specific transposition, and so on, are easily implemented and widely used.

The GEP-RNC Algorithm

Numerical constants are essential elements of mathematical and statistical models and therefore it is important to allow their integration in the models designed by evolutionary algorithms.

Gene expression programming solves this problem very elegantly through the use of an extra gene domain – the Dc – for handling random numerical constants (RNC). By combining this domain with a special terminal placeholder for the RNCs, a richly expressive system can be created.

Structurally, the Dc comes after the tail, has a length equal to the size of the tail t, and is composed of the symbols used to represent the RNCs.

For example, below is shown a simple chromosome composed of only one gene a head size of 7 (the Dc stretches over positions 15–22):

```
0123456789012345678901 2
+?*+?**aaa??aaa68083295
```

where the terminal "?" represents the placeholder for the RNCs. This kind of chromosome is expressed exactly as shown above, giving:

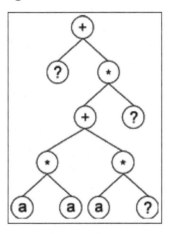

Then the ?'s in the expression tree are replaced from left to right and from top to bottom by the symbols (for simplicity represented by numerals) in the Dc, giving:

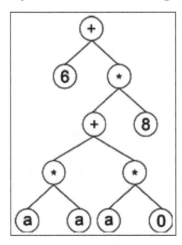

This elegant structure for handling random numerical constants is at the heart of different GEP systems, such as GEP neural networks and GEP decision trees.

Like the basic gene expression algorithm, the GEP-RNC algorithm is also multigenic and its chromosomes are decoded as usual by expressing one gene after another and then linking them all together by the same kind of linking process.

The genetic operators used in the GEP-RNC system are an extension to the genetic operators of the basic GEP algorithm, and they all can be straightforwardly implemented in these new chromosomes. On the other hand, the basic operators of mutation, inversion, transposition, and recombination are also used in the GEP-RNC algorithm. Furthermore, special Dc-specific operators such as mutation, inversion, and transposition, are also used to aid in a more efficient circulation of the RNCs among individual programs. In addition, there is also a special mutation operator that allows the permanent introduction of variation in the set of RNCs. The initial set of RNCs is randomly created at the beginning of a run, which means that, for each gene in the initial population, a specified number of numerical constants, chosen from a certain range, are randomly generated. Then their circulation and mutation is enabled by the genetic operators.

Neural Networks

An artificial neural network (ANN or NN) is a computational device that consists of many simple connected units or neurons. The connections between the units are usually weighted by real-valued weights. These weights are the primary means of learning in neural networks and a learning algorithm is usually used to adjust them.

Structurally, a neural network has three different classes of units: input units, hidden units, and output units. An activation pattern is presented at the input units and then spreads in a forward direction from the input units through one or more layers of hidden units to the output units. The activation coming into one unit from other unit is multiplied by the weights on the links over which it spreads. All incoming activation is then added together and the unit becomes activated only if the incoming result is above the unit's threshold.

In summary, the basic components of a neural network are the units, the connections between the units, the weights, and the thresholds. So, in order to fully simulate an artificial neural network one must somehow encode these components in a linear chromosome and then be able to express them in a meaningful way.

In GEP neural networks (GEP-NN or GEP nets), the network architecture is encoded in the usual structure of a head/tail domain. The head contains special functions/neurons that activate the hidden and output units (in the GEP context, all these units are more appropriately called functional units) and terminals that represent the input units. The tail, as usual, contains only terminals/input units.

Besides the head and the tail, these neural network genes contain two additional domains, Dw and Dt, for encoding the weights and thresholds of the neural network. Structurally, the Dw comes after the tail and its length d_w depends on the head size h and maximum arity n_{max} and is evaluated by the formula:

$$d_w = hn_{max}$$

The Dt comes after Dw and has a length d_t equal to t. Both domains are composed of symbols representing the weights and thresholds of the neural network.

For each NN-gene, the weights and thresholds are created at the beginning of each run, but their circulation and adaptation are guaranteed by the usual genetic operators of mutation, transposition, inversion, and recombination. In addition, special operators are also used to allow a constant flow of genetic variation in the set of weights and thresholds.

For example, below is shown a neural network with two input units (i_1 and i_2), two hidden units (h_1 and h_2), and one output unit (o_1). It has a total of six connections with six corresponding weights represented by the numerals 1–6 (for simplicity, the thresholds are all equal to 1 and are omitted):

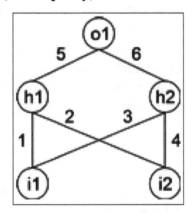

This representation is the canonical neural network representation, but neural networks can also be represented by a tree, which, in this case, corresponds to:

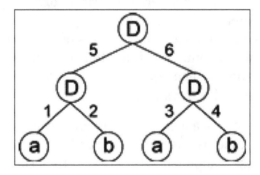

where "a" and "b" represent the two inputs i_1 and i_2 and "D" represents a function with connectivity two. This function adds all its weighted arguments and then thresholds this activation in order to determine the forwarded output. This output (zero or one in this simple case) depends on the threshold of each unit, that is, if the total incoming activation is equal to or greater than the threshold, then the output is one, zero otherwise.

The above NN-tree can be linearized as follows:

```
0123456789012
```

```
DDDabab654321
```

where the structure in positions 7–12 (Dw) encodes the weights. The values of each weight are kept in an array and retrieved as necessary for expression.

As a more concrete example, below is shown a neural net gene for the exclusive-or problem. It has a head size of 3 and Dw size of 6:

```
0123456789012

DDDabab393257
```

Its expression results in the following neural network:

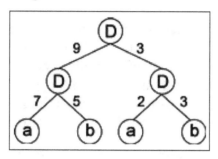

which, for the set of weights:

$W = \{-1.978, 0.514, -0.465, 1.22, -1.686, -1.797, 0.197, 1.606, 0, 1.753\}$

it gives:

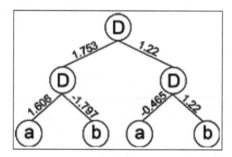

which is a perfect solution to the exclusive-or function.

Besides simple Boolean functions with binary inputs and binary outputs, the GEP-nets algorithm can handle all kinds of functions or neurons (linear neuron, tanh neuron, atan neuron, logistic neuron, limit neuron, radial basis and triangular basis neurons, all kinds of step neurons, and so on). Also interesting is that the GEP-nets algorithm can use all these neurons together and let evolution decide which ones work best to solve the problem at hand. So, GEP-nets can be used not only in Boolean problems but also in logistic regression, classification, and regression. In all cases, GEP-nets can be implemented not only with multigenic systems but also cellular systems, both unicellular and multicellular. Furthermore, multinomial classification problems can also be tackled in one go by GEP-nets both with multigenic systems and multicellular systems.

Automated Reasoning

Automated reasoning is the area of computer science that is concerned with applying reasoning in the form of logic to computing systems. If given a set of assumptions and a goal, an automated reasoning system should be able to make logical inferences towards that goal automatically. Computers that use automated reasoning can be used to automate and apply logical reasoning to activities such as proving theorems, checking proofs or designing circuits. Automated reasoning can also use logic in the form of reasoning through analogy, induction, abduction and non-monotonic reasoning. However, the term automated reasoning is mostly used when referring to deductive reasoning in mathematics and logic.

The term "problem domain" is used to describe the class of problems presented to an automated reasoning program. Problem domains include problem assumptions, which are statements that provide relevant information to the automated reasoning system, and problem conclusions, which are the questions being asked of the system. The reasoning program will receive the problem domain as input and provide a solution as output, such as the accuracy of a proof. An automated reasoning program will terminate when a solution is found or resources are depleted.

The most common use of automated reasoning programs, to prove theorems, is accomplished through providing algorithmic descriptions to the calculus being used. Users are also required to define the class of problems the automated reasoning program will need to solve, the language the program will use to represent given information and what the program will use to implement deductive inferences.

The term automated deduction can also be used to refer to automated reasoning; however, automated deduction is used more narrowly in reference to using deduction logic in mathematics.

Uses

Automated reasoning is mostly used with deductive reasoning to find, check and verify mathematical proofs using a computing system. Using an automated reasoning system to check proofs ensures that the user has not made a mistake in their calculations. Automated reasoning can also be used for applications in mathematics, engineering, computer science or non-mathematical purposes such as asking questions in exact philosophy. However, many of these other subjects still must be represented using a language the program can understand.

Automated Reasoning and AI

Automated reasoning is considered to be a sub-field of artificial intelligence (AI). However, the methods and implementation of both are unique enough that they can be thought of as separate entities. For example, AI typically uses a type logic called modal logic, which uses classical logic while also expressing modality (possibilities or impossibilities). The phrase AI also has connotations denoting a computer which works like a person, which opposes how automated reasoning operates.

Evolutionary Computation

In computer science, evolutionary computation is a family of algorithms for global optimization inspired by biological evolution, and the subfield of artificial intelligence and soft computing studying these algorithms. In technical terms, they are a family of population-based trial and error problem solvers with a metaheuristic or stochastic optimization character.

In evolutionary computation, an initial set of candidate solutions is generated and iteratively updated. Each new generation is produced by stochastically removing less desired solutions, and introducing small random changes. In biological terminology, a population of solutions is subjected to natural selection (or artificial selection) and mutation. As a result, the population will gradually evolve to increase in fitness, in this case the chosen fitness function of the algorithm.

Evolutionary computation techniques can produce highly optimized solutions in a wide range of problem settings, making them popular in computer science. Many variants and extensions exist, suited to more specific families of problems and data structures. Evolutionary computation is also sometimes used in evolutionary biology as an *in silico* experimental procedure to study common aspects of general evolutionary processes.

The use of evolutionary principles for automated problem solving originated in the 1950s. It was not until the 1960s that three distinct interpretations of this idea started to be developed in three different places.

Evolutionary programming was introduced by Lawrence J. Fogel in the US, while John Henry Holland called his method a *genetic algorithm*. In Germany Ingo Rechenberg and Hans-Paul Schwefel introduced *evolution strategies*. These areas developed separately for about 15 years. From the early nineties on they are unified as different representatives ("dialects") of one technology, called *evolutionary computing*. Also in the early nineties, a fourth stream following the general ideas had emerged – *genetic programming*. Since the 1990s, nature-inspired algorithms are becoming an increasingly significant part of the evolutionary computation.

These terminologies denote the field of evolutionary computing and consider evolutionary programming, evolution strategies, genetic algorithms, and genetic programming as sub-areas.

Simulations of evolution using evolutionary algorithms and artificial life started with the work of Nils Aall Barricelli in the 1960s, and was extended by Alex Fraser, who published a series of papers on simulation of artificial selection. Artificial evolution became a widely recognised optimisation method as a result of the work of Ingo Rechenberg in the 1960s and early 1970s, who used evolution strategies to solve complex engineering problems. Genetic algorithms in particular became popular through the writing of John Holland. As academic interest grew, dramatic increases in the power of computers allowed practical applications, including the automatic evolution of computer programs. Evolutionary algorithms are now used to solve multi-dimensional problems more efficiently than software produced by human designers, and also to optimise the design of systems.

Techniques

Evolutionary computing techniques mostly involve metaheuristic optimization algorithms. Broadly speaking, the field includes:

- Ant colony optimization,
- Artificial immune systems,
- Artificial life,
- Cultural algorithms,

- Differential evolution,
- Dual-phase evolution,
- Estimation of distribution algorithms,
- Evolutionary algorithms,
- Evolutionary programming,
- Evolution strategy,
- Gene expression programming,
- Genetic algorithm,
- Genetic programming,
- Grammatical evolution,
- Learnable evolution model,
- Learning classifier systems,
- Memetic algorithms,
- Neuroevolution,
- Particle swarm optimization,
- Synergistic Fibroblast Optimization,
- Self-organization such as self-organizing maps, competitive learning,
- Swarm intelligence.

Evolutionary Algorithms

Evolutionary algorithms form a subset of evolutionary computation in that they generally only involve techniques implementing mechanisms inspired by biological evolution such as reproduction, mutation, recombination, natural selection and survival of the fittest. Candidate solutions to the optimization problem play the role of individuals in a population, and the cost function determines the environment within which the solutions "live". Evolution of the population then takes place after the repeated application of the above operators.

In this process, there are two main forces that form the basis of evolutionary systems: Recombination mutation and crossover create the necessary diversity and thereby facilitate novelty, while selection acts as a force increasing quality.

Many aspects of such an evolutionary process are stochastic. Changed pieces of information due to recombination and mutation are randomly chosen. On the other hand, selection operators can be either deterministic, or stochastic. In the latter case, individuals with a higher fitness have a higher chance to be selected than individuals with a lower fitness, but typically even the weak individuals have a chance to become a parent or to survive.

Evolutionary Algorithms and Biology

Genetic algorithms deliver methods to model biological systems and systems biology that are linked to the theory of dynamical systems, since they are used to predict the future states of the system. This is just a vivid (but perhaps misleading) way of drawing attention to the orderly, well-controlled and highly structured character of development in biology.

However, the use of algorithms and informatics, in particular of computational theory, beyond the analogy to dynamical systems, is also relevant to understand evolution itself.

This view has the merit of recognizing that there is no central control of development; organisms develop as a result of local interactions within and between cells. The most promising ideas about program-development parallels seem to us to be ones that point to an apparently close analogy between processes within cells, and the low-level operation of modern computers . Thus, biological systems are like computational machines that process input information to compute next states, such that biological systems are closer to a computation than classical dynamical system.

Furthermore, following concepts from computational theory, micro processes in biological organisms are fundamentally incomplete and undecidable, implying that "there is more than a crude metaphor behind the analogy between cells and computers.

The analogy to computation extends also to the relationship between inheritance systems and biological structure, which is often thought to reveal one of the most pressing problems in explaining the origins of life.

References

- Simionescu, P.A. (2014). Computer Aided Graphing and Simulation Tools for AutoCAD Users (1st ed.). Boca Raton, FL: CRC Press. ISBN 978-1-4822-5290-3

- Tools-framework-machinelearning: edoramedia.com, Retrieved 14 June, 2019

- French, jordan (2016). "the time traveller's capm". Investment analysts journal. 46 (2): 81–96. Doi:10.1080/1 0293523.2016.1255469

- Ten-popular-tools-frameworks-artificial-intelligence: opensourceforu.com, Retrieved 28 February, 2019

- Deng, geng; ferris, m.c. (2008). Neuro-dynamic programming for fractionated radiotherapy planning. Springer optimization and its applications. 12. Pp. 47–70. Citeseerx 10.1.1.137.8288. Doi:10.1007/978-0-387-73299-2_3. Isbn 978-0-387-73298-5

- Automated-reasoning, definition: techtarget.com, Retrieved 19 May, 2019

- Alizadeh, elaheh; lyons, samanthe m; castle, jordan m; prasad, ashok (2016). "measuring systematic changes in invasive cancer cell shape using zernike moments". Integrative biology. 8 (11): 1183–1193. Doi:10.1039/c6i-b00100a. Pmid 27735002

3

Applications

Artificial intelligence finds applications in numerous areas. A few of them are speech recognition, face recognition, computer vision, data mining and automation. The diverse applications of artificial intelligence in these fields have been extensively discussed in this chapter.

Artificial intelligence, defined as intelligence exhibited by machines, has many applications in today's society. More specifically, it is Weak AI, the form of AI where programs are developed to perform specific tasks, that is being utilized for a wide range of activities including medical diagnosis, electronic trading platforms, robot control, and remote sensing. AI has been used to develop and advance numerous fields and industries, including finance, healthcare, education, transportation, and more. AI has impacted our human life positively in various fields like marketing, finance, banking etc. and their applications are given below:

- AI in Marketing,

- AI in Banking,

- AI in Finance,

- AI in Agriculture,

- AI in HealthCare,

- AI in Gaming,

- AI in Space Exploration,

- AI in Autonomous Vehicles,

- AI in Chatbots,

- AI in Artificial Creativity.

Artificial Intelligence Applications

Marketing

Marketing is a way to sugar coat your products to attract more customers. We, humans, are pretty good at sugar coating, but what if an algorithm or a bot is built solely for the purpose of marketing a brand or a company? It would do a pretty awesome job.

In the early 2000s, if we searched an online store to find a product without knowing it's exact name, it would become a nightmare to find the product. But now when we search for an item on any e-commerce store, we get all possible results related to the item. It's like these search engines read our minds! In a matter of seconds, we get a list of all relevant items. An example of this is finding the right movies on Netflix.

One reason why we're all obsessed with Netflix and chill is because, Netflix provides highly accurate predictive technology based on customer's reactions to films. It examines millions of records to suggest shows and films that you might like based on your previous actions and choices of films. As the data set grows, this technology is getting smarter and smarter every day.

With the growing advancement in AI, in the near future, it may be possible for consumers on the web to buy products by snapping a photo of it. Companies like CamFind and their competitors are experimenting this already.

Banking

A lot of banks have already adopted AI-based systems to provide customer support, detect anomalies and credit card frauds. An example of this is HDFC Bank.

HDFC Bank has developed an AI-based chatbot called EVA (Electronic Virtual Assistant), built by Bengaluru-based Senseforth AI Research.

Since its launch, Eva has addressed over 3 million customer queries, interacted with over half a million unique users, and held over a million conversations. Eva can collect knowledge from thousands of sources and provide simple answers in less than 0.4 seconds.

Artificial Intelligence Applications - AI in BankingArtificial Intelligence Applications – AI in Banking.

The use of AI for fraud prevention is not a new concept. In fact, AI solutions can be used to enhance security across a number of business sectors, including retail and finance.

By tracing card usage and endpoint access, security specialists are more effectively preventing fraud. Organizations rely on AI to trace those steps by analyzing the behaviors of transactions.

Companies such as MasterCard and RBS WorldPay have relied on AI and Deep Learning to detect fraudulent transaction patterns and prevent card fraud for years now. This has saved millions of dollars.

Finance

Ventures have been relying on computers and data scientists to determine future patterns in the market. Trading mainly depends on the ability to predict the future accurately.

Machines are great at this because they can crunch a huge amount of data in a short span. Machines can also learn to observe patterns in past data and predict how these patterns might repeat in the future.

In the age of ultra-high-frequency trading, financial organizations are turning to AI to improve their stock trading performance and boost profit.

One such organization is Japan's leading brokerage house, Nomura Securities. The company has been reluctantly pursuing one goal, i.e. to analyze the insights of experienced stock traders with the help of computers. After years of research, Nomura is set to introduce a new stock trading system.

The new system stores a vast amount of price and trading data in its computer. By tapping into this reservoir of information, it will make assessments, for example, it may determine that current market conditions are similar to the conditions two weeks ago and predict how share prices will be changing a few minutes down the line. This will help to take better trading decisions based on the predicted market prices.

Agriculture

Here's an alarming fact, the world will need to produce 50 percent more food by 2050 because we're literally eating up everything! The only way this can be possible is if we use our resources more carefully. With that being said, AI can help farmers get more from the land while using resources more sustainably.

Issues such as climate change, population growth, and food security concerns have pushed the industry into seeking more innovative approaches to improve crop yield.

Organizations are using automation and robotics to help farmers find more efficient ways to protect their crops from weeds.

Blue River Technology has developed a robot called See & Spray which uses computer vision technologies like object detection to monitor and precisely spray weedicide on cotton plants. Precision spraying can help prevent herbicide resistance.

Apart from this, Berlin-based agricultural tech start-up called PEAT, has developed an application called Plantix that identifies potential defects and nutrient deficiencies in the soil through images.

The image recognition app identifies possible defects through images captured by the user's smartphone camera. Users are then provided with soil restoration techniques, tips, and other possible solutions. The company claims that its software can achieve pattern detection with an estimated accuracy of up to 95%.

Health Care

When it comes to saving our lives, a lot of organizations and medical care centers are relying on AI. There are many examples of how AI in healthcare has helped patients all over the world.

An organization called Cambio Health Care developed a clinical decision support system for stroke prevention that can give the physician a warning when there's a patient at risk of having a heart stroke.

Another such example is Coala life which is a company that has a digitalized device that can find cardiac diseases.

Similarly, Aifloo is developing a system for keeping track of how people are doing in nursing homes, home care, etc. The best thing about AI in healthcare is that you don't even need to develop a new medication. Just by using an existing medication in the right way, you can also save lives.

Gaming

Over the past few years, Artificial Intelligence has become an integral part of the gaming industry. In fact, one of the biggest accomplishments of AI is in the gaming industry.

DeepMind's AI-based AlphaGo software, which is known for defeating Lee Sedol, the world champion in the game of GO, is considered to be one of the most significant accomplishment in the field of AI.

Shortly after the victory, DeepMind created an advanced version of AlphaGo called AlphaGo Zero which defeated the predecessor in an AI-AI face off. Unlike the original AlphaGo, which DeepMind trained over time by using a large amount of data and supervision, the advanced system, AlphaGo Zero taught itself to master the game.

Other examples of Artificial Intelligence in gaming include the First Encounter Assault Recon, popularly known as F.E.A.R, which is a first-person shooter video game.

But, what makes this Game so special?

The actions taken by the opponent AI are unpredictable because the game is designed in such a way that the opponents are trained throughout the game and never repeat the same mistakes. They get better as the game gets harder. This makes the game very challenging and prompts the players to constantly switch strategies and never sit in the same position.

Space Exploration

Space expeditions and discoveries always require analyzing vast amounts of data. Artificial Intelligence and Machine learning is the best way to handle and process data on this scale. After rigorous research, astronomers used Artificial Intelligence to sift through years of data obtained by the Kepler telescope in order to identify a distant eight-planet solar system.

Artificial Intelligence is also being used for NASA's next rover mission to Mars, the Mars 2020 Rover. The AEGIS, which is an AI-based Mars rover is already on the red planet. The rover is responsible for autonomous targeting of cameras in order to perform investigations on Mars.

Autonomous Vehicles

For the longest time, self-driving cars have been a buzzword in the AI industry. The development of autonomous vehicles will definitely revolutionaries the transport system.

Companies like Waymo conducted several test drives in Phoenix before deploying their first AI-based public ride-hailing service. The AI system collects data from the vehicles radar, cameras, GPS, and cloud services to produce control signals that operate the vehicle.

Advanced Deep Learning algorithms can accurately predict what objects in the vehicle's vicinity are likely to do. This makes Waymo cars more effective and safer.

Another famous example of an autonomous vehicle is Tesla's self-driving car. Artificial Intelligence implements computer vision, image detection and deep learning to build cars that can automatically detect objects and drive around without human intervention.

Elon Musk talks a ton about how AI is implemented in tesla's self-driving cars and autopilot features. He quoted that,

"Tesla will have fully self-driving cars ready by the end of the year and a "robotaxi" version – one that can ferry passengers without anyone behind the wheel – ready for the streets next year".

Chatbots

These days Virtual assistants have become a very common technology. Almost every household has a virtual assistant that controls the appliances at home. A few examples include Siri, Cortana, which are gaining popularity because of the user experience they provide.

Amazon's Echo is an example of how Artificial Intelligence can be used to translate human language into desirable actions. This device uses speech recognition and NLP to perform a wide range of tasks on your command. It can do more than just play your favorite songs. It can be used to control the devices at your house, book cabs, make phone calls, order your favorite food, check the weather conditions and so on.

Another example is the newly released Google's virtual assistant called Google Duplex, that has astonished millions of people. Not only can it respond to calls and book appointments for you, but it also adds a human touch.

The device uses Natural language processing and machine learning algorithms to process human language and perform tasks such as manage your schedule, control your smart home, make a reservation and so on.

Social Media

Ever since social media has become our identity, we've been generating an immeasurable amount of data through chats, tweets, posts and so on. And wherever there is an abundance of data, AI and Machine Learning are always involved.

In social media platforms like Facebook, AI is used for face verification wherein machine learning and deep learning concepts are used to detect facial features and tag your friends. Deep Learning is used to extract every minute detail from an image by using a bunch of deep neural networks. On the other hand, Machine learning algorithms are used to design your feed based on your interests.

Another such example is Twitter's AI, which is being used to identify hate speech and terroristic language in tweets. It makes use of Machine Learning, Deep Learning, and Natural language processing to filter out offensive content. The company discovered and banned 300,000 terrorist-linked accounts, 95% of which were found by non-human, artificially intelligent machines.

Artificial Creativity

An AI-based system called MuseNet can now compose classical music that echoes the classical legends, Bach and Mozart.

MuseNet is a deep neural network that is capable of generating 4-minute musical compositions with 10 different instruments and can combine styles from country to Mozart to the Beatles.

MuseNet was not explicitly programmed with an understanding of music, but instead discovered patterns of harmony, rhythm, and style by learning on its own.

Another creative product of Artificial Intelligence is a content automation tool called Wordsmith. Wordsmith is a natural language generation platform that can transform your data into insightful narratives.

Computer Vision

Computer vision is an interdisciplinary scientific field that deals with how computers can be made to gain high-level understanding from digital images or videos. From the perspective of engineering, it seeks to automate tasks that the human visual system can do.

Computer vision tasks include methods for acquiring, processing, analyzing and understanding digital images, and extraction of high-dimensional data from the real world in order to produce numerical or symbolic information, e.g., in the forms of decisions.Understanding in this context means the transformation of visual images (the input of the retina) into descriptions of the world that can interface with other thought processes and elicit appropriate action. This image understanding can be seen as the disentangling of symbolic information from image data using models constructed with the aid of geometry, physics, statistics, and learning theory.

As a scientific discipline, computer vision is concerned with the theory behind artificial systems that extract information from images. The image data can take many forms, such as video sequences, views from multiple cameras, or multi-dimensional data from a medical scanner. As a technological discipline, computer vision seeks to apply its theories and models for the construction of computer vision systems.

Sub-domains of computer vision include scene reconstruction, event detection, video tracking, object recognition, 3D pose estimation, learning, indexing, motion estimation, and image restoration.

Computer vision is an interdisciplinary field that deals with how computers can be made to gain high-level understanding from digital images or videos. From the perspective of engineering, it seeks to automate tasks that the human visual system can do. "Computer vision is concerned with the automatic extraction, analysis and understanding of useful information from a single image or a sequence of images. It involves the development of a theoretical and algorithmic basis to achieve automatic visual understanding." As a scientific discipline, computer vision is concerned with the theory behind artificial systems that extract information from images. The image data can take many forms, such as video sequences, views from multiple cameras, or multi-dimensional data from a medical scanner. As a technological discipline, computer vision seeks to apply its theories and models for the construction of computer vision systems.

Related Fields

Artificial Intelligence

Areas of artificial intelligence deal with autonomous planning or deliberation for robotical systems to navigate through an environment. A detailed understanding of these environments is required to navigate through them. Information about the environment could be provided by a computer vision system, acting as a vision sensor and providing high-level information about the environment and the robot.

Artificial intelligence and computer vision share other topics such as pattern recognition and learning techniques. Consequently, computer vision is sometimes seen as a part of the artificial intelligence field or the computer science field in general.

Information Engineering

Computer vision is often considered to be part of information engineering.

Solid-state Physics

Solid-state physics is another field that is closely related to computer vision. Most computer vision systems rely on image sensors, which detect electromagnetic radiation, which is typically in the form of either visible or infra-red light. The sensors are designed using quantum physics. The process by which light interacts with surfaces is explained using physics. Physics explains the behavior of optics which are a core part of most imaging systems. Sophisticated image sensors even require quantum mechanics to provide a complete understanding of the image formation process. Also, various measurement problems in physics can be addressed using computer vision, for example motion in fluids.

Neurobiology

A third field which plays an important role is neurobiology, specifically the study of the biological vision system. Over the last century, there has been an extensive study of eyes, neurons, and the brain structures devoted to processing of visual stimuli in both humans and various animals. This has led to a coarse, yet complicated, description of how "real" vision systems operate in order to solve certain vision-related tasks. These results have led to a subfield within computer vision where artificial systems are designed to mimic the processing and behavior of biological systems, at different levels of complexity. Also, some of the learning-based methods developed within computer vision (*e.g.* neural net and deep learning based image and feature analysis and classification) have their background in biology.

Some strands of computer vision research are closely related to the study of biological vision – indeed, just as many strands of AI research are closely tied with research into human consciousness, and the use of stored knowledge to interpret, integrate and utilize visual information. The field of biological vision studies and models the physiological processes behind visual perception in humans and other animals. Computer vision, on the other hand, studies and describes the processes implemented in software and hardware behind artificial vision systems. Interdisciplinary exchange between biological and computer vision has proven fruitful for both fields.

Signal Processing

Yet another field related to computer vision is signal processing. Many methods for processing of one-variable signals, typically temporal signals, can be extended in a natural way to processing of two-variable signals or multi-variable signals in computer vision. However, because of the specific nature of images there are many methods developed within computer vision which have no counterpart in processing of one-variable signals. Together with the multi-dimensionality of the signal, this defines a subfield in signal processing as a part of computer vision.

Other Fields

Beside the above-mentioned views on computer vision, many of the related research topics can also be studied from a purely mathematical point of view. For example, many methods in computer vision are based on statistics, optimization or geometry. Finally, a significant part of the field is devoted to the implementation aspect of computer vision; how existing methods can be realized in various combinations of software and hardware, or how these methods can be modified in order to gain processing speed without losing too much performance. Computer vision is also used in fashion ecommerce, inventory management, patent search, furniture, and the beauty industry.

Distinctions

The fields most closely related to computer vision are image processing, image analysis and machine vision. There is a significant overlap in the range of techniques and applications that these cover. This implies that the basic techniques that are used and developed in these fields are similar, something which can be interpreted as there is only one field with different names. On the other hand, it appears to be necessary for research groups, scientific journals, conferences and companies to present or market themselves as belonging specifically to one of these fields and, hence, various characterizations which distinguish each of the fields from the others have been presented.

Computer graphics produces image data from 3D models, computer vision often produces 3D models from image data. There is also a trend towards a combination of the two disciplines, *e.g.*, as explored in augmented reality.

The following characterizations appear relevant but should not be taken as universally accepted:

- Image processing and image analysis tend to focus on 2D images, how to transform one image to another, *e.g.*, by pixel-wise operations such as contrast enhancement, local operations such as edge extraction or noise removal, or geometrical transformations such as rotating the image. This characterization implies that image processing/analysis neither require assumptions nor produce interpretations about the image content.

- Computer vision includes 3D analysis from 2D images. This analyzes the 3D scene projected onto one or several images, *e.g.*, how to reconstruct structure or other information about the 3D scene from one or several images. Computer vision often relies on more or less complex assumptions about the scene depicted in an image.

- Machine vision is the process of applying a range of technologies & methods to provide imaging-based automatic inspection, process control and robot guidance in industrial applications. Machine vision tends to focus on applications, mainly in manufacturing, *e.g.*, vision-based robots and systems for vision-based inspection, measurement, or picking (such as bin picking). This implies that image sensor technologies and control theory often are integrated with the processing of image data to control a robot and that real-time processing is emphasised by means of efficient implementations in hardware and software. It also implies that the external conditions such as lighting can be and are often more controlled in machine vision than they are in general computer vision, which can enable the use of different algorithms.

- There is also a field called imaging which primarily focuses on the process of producing images, but sometimes also deals with processing and analysis of images. For example, medical imaging includes substantial work on the analysis of image data in medical applications.

- Finally, pattern recognition is a field which uses various methods to extract information from signals in general, mainly based on statistical approaches and artificial neural networks. A significant part of this field is devoted to applying these methods to image data.

Photogrammetry also overlaps with computer vision, e.g., stereophotogrammetry vs. computer stereo vision.

Applications

Applications range from tasks such as industrial machine vision systems which, say, inspect bottles speeding by on a production line, to research into artificial intelligence and computers or robots that can comprehend the world around them. The computer vision and machine vision fields have significant overlap. Computer vision covers the core technology of automated image analysis which is used in many fields. Machine vision usually refers to a process of combining automated image analysis with other methods and technologies to provide automated inspection and robot guidance in industrial applications. In many computer-vision applications, the computers are pre-programmed to solve a particular task, but methods based on learning are now becoming increasingly common. Examples of applications of computer vision include systems for:

- Automatic inspection, *e.g.*, in manufacturing applications.
- Assisting humans in identification tasks, e.g., a species identification system.
- Controlling processes, *e.g.*, an industrial robot.
- Detecting events, *e.g.*, for visual surveillance or people counting.
- Interaction, *e.g.*, as the input to a device for computer-human interaction.
- Modeling objects or environments, *e.g.*, medical image analysis or topographical modeling.

- Navigation, *e.g.*, by an autonomous vehicle or mobile robot.

- Organizing information, *e.g.*, for indexing databases of images and image sequences.

One of the most prominent application fields is medical computer vision, or medical image processing, characterized by the extraction of information from image data to diagnose a patient. An example of this is detection of tumours, arteriosclerosis or other malign changes; measurements of organ dimensions, blood flow, etc. are another example. It also supports medical research by providing new information: *e.g.*, about the structure of the brain, or about the quality of medical treatments. Applications of computer vision in the medical area also includes enhancement of images interpreted by humans—ultrasonic images or X-ray images for example—to reduce the influence of noise.

A second application area in computer vision is in industry, sometimes called machine vision, where information is extracted for the purpose of supporting a manufacturing process. One example is quality control where details or final products are being automatically inspected in order to find defects. Another example is measurement of position and orientation of details to be picked up by a robot arm. Machine vision is also heavily used in agricultural process to remove undesirable food stuff from bulk material, a process called optical sorting.

Military applications are probably one of the largest areas for computer vision. The obvious examples are detection of enemy soldiers or vehicles and missile guidance. More advanced systems for missile guidance send the missile to an area rather than a specific target, and target selection is made when the missile reaches the area based on locally acquired image data. Modern military concepts, such as "battlefield awareness", imply that various sensors, including image sensors, provide a rich set of information about a combat scene which can be used to support strategic decisions. In this case, automatic processing of the data is used to reduce complexity and to fuse information from multiple sensors to increase reliability.

Artist's concept of a Mars Exploration Rover, an example of an unmanned land-based vehicle. Notice the stereo cameras mounted on top of the rover.

One of the newer application areas is autonomous vehicles, which include submersibles, land-based vehicles (small robots with wheels, cars or trucks), aerial vehicles, and unmanned aerial vehicles (UAV). The level of autonomy ranges from fully autonomous (unmanned) vehicles to vehicles where computer-vision-based systems support a driver or a pilot in various situations. Fully autonomous vehicles typically use computer vision for navigation, *e.g.* for knowing where it is, or for producing a map of its environment (SLAM) and for detecting obstacles. It can also be used for detecting certain task specific events, *e.g.*, a UAV looking for forest fires. Examples of supporting systems are obstacle warning systems in cars, and systems for autonomous landing of aircraft. Several car manufacturers have demonstrated systems for autonomous driving of cars, but this technology has still not reached a level where it can be put on the market. There are ample examples of military autonomous vehicles ranging from advanced missiles to UAVs for recon missions or missile guidance. Space exploration is already being made with autonomous vehicles using computer vision, *e.g.*, NASA's Mars Exploration Rover and ESA's ExoMars Rover.

Other application areas include:

- Support of visual effects creation for cinema and broadcast, *e.g.*, camera tracking (matchmoving).

- Surveillance.

- Tracking and counting organisms in the biological sciences.

Typical Tasks

Each of the application areas described above employ a range of computer vision tasks; more or less well-defined measurement problems or processing problems, which can be solved using a variety of methods. Some examples of typical computer vision tasks are presented below.

Computer vision tasks include methods for acquiring, processing, analyzing and understanding digital images, and extraction of high-dimensional data from the real world in order to produce numerical or symbolic information, *e.g.*, in the forms of decisions.Understanding in this context means the transformation of visual images (the input of the retina) into descriptions of the world that can interface with other thought processes and elicit appropriate action. This image understanding can be seen as the disentangling of symbolic information from image data using models constructed with the aid of geometry, physics, statistics, and learning theory.

Recognition

The classical problem in computer vision, image processing, and machine vision is that of determining whether or not the image data contains some specific object, feature, or activity. Different varieties of the recognition problem are described in the literature:

- Object recognition (also called object classification): One or several pre-specified or learned objects or object classes can be recognized, usually together with their 2D positions in the image or 3D poses in the scene. Blippar, Google Goggles and LikeThat provide stand-alone programs that illustrate this functionality.

- Identification: An individual instance of an object is recognized. Examples include identification of a specific person's face or fingerprint, identification of handwritten digits, or identification of a specific vehicle.

- Detection: The image data are scanned for a specific condition. Examples include detection of possible abnormal cells or tissues in medical images or detection of a vehicle in an automatic road toll system. Detection based on relatively simple and fast computations is sometimes used for finding smaller regions of interesting image data which can be further analyzed by more computationally demanding techniques to produce a correct interpretation.

Currently, the best algorithms for such tasks are based on convolutional neural networks. An illustration of their capabilities is given by the ImageNet Large Scale Visual Recognition Challenge; this is a benchmark in object classification and detection, with millions of images and hundreds of object classes. Performance of convolutional neural networks, on the ImageNet tests, is now close to that of humans. The best algorithms still struggle with objects that are small or thin, such as a small ant on a stem of a flower or a person holding a quill in their hand. They also have trouble with images that have been distorted with filters (an increasingly common phenomenon with modern digital cameras). By contrast, those kinds of images rarely trouble humans. Humans, however, tend to have trouble with other issues. For example, they are not good at classifying objects into fine-grained classes, such as the particular breed of dog or species of bird, whereas convolutional neural networks handle this with ease.

Several specialized tasks based on recognition exist, such as:

- Content-based image retrieval: Finding all images in a larger set of images which have a specific content. The content can be specified in different ways, for example in terms of similarity relative a target image (give me all images similar to image X), or in terms of high-level search criteria given as text input (give me all images which contains many houses, are taken during winter, and have no cars in them).

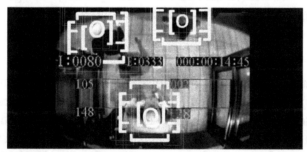

Computer vision for people counterpurposes in public places, malls, shopping centres.

- Pose estimation: Estimating the position or orientation of a specific object relative to the camera. An example application for this technique would be assisting a robot arm in retrieving objects from a conveyor belt in an assembly line situation or picking parts from a bin.

- Optical character recognition (OCR): Identifying characters in images of printed or handwritten text, usually with a view to encoding the text in a format more amenable to editing or indexing (e.g. ASCII).

- 2D code reading: Reading of 2D codes such as data matrix and QR codes.

- Facial recognition.

- Shape Recognition Technology (SRT) in people counter systems differentiating human beings (head and shoulder patterns) from objects.

Motion Analysis

Several tasks relate to motion estimation where an image sequence is processed to produce an estimate of the velocity either at each points in the image or in the 3D scene, or even of the camera that produces the images . Examples of such tasks are:

- Egomotion: Determining the 3D rigid motion (rotation and translation) of the camera from an image sequence produced by the camera.

- Tracking: Following the movements of a (usually) smaller set of interest points or objects (e.g., vehicles, humans or other organisms) in the image sequence.

- Optical flow: To determine, for each point in the image, how that point is moving relative to the image plane, i.e., its apparent motion. This motion is a result both of how the corresponding 3D point is moving in the scene and how the camera is moving relative to the scene.

Scene Reconstruction

Given one or (typically) more images of a scene, or a video, scene reconstruction aims at computing a 3D model of the scene. In the simplest case the model can be a set of 3D points. More sophisticated methods produce a complete 3D surface model. The advent of 3D imaging not requiring motion or scanning, and related processing algorithms is enabling rapid advances in this field. Grid-based 3D sensing can be used to acquire 3D images from multiple angles. Algorithms are now available to stitch multiple 3D images together into point clouds and 3D models.

Image Restoration

The aim of image restoration is the removal of noise (sensor noise, motion blur, etc.) from images. The simplest possible approach for noise removal is various types of filters such as low-pass filters or median filters. More sophisticated methods assume a model of how the local image structures look, to distinguish them from noise. By first analysing the image data in terms of the local image structures, such as lines or edges, and then controlling the filtering based on local information from the analysis step, a better level of noise removal is usually obtained compared to the simpler approaches. An example in this field is inpainting.

System Methods

The organization of a computer vision system is highly application-dependent. Some systems are stand-alone applications that solve a specific measurement or detection problem, while others constitute a sub-system of a larger design which, for example, also contains sub-systems for control of mechanical actuators, planning, information databases, man-machine interfaces, etc. The specific implementation of a computer vision system also depends on whether its functionality is pre-specified or if some part of it can be learned or modified during operation. Many functions are unique to the application. There are, however, typical functions that are found in many computer vision systems.

- Image acquisition: A digital image is produced by one or several image sensors, which, besides various types of light-sensitive cameras, include range sensors, tomography devices, radar, ultra-sonic cameras, etc. Depending on the type of sensor, the resulting image data is an ordinary 2D image, a 3D volume, or an image sequence. The pixel values typically correspond to light intensity in one or several spectral bands (gray images or colour images), but can also be related to various physical measures, such as depth, absorption or reflectance of sonic or electromagnetic waves, or nuclear magnetic resonance.

- Pre-processing: Before a computer vision method can be applied to image data in order to extract some specific piece of information, it is usually necessary to process the data in order to assure that it satisfies certain assumptions implied by the method. Examples are:

  - Re-sampling to assure that the image coordinate system is correct.

  - Noise reduction to assure that sensor noise does not introduce false information.

  - Contrast enhancement to assure that relevant information can be detected.

  - Scale space representation to enhance image structures at locally appropriate scales.

- Feature extraction: Image features at various levels of complexity are extracted from the image data. Typical examples of such features are:

  - Lines, edges and ridges.

  - Localized interest points such as corners, blobs or points.

More complex features may be related to texture, shape or motion:

- Detection/segmentation: At some point in the processing a decision is made about which image points or regions of the image are relevant for further processing. Examples are:

  - Selection of a specific set of interest points.

  - Segmentation of one or multiple image regions that contain a specific object of interest.

  - Segmentation of image into nested scene architecture comprising foreground, object groups, single objects or salient object parts (also referred to as spatial-taxon scene hierarchy), while the visual salience is often implemented as spatial and temporal attention.

  - Segmentation or co-segmentation of one or multiple videos into a series of per-frame foreground masks, while maintaining its temporal semantic continuity.

- High-level processing: At this step the input is typically a small set of data, for example a set of points or an image region which is assumed to contain a specific object. The remaining processing deals with, for example:

  - Verification that the data satisfy model-based and application-specific assumptions.

  - Estimation of application-specific parameters, such as object pose or object size.

  - Image recognition: Classifying a detected object into different categories.

- ○   Image registration: Comparing and combining two different views of the same object.
- Decision making Making the final decision required for the application, for example:
  - ○   Pass/fail on automatic inspection applications.
  - ○   Match/no-match in recognition applications.
  - ○   Flag for further human review in medical, military, security and recognition applications.

Image-Understanding Systems

Image-understanding systems (IUS) include three levels of abstraction as follows: low level includes image primitives such as edges, texture elements, or regions; intermediate level includes boundaries, surfaces and volumes; and high level includes objects, scenes, or events. Many of these requirements are really topics for further research.

The representational requirements in the designing of IUS for these levels are: representation of prototypical concepts, concept organization, spatial knowledge, temporal knowledge, scaling, and description by comparison and differentiation.

While inference refers to the process of deriving new, not explicitly represented facts from currently known facts, control refers to the process that selects which of the many inference, search, and matching techniques should be applied at a particular stage of processing. Inference and control requirements for IUS are: search and hypothesis activation, matching and hypothesis testing, generation and use of expectations, change and focus of attention, certainty and strength of belief, inference and goal satisfaction.

Hardware

There are many kinds of computer vision systems; however, all of them contain these basic elements: a power source, at least one image acquisition device (camera, ccd, etc.), a processor, and control and communication cables or some kind of wireless interconnection mechanism. In addition, a practical vision system contains software, as well as a display in order to monitor the system. Vision systems for inner spaces, as most industrial ones, contain an illumination system and may be placed in a controlled environment. Furthermore, a completed system includes many accessories such as camera supports, cables and connectors.

Most computer vision systems use visible-light cameras passively viewing a scene at frame rates of at most 60 frames per second (usually far slower).

A few computer vision systems use image-acquisition hardware with active illumination or something other than visible light or both, such as structured-light 3D scanners, thermographic cameras, hyperspectral imagers, radar imaging, lidar scanners, magnetic resonance images, side-scan sonar, synthetic aperture sonar, etc. Such hardware captures "images" that are then processed often using the same computer vision algorithms used to process visible-light images.

While traditional broadcast and consumer video systems operate at a rate of 30 frames per second, advances in digital signal processingand consumer graphics hardware has made high-speed image acquisition, processing, and display possible for real-time systems on the order of hundreds to thousands of frames per second. For applications in robotics, fast, real-time video systems are critically important and often can simplify the processing needed for certain algorithms. When combined with a high-speed projector, fast image acquisition allows 3D measurement and feature tracking to be realised.

Egocentric vision systems are composed of a wearable camera that automatically take pictures from a first-person perspective. Vision processing units are emerging as a new class of processor, to complement CPUs and graphics processing units (GPUs) in this role.

Speech Recognition

Speech recognition is the interdisciplinary subfield of computational linguistics that develops methodologies and technologies that enables the recognition and translation of spoken language into text by computers. It is also known as automatic speech recognition (ASR), computer speech recognition or speech to text (STT). It incorporates knowledge and research in the linguistics, computer science, and electrical engineering fields.

Some speech recognition systems require "training" (also called "enrollment") where an individual speaker reads text or isolated vocabulary into the system. The system analyzes the person's specific voice and uses it to fine-tune the recognition of that person's speech, resulting in increased accuracy. Systems that do not use training are called "speaker independent" systems. Systems that use training are called "speaker dependent".

Speech recognition applications include voice user interfaces such as voice dialing (e.g. "call home"), call routing (e.g. "I would like to make a collect call"), domotic appliance control, search (e.g. find a podcast where particular words were spoken), simple data entry (e.g., entering a credit card number), preparation of structured documents (e.g. a radiology report), determining speaker characteristics, speech-to-text processing (e.g., word processors or emails), and aircraft (usually termed direct voice input).

The term *voice recognition* or *speaker identification* refers to identifying the speaker, rather than what they are saying. Recognizing the speaker can simplify the task of translating speech in systems that have been trained on a specific person's voice or it can be used to authenticate or verify the identity of a speaker as part of a security process.

From the technology perspective, speech recognition has a long history with several waves of major innovations. Most recently, the field has benefited from advances in deep learning and big data. The advances are evidenced not only by the surge of academic papers published in the field, but more importantly by the worldwide industry adoption of a variety of deep learning methods in designing and deploying speech recognition systems.

Models, Methods and Algorithms

Both acoustic modeling and language modeling are important parts of modern statistically-based speech recognition algorithms. Hidden Markov models (HMMs) are widely used in many systems.

Language modeling is also used in many other natural language processing applications such as document classification or statistical machine translation.

Hidden Markov Models

Modern general-purpose speech recognition systems are based on Hidden Markov Models. These are statistical models that output a sequence of symbols or quantities. HMMs are used in speech recognition because a speech signal can be viewed as a piecewise stationary signal or a short-time stationary signal. In a short time-scale (e.g., 10 milliseconds), speech can be approximated as a stationary process. Speech can be thought of as a Markov model for many stochastic purposes.

Another reason why HMMs are popular is because they can be trained automatically and are simple and computationally feasible to use. In speech recognition, the hidden Markov model would output a sequence of n-dimensional real-valued vectors (with n being a small integer, such as 10), outputting one of these every 10 milliseconds. The vectors would consist of cepstral coefficients, which are obtained by taking a Fourier transform of a short time window of speech and decorrelating the spectrum using a cosine transform, then taking the first (most significant) coefficients. The hidden Markov model will tend to have in each state a statistical distribution that is a mixture of diagonal covariance Gaussians, which will give a likelihood for each observed vector. Each word, or (for more general speech recognition systems), each phoneme, will have a different output distribution; a hidden Markov model for a sequence of words or phonemes is made by concatenating the individual trained hidden Markov models for the separate words and phonemes.

Modern speech recognition systems use various combinations of a number of standard techniques in order to improve results over the basic approach described above. A typical large-vocabulary system would need context dependency for the phonemes (so phonemes with different left and right context have different realizations as HMM states); it would use cepstral normalization to normalize for different speaker and recording conditions; for further speaker normalization it might use vocal tract length normalization (VTLN) for male-female normalization and maximum likelihood linear regression (MLLR) for more general speaker adaptation. The features would have so-called delta and delta-delta coefficients to capture speech dynamics and in addition might use heteroscedastic linear discriminant analysis (HLDA); or might skip the delta and delta-delta coefficients and use splicing and an LDA-based projection followed perhaps by heteroscedastic linear discriminant analysis or a global semi-tied co variance transform (also known as maximum likelihood linear transform, or MLLT). Many systems use so-called discriminative training techniques that dispense with a purely statistical approach to HMM parameter estimation and instead optimize some classification-related measure of the training data. Examples are maximum mutual information (MMI), minimum classification error (MCE) and minimum phone error (MPE).

Decoding of the speech (the term for what happens when the system is presented with a new utterance and must compute the most likely source sentence) would probably use the Viterbi algorithm to find the best path, and here there is a choice between dynamically creating a combination hidden Markov model, which includes both the acoustic and language model information, and combining it statically beforehand (the finite state transducer, or FST, approach).

A possible improvement to decoding is to keep a set of good candidates instead of just keeping the best candidate, and to use a better scoring function (re scoring) to rate these good candidates so that we may pick the best one according to this refined score. The set of candidates can be kept either as a list (the N-best list approach) or as a subset of the models (a lattice). Re scoring is usually done by trying to minimize the Bayes risk (or an approximation thereof): Instead of taking the source sentence with maximal probability, we try to take the sentence that minimizes the expectancy of a given loss function with regards to all possible transcriptions (i.e., we take the sentence that minimizes the average distance to other possible sentences weighted by their estimated probability). The loss function is usually the Levenshtein distance, though it can be different distances for specific tasks; the set of possible transcriptions is, of course, pruned to maintain tractability. Efficient algorithms have been devised to re score lattices represented as weighted finite state transducers with edit distances represented themselves as a finite state transducer verifying certain assumptions.

Dynamic Time Warping (DTW)-based Speech Recognition

Dynamic time warping is an approach that was historically used for speech recognition but has now largely been displaced by the more successful HMM-based approach.

Dynamic time warping is an algorithm for measuring similarity between two sequences that may vary in time or speed. For instance, similarities in walking patterns would be detected, even if in one video the person was walking slowly and if in another he or she were walking more quickly, or even if there were accelerations and deceleration during the course of one observation. DTW has been applied to video, audio, and graphics – indeed, any data that can be turned into a linear representation can be analyzed with DTW.

A well-known application has been automatic speech recognition, to cope with different speaking speeds. In general, it is a method that allows a computer to find an optimal match between two given sequences (e.g., time series) with certain restrictions. That is, the sequences are "warped" non-linearly to match each other. This sequence alignment method is often used in the context of hidden Markov models.

Neural Networks

Neural networks emerged as an attractive acoustic modeling approach in ASR in the late 1980s. Since then, neural networks have been used in many aspects of speech recognition such as phoneme classification, isolated word recognition, audiovisual speech recognition, audiovisual speaker recognition and speaker adaptation.

Neural networks make fewer explicit assumptions about feature statistical properties than HMMs and have several qualities making them attractive recognition models for speech recognition. When used to estimate the probabilities of a speech feature segment, neural networks allow discriminative training in a natural and efficient manner. However, in spite of their effectiveness in classifying short-time units such as individual phonemes and isolated words, early neural networks were rarely successful for continuous recognition tasks because of their limited ability to model temporal dependencies.

One approach to this limitation was to use neural networks as a pre-processing, feature transformation or dimensionality reduction, step prior to HMM based recognition. However, more recently, LSTM and related recurrent neural networks (RNNs) and Time Delay Neural Networks (TDNN's) have demonstrated improved performance in this area.

Deep Feedforward and Recurrent Neural Networks

Deep Neural Networks and Denoising Autoencoders are also under investigation. A deep feed-forward neural network (DNN) is an artificial neural network with multiple hidden layers of units between the input and output layers. Similar to shallow neural networks, DNNs can model complex non-linear relationships. DNN architectures generate compositional models, where extra layers enable composition of features from lower layers, giving a huge learning capacity and thus the potential of modeling complex patterns of speech data.

A success of DNNs in large vocabulary speech recognition occurred in 2010 by industrial researchers, in collaboration with academic researchers, where large output layers of the DNN based on context dependent HMM states constructed by decision trees were adopted.

One fundamental principle of deep learning is to do away with hand-crafted feature engineering and to use raw features. This principle was first explored successfully in the architecture of deep autoencoder on the "raw" spectrogram or linear filter-bank features, showing its superiority over the Mel-Cepstral features which contain a few stages of fixed transformation from spectrograms. The true "raw" features of speech, waveforms, have more recently been shown to produce excellent larger-scale speech recognition results.

End-to-end Automatic Speech Recognition

Since 2014, there has been much research interest in "end-to-end" ASR. Traditional phonetic-based (i.e., all HMM-based model) approaches required separate components and training for the pronunciation, acoustic and language model. End-to-end models jointly learn all the components of the speech recognizer. This is valuable since it simplifies the training process and deployment process. For example, a n-gram language model is required for all HMM-based systems, and a typical n-gram language model often takes several gigabytes in memory making them impractical to deploy on mobile devices. Consequently, modern commercial ASR systems from Google and Apple (as of 2017) are deployed on the cloud and require a network connection as opposed to the device locally.

The first attempt at end-to-end ASR was with Connectionist Temporal Classification (CTC)-based systems introduced by Alex Graves of Google DeepMind and Navdeep Jaitly of the University of Toronto in 2014. The model consisted of recurrent neural networks and a CTC layer. Jointly, the RNN-CTC model learns the pronunciation and acoustic model together, however it is incapable of learning the language due to conditional independence assumptions similar to a HMM. Consequently, CTC models can directly learn to map speech acoustics to English characters, but the models make many common spelling mistakes and must rely on a separate language model to clean up the transcripts. Later, Baidu expanded on the work with extremely large datasets and demonstrated some commercial success in Chinese Mandarin and English. In 2016, University of Oxford presented LipNet, the first end-to-end sentence-level lip reading model, using spatiotemporal convolutions coupled with an RNN-CTC architecture, surpassing human-level performance in a restricted grammar dataset. A large-scale CNN-RNN-CTC architecture was presented in 2018 by Google DeepMind achieving 6 times better performance than human experts.

An alternative approach to CTC-based models are attention-based models. Attention-based ASR models were introduced simultaneously by Chan et al. of Carnegie Mellon University and Google Brain and Bahdanau et al. of the University of Montreal in 2016. The model named "Listen, Attend and Spell" (LAS), literally "listens" to the acoustic signal, pays "attention" to different parts of the signal and "spells" out the transcript one character at a time. Unlike CTC-based models, attention-based models do not have conditional-independence assumptions and can learn all the components of a speech recognizer including the pronunciation, acoustic and language model directly. This means, during deployment, there is no need to carry around a language model making it very practical for deployment onto applications with limited memory. By the end of 2016, the attention-based models have seen considerable success including outperforming the CTC models (with or without an external language model). Various extensions have been proposed since the original LAS model. Latent Sequence Decompositions (LSD) was proposed by Carnegie Mellon University, MIT and Google Brain to directly emit sub-word units which are more natural than English characters; University of Oxford and Google DeepMind extended LAS to "Watch, Listen, Attend and Spell" (WLAS) to handle lip reading surpassing human-level performance.

Applications

In-car Systems

Typically a manual control input, for example by means of a finger control on the steering-wheel, enables the speech recognition system and this is signalled to the driver by an audio prompt. Following the audio prompt, the system has a "listening window" during which it may accept a speech input for recognition.

Simple voice commands may be used to initiate phone calls, select radio stations or play music from a compatible smartphone, MP3 player or music-loaded flash drive. Voice recognition capabilities vary between car make and model. Some of the most recentcar models offer natural-language speech recognition in place of a fixed set of commands, allowing the driver to use full sentences and common phrases. With such systems there is, therefore, no need for the user to memorize a set of fixed command words.

Health Care

Medical Documentation

In the health care sector, speech recognition can be implemented in front-end or back-end of the medical documentation process. Front-end speech recognition is where the provider dictates into a speech-recognition engine, the recognized words are displayed as they are spoken, and the dictator is responsible for editing and signing off on the document. Back-end or deferred speech recognition is where the provider dictates into a digital dictation system, the voice is routed through a speech-recognition machine and the recognized draft document is routed along with the original voice file to the editor, where the draft is edited and report finalized. Deferred speech recognition is widely used in the industry currently.

One of the major issues relating to the use of speech recognition in healthcare is that the American Recovery and Reinvestment Act (ARRA) provides for substantial financial benefits to physicians who utilize an EMR according to "Meaningful Use" standards. These standards require that a substantial amount of data be maintained by the EMR (now more commonly referred to as an Electronic Health Record or EHR). The use of speech recognition is more naturally suited to the generation of narrative text, as part of a radiology/pathology interpretation, progress note or discharge summary: the ergonomic gains of using speech recognition to enter structured discrete data (e.g., numeric values or codes from a list or a controlled vocabulary) are relatively minimal for people who are sighted and who can operate a keyboard and mouse.

A more significant issue is that most EHRs have not been expressly tailored to take advantage of voice-recognition capabilities. A large part of the clinician's interaction with the EHR involves navigation through the user interface using menus, and tab/button clicks, and is heavily dependent on keyboard and mouse: voice-based navigation provides only modest ergonomic benefits. By contrast, many highly customized systems for radiology or pathology dictation implement voice "macros", where the use of certain phrases – e.g., "normal report", will automatically fill in a large number of default values and/or generate boilerplate, which will vary with the type of the exam – e.g., a chest X-ray vs. a gastrointestinal contrast series for a radiology system.

As an alternative to this navigation by hand, cascaded use of speech recognition and information extraction has been studied as a way to fill out a handover form for clinical proofing and sign-off. The results are encouraging, and the paper also opens data, together with the related performance benchmarks and some processing software, to the research and development community for studying clinical documentation and language-processing.

Therapeutic Use

Prolonged use of speech recognition software in conjunction with word processors has shown benefits to short-term-memory restrengthening in brain AVM patients who have been treated with resection. Further research needs to be conducted to determine cognitive benefits for individuals whose AVMs have been treated using radiologic techniques.

Military

High-Performance Fighter Aircraft

Substantial efforts have been devoted in the last decade to the test and evaluation of speech recognition in fighter aircraft. Of particular note have been the US program in speech recognition for the Advanced Fighter Technology Integration (AFTI)/F-16 aircraft (F-16 VISTA), the program in France for Mirage aircraft, and other programs in the UK dealing with a variety of aircraft platforms. In these programs, speech recognizers have been operated successfully in fighter aircraft, with applications including: setting radio frequencies, commanding an autopilot system, setting steer-point coordinates and weapons release parameters, and controlling flight display.

Working with Swedish pilots flying in the JAS-39 Gripen cockpit, Englund found recognition deteriorated with increasing g-loads. The report also concluded that adaptation greatly improved the results in all cases and that the introduction of models for breathing was shown to improve recognition scores significantly. Contrary to what might have been expected, no effects of the broken English of the speakers were found. It was evident that spontaneous speech caused problems for the recognizer, as might have been expected. A restricted vocabulary, and above all, a proper syntax, could thus be expected to improve recognition accuracy substantially.

The Eurofighter Typhoon, currently in service with the UK RAF, employs a speaker-dependent system, requiring each pilot to create a template. The system is not used for any safety-critical or weapon-critical tasks, such as weapon release or lowering of the undercarriage, but is used for a wide range of other cockpit functions. Voice commands are confirmed by visual and/or aural feedback. The system is seen as a major design feature in the reduction of pilot workload, and even allows the pilot to assign targets to his aircraft with two simple voice commands or to any of his wingmen with only five commands.

Speaker-independent systems are also being developed and are under test for the F35 Lightning II (JSF) and the Alenia Aermacchi M-346 Master lead-in fighter trainer. These systems have produced word accuracy scores in excess of 98%.

Helicopters

The problems of achieving high recognition accuracy under stress and noise pertain strongly to the helicopter environment as well as to the jet fighter environment. The acoustic noise problem is actually more severe in the helicopter environment, not only because of the high noise levels but also because the helicopter pilot, in general, does not wear a facemask, which would reduce acoustic noise in the microphone. Substantial test and evaluation programs have been carried out in the past decade in speech recognition systems applications in helicopters, notably by the U.S. Army Avionics Research and Development Activity (AVRADA) and by the Royal Aerospace Establishment (RAE) in the UK. Work in France has included speech recognition in the Puma helicopter. There has also been much useful work in Canada. Results have been encouraging, and voice applications have included: control of communication radios, setting of navigation systems, and control of an automated target handover system.

As in fighter applications, the overriding issue for voice in helicopters is the impact on pilot effectiveness. Encouraging results are reported for the AVRADA tests, although these represent only a feasibility demonstration in a test environment. Much remains to be done both in speech recognition and in overall speech technology in order to consistently achieve performance improvements in operational settings.

Training Air Traffic Controllers

Training for air traffic controllers (ATC) represents an excellent application for speech recognition systems. Many ATC training systems currently require a person to act as a "pseudo-pilot", engaging in a voice dialog with the trainee controller, which simulates the dialog that the controller would have to conduct with pilots in a real ATC situation. Speech recognition and synthesis techniques offer the potential to eliminate the need for a person to act as pseudo-pilot, thus reducing training and support personnel. In theory, Air controller tasks are also characterized by highly structured speech as the primary output of the controller, hence reducing the difficulty of the speech recognition task should be possible. In practice, this is rarely the case. The FAA document 7110.65 details the phrases that should be used by air traffic controllers. While this document gives less than 150 examples of such phrases, the number of phrases supported by one of the simulation vendors speech recognition systems is in excess of 500,000.

The USAF, USMC, US Army, US Navy, and FAA as well as a number of international ATC training organizations such as the Royal Australian Air Force and Civil Aviation Authorities in Italy, Brazil, and Canada are currently using ATC simulators with speech recognition from a number of different vendors.

Telephony and other Domains

ASR is now commonplace in the field of telephony and is becoming more widespread in the field of computer gaming and simulation. In telephony systems, ASR is now being predominantly used in contact centers by integrating it with IVR systems. Despite the high level of integration with word processing in general personal computing, in the field of document production, ASR has not seen the expected increases in use.

The improvement of mobile processor speeds has made speech recognition practical in smartphones. Speech is used mostly as a part of a user interface, for creating predefined or custom speech commands.

Usage in Education and Daily Life

For language learning, speech recognition can be useful for learning a second language. It can teach proper pronunciation, in addition to helping a person develop fluency with their speaking skills.

Students who are blind or have very low vision can benefit from using the technology to convey words and then hear the computer recite them, as well as use a computer by commanding with their voice, instead of having to look at the screen and keyboard.

Students who are physically disabled or suffer from Repetitive strain injury/other injuries to the upper extremities can be relieved from having to worry about handwriting, typing, or working with scribe on school assignments by using speech-to-text programs. They can also utilize speech recognition technology to freely enjoy searching the Internet or using a computer at home without having to physically operate a mouse and keyboard.

Speech recognition can allow students with learning disabilities to become better writers. By saying the words aloud, they can increase the fluidity of their writing, and be alleviated of concerns regarding spelling, punctuation, and other mechanics of writing.

Use of voice recognition software, in conjunction with a digital audio recorder and a personal computer running word-processing software has proven to be positive for restoring damaged short-term-memory capacity, in stroke and craniotomy individuals.

People with Disabilities

People with disabilities can benefit from speech recognition programs. For individuals that are Deaf or Hard of Hearing, speech recognition software is used to automatically generate a closed-captioning of conversations such as discussions in conference rooms, classroom lectures, and/or religious services.

Speech recognition is also very useful for people who have difficulty using their hands, ranging from mild repetitive stress injuries to involve disabilities that preclude using conventional computer input devices. In fact, people who used the keyboard a lot and developed RSI became an urgent early market for speech recognition. Speech recognition is used in deaf telephony, such as voicemail to text, relay services, and captioned telephone. Individuals with learning disabilities who have problems with thought-to-paper communication (essentially they think of an idea but it is processed incorrectly causing it to end up differently on paper) can possibly benefit from the software but the technology is not bug proof. Also the whole idea of speak to text can be hard for intellectually disabled person's due to the fact that it is rare that anyone tries to learn the technology to teach the person with the disability.

This type of technology can help those with dyslexia but other disabilities are still in question. The effectiveness of the product is the problem that is hindering it being effective. Although a kid may be able to say a word depending on how clear they say it the technology may think they are saying another word and input the wrong one. Giving them more work to fix, causing them to have to take more time with fixing the wrong word.

Further Applications

- Aerospace (e.g. space exploration, spacecraft, etc.) NASA's Mars Polar Lander used speech recognition technology from Sensory, Inc. in the Mars Microphone on the Lander,

- Automatic subtitling with speech recognition,

- Automatic emotion recognition,

- Automatic translation,

- Court reporting (Real time Speech Writing),

- eDiscovery (Legal discovery),

- Hands-free computing: Speech recognition computer user interface,

- Home automation,

- Interactive voice response,

- Mobile telephony, including mobile email,

- Multimodal interaction,

- Pronunciation evaluation in computer-aided language learning applications,

- Real Time Captioning,

- Robotics,

- Speech to text (transcription of speech into text, real time video captioning, Court reporting),

- Telematics (e.g. vehicle Navigation Systems),

- Transcription (digital speech-to-text),

- Video games, with *Tom Clancy's EndWar* and *Lifeline* as working examples,

- Virtual assistant (e.g. Apple's Siri).

Data Mining

Data mining is the process of discovering patterns in large data sets involving methods at the intersection of machine learning, statistics, and database systems. Data mining is an interdisciplinary subfield of computer science and statistics with an overall goal to extract information (with intelligent methods) from a data set and transform the information into a comprehensible structure for further use. Data mining is the analysis step of the "knowledge discovery in databases" process, or KDD. Aside from the raw analysis step, it also involves database and data management aspects, data pre-processing, model and inference considerations, interestingness metrics, complexity considerations, post-processing of discovered structures, visualization, and online updating. The difference between data analysis and data mining is that data analysis is used to test models and hypotheses on the dataset, e.g., analyzing the effectiveness of a marketing campaign, regardless of the amount of data; in contrast, data mining uses machine-learning and statistical models to uncover clandestine or hidden patterns in a large volume of data.

The term "data mining" is in fact a misnomer, because the goal is the extraction of patterns and knowledge from large amounts of data, not the extraction (*mining*) of data itself. It also is a buzzword and is frequently applied to any form of large-scale data or information processing(collection, extraction, warehousing, analysis, and statistics) as well as any application of computer decision support system, including artificial intelligence (e.g., machine learning) and business intelligence. The book *Data mining: Practical machine learning tools and techniques with Java* (which covers mostly machine learning material) was originally to be named just *Practical machine learning*, and the term *data mining* was only added for marketing reasons. Often the more general terms (*large scale*) *data analysis* and *analytics* – or, when referring to actual methods, *artificial intelligence* and *machine learning* – are more appropriate.

The actual data mining task is the semi-automatic or automatic analysis of large quantities of data to extract previously unknown, interesting patterns such as groups of data records (cluster analysis), unusual records (anomaly detection), and dependencies (association rule mining, sequential pattern mining). This usually involves using database techniques such as spatial indices. These patterns can then be seen as a kind of summary of the input data, and may be used in further analysis or, for example, in machine learning and predictive analytics. For example, the data mining step might identify multiple groups in the data, which can then be used to obtain more accurate prediction results by a decision support system. Neither the data collection, data preparation, nor result interpretation and reporting is part of the data mining step, but do belong to the overall KDD process as additional steps.

The related terms *data dredging*, *data fishing*, and *data snooping* refer to the use of data mining methods to sample parts of a larger population data set that are (or may be) too small for reliable statistical inferences to be made about the validity of any patterns discovered. These methods can, however, be used in creating new hypotheses to test against the larger data populations.

Process

The knowledge discovery in databases (KDD) *process* is commonly defined with the stages:

- Selection,
- Pre-processing,
- Transformation,
- Data mining,
- Interpretation/evaluation.

It exists, however, in many variations on this theme, such as the Cross-industry standard process for data mining (CRISP-DM) which defines six phases:

- Business understanding,
- Data understanding,
- Data preparation,
- Modeling,
- Evaluation,
- Deployment.

or a simplified process such as (1) Pre-processing, (2) Data Mining, and (3) Results Validation.

Polls conducted show that the CRISP-DM methodology is the leading methodology used by data miners.The only other data mining standard named in these polls was SEMMA. However, 3–4 times as many people reported using CRISP-DM. Several teams of researchers have published reviews of data mining process models, and Azevedo and Santos conducted a comparison of CRISP-DM and SEMMA in 2008.

Pre-processing

Before data mining algorithms can be used, a target data set must be assembled. As data mining can only uncover patterns actually present in the data, the target data set must be large enough to contain these patterns while remaining concise enough to be mined within an acceptable time limit. A common source for data is a data mart or data warehouse. Pre-processing is essential to analyze the multivariatedata sets before data mining. The target set is then cleaned. Data cleaning removes the observations containing noise and those with missing data.

Data Mining

Data mining involves six common classes of tasks:

- Anomaly detection (outlier/change/deviation detection): The identification of unusual data records, that might be interesting or data errors that require further investigation.

- Association rule learning (dependency modelling): Searches for relationships between variables. For example, a supermarket might gather data on customer purchasing habits. Using association rule learning, the supermarket can determine which products are frequently bought together and use this information for marketing purposes. This is sometimes referred to as market basket analysis.

- Clustering: Is the task of discovering groups and structures in the data that are in some way or another "similar", without using known structures in the data.

- Classification: Is the task of generalizing known structure to apply to new data. For example, an e-mail program might attempt to classify an e-mail as "legitimate" or as "spam".

- Regression: Attempts to find a function which models the data with the least error that is, for estimating the relationships among data or datasets.

- Summarization: Providing a more compact representation of the data set, including visualization and report generation.

Results Validation

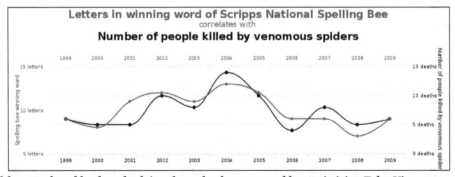

An example of data produced by data dredging through a bot operated by statistician Tyler Vigen, apparently showing a close link between the best word winning a spelling bee competition and the number of people in the United States killed by venomous spiders. The similarity in trends is obviously a coincidence.

Data mining can unintentionally be misused, and can then produce results which appear to be significant; but which do not actually predict future behavior and cannot be reproduced on a new sample of data and bear little use. Often this results from investigating too many hypotheses and not performing proper statistical hypothesis testing. A simple version of this problem in machine learningis known as overfitting, but the same problem can arise at different phases of the process and thus a train/test split - when applicable at all - may not be sufficient to prevent this from happening.

The final step of knowledge discovery from data is to verify that the patterns produced by the data mining algorithms occur in the wider data set. Not all patterns found by the data mining algorithms are necessarily valid. It is common for the data mining algorithms to find patterns in the training set which are not present in the general data set. This is called overfitting. To overcome this, the evaluation uses a test set of data on which the data mining algorithm was not trained. The learned patterns are applied to this test set, and the resulting output is compared to the desired output. For example, a data mining algorithm trying to distinguish "spam" from "legitimate" emails would be trained on a training set of sample e-mails. Once trained, the learned patterns would be applied to the test set of e-mails on which it had *not* been trained. The accuracy of the patterns can then be measured from how many e-mails they correctly classify. A number of statistical methods may be used to evaluate the algorithm, such as ROC curves.

If the learned patterns do not meet the desired standards, subsequently it is necessary to re-evaluate and change the pre-processing and data mining steps. If the learned patterns do meet the desired standards, then the final step is to interpret the learned patterns and turn them into knowledge.

The premier professional body in the field is the Association for Computing Machinery's (ACM) Special Interest Group (SIG) on Knowledge Discovery and Data Mining (SIGKDD). Since 1989, this ACM SIG has hosted an annual international conference and published its proceedings, and since 1999 it has published a biannual academic journal titled "SIGKDD Explorations".

Computer science conferences on data mining include:

- CIKM Conference: ACM Conference on Information and Knowledge Management.

- European Conference on Machine Learning and Principles and Practice of Knowledge Discovery in Databases.

- KDD Conference: ACM SIGKDD Conference on Knowledge Discovery and Data Mining.

Data mining topics are also present on many data management/database conferences such as the ICDE Conference, SIGMOD Conferenceand International Conference on Very Large Data Bases.

Standards

There have been some efforts to define standards for the data mining process, for example the 1999 European Cross Industry Standard Process for Data Mining (CRISP-DM 1.0) and the 2004 Java Data Mining standard (JDM 1.0). Development on successors to these processes (CRISP-DM 2.0 and JDM 2.0) was active in 2006, but has stalled since. JDM 2.0 was withdrawn without reaching a final draft.

For exchanging the extracted models – in particular for use in predictive analytics – the key standard is the Predictive Model Markup Language (PMML), which is an XML-based language developed by the Data Mining Group (DMG) and supported as exchange format by many data mining applications. As the name suggests, it only covers prediction models, a particular data mining task of high importance to business applications. However, extensions to cover (for example) subspace clustering have been proposed independently of the DMG.

Privacy Concerns and Ethics

While the term "data mining" itself may have no ethical implications, it is often associated with the mining of information in relation to peoples' behavior.

The ways in which data mining can be used can in some cases and contexts raise questions regarding privacy, legality, and ethics. In particular, data mining government or commercial data sets for national security or law enforcement purposes, such as in the Total Information Awareness Program or in ADVISE, has raised privacy concerns.

Data mining requires data preparation which can uncover information or patterns which may compromise confidentiality and privacy obligations. A common way for this to occur is through data aggregation. Data aggregation involves combining data together (possibly from various sources) in a way that facilitates analysis (but that also might make identification of private, individual-level data deducible or otherwise apparent). This is not data mining *per se*, but a result of the preparation of data before – and for the purposes of – the analysis. The threat to an individual's privacy comes into play when the data, once compiled, cause the data miner, or anyone who has access to the newly compiled data set, to be able to identify specific individuals, especially when the data were originally anonymous.

It is recommended that an individual is made aware of the following before data are collected:

- The purpose of the data collection and any (known) data mining projects;
- How the data will be used;
- Who will be able to mine the data and use the data and their derivatives;
- The status of security surrounding access to the data;
- How collected data can be updated.

Data may also be modified so as to *become* anonymous, so that individuals may not readily be identified. However, even "de-identified"/"anonymized" data sets can potentially contain enough information to allow identification of individuals, as occurred when journalists were able to find several individuals based on a set of search histories that were inadvertently released by AOL.

The inadvertent revelation of personally identifiable information leading to the provider violates Fair Information Practices. This indiscretion can cause financial, emotional, or bodily harm to the indicated individual. In one instance of privacy violation, the patrons of Walgreens filed a lawsuit against the company in 2011 for selling prescription information to data mining companies who in turn provided the data to pharmaceutical companies.

Situation in Europe

Europe has rather strong privacy laws, and efforts are underway to further strengthen the rights of the consumers. However, the U.S.-E.U. Safe Harbor Principles currently effectively expose European users to privacy exploitation by U.S. companies. As a consequence of Edward Snowden's global surveillance disclosure, there has been increased discussion to revoke this agreement, as in particular the data will be fully exposed to the National Security Agency, and attempts to reach an agreement have failed.

Situation in the United States

In the United States, privacy concerns have been addressed by the US Congress via the passage of regulatory controls such as the Health Insurance Portability and Accountability Act (HIPAA). The HIPAA requires individuals to give their "informed consent" regarding information they provide and its intended present and future uses. According to an article in *Biotech Business Week*, in practice, HIPAA may not offer any greater protection than the longstanding regulations in the research arena,' says the AAHC. More importantly, the rule's goal of protection through informed consent is approach a level of incomprehensibility to average individuals." This underscores the necessity for data anonymity in data aggregation and mining practices.

U.S. information privacy legislation such as HIPAA and the Family Educational Rights and Privacy Act (FERPA) applies only to the specific areas that each such law addresses. Use of data mining by the majority of businesses in the U.S. is not controlled by any legislation.

Copyright Law

Situation in Europe

Due to a lack of flexibilities in European copyright and database law, the mining of in-copyright works such as web mining without the permission of the copyright owner is not legal. Where a database is pure data in Europe there is likely to be no copyright, but database rights may exist so data mining becomes subject to regulations by the Database Directive. On the recommendation of the Hargreaves review this led to the UK government to amend its copyright law in 2014 to allow content mining as a limitation and exception. Only the second country in the world to do so after Japan, which introduced an exception in 2009 for data mining. However, due to the restriction of the Copyright Directive, the UK exception only allows content mining for non-commercial purposes. UK copyright law also does not allow this provision to be overridden by contractual terms and conditions. The European Commission facilitated stakeholder discussion on text and data mining in 2013, under the title of Licences for Europe. The focus on the solution to this legal issue being licences and not limitations and exceptions led to representatives of universities, researchers, libraries, civil society groups and open access publishers to leave the stakeholder dialogue in May 2013.

Situation in the United States

By contrast to Europe, the flexible nature of US copyright law, and in particular fair use means that content mining in America, as well as other fair use countries such as Israel, Taiwan and South Korea is viewed as being legal. As content mining is transformative, that is it does not supplant the original work, it is viewed as being lawful under fair use. For example, as part of the Google Book settlement the presiding judge on the case ruled that Google's digitisation project of in-copyright books was lawful, in part because of the transformative uses that the digitization project displayed - one being text and data mining.

Software

Free Open-source Data Mining Software and Applications

The following applications are available under free/open source licenses. Public access to application source code is also available:

- Carrot2: Text and search results clustering framework.

- Chemicalize.org: A chemical structure miner and web search engine.

- ELKI: A university research project with advanced cluster analysis and outlier detection methods written in the Java language.

- GATE: A natural language processing and language engineering tool.

- KNIME: The Konstanz Information Miner, a user friendly and comprehensive data analytics framework.

- Massive Online Analysis (MOA): A real-time big data stream mining with concept drift tool in the Java programming language.

- MEPX: cross platform tool for regression and classification problems based on a Genetic Programming variant.

- ML-Flex: A software package that enables users to integrate with third-party machine-learning packages written in any programming language, execute classification analyses in parallel across multiple computing nodes, and produce HTML reports of classification results.

- Mlpack: A collection of ready-to-use machine learning algorithms written in the C++ language.

- NLTK (Natural Language Toolkit): A suite of libraries and programs for symbolic and statistical natural language processing (NLP) for the Python language.

- OpenNN: Open neural networks library.

- Orange: A component-based data mining and machine learning software suite written in the Python language.

- R: A programming language and software environment for statistical computing, data mining, and graphics. It is part of the GNU Project.

- Scikit-learn is an open source machine learning library for the Python programming language.

- Torch: An open-source deep learning library for the Lua programming language and scientific computing framework with wide support for machine learning algorithms.

- UIMA: The UIMA (Unstructured Information Management Architecture) is a component framework for analyzing unstructured content such as text, audio and video – originally developed by IBM.

- Weka: A suite of machine learning software applications written in the Java programming language.

Proprietary Data-mining Software and Applications

The following applications are available under proprietary licenses:

- Angoss Knowledge STUDIO: Data mining tool.

- Clarabridge: Text analytics product.

- KXEN Modeler: Data mining tool provided by KXEN Inc.

- LIONsolver: An integrated software application for data mining, business intelligence, and modeling that implements the Learning and Intelligent OptimizatioN (LION) approach.

- Megaputer Intelligence: Data and text mining software is called PolyAnalyst.

- Microsoft Analysis Services: Data mining software provided by Microsoft.

- NetOwl: Suite of multilingual text and entity analytics products that enable data mining.

- OpenText Big Data Analytics: Visual Data Mining & Predictive Analysis by Open Text Corporation.

- Oracle Data Mining: Data mining software by Oracle Corporation.

- PSeven: Platform for automation of engineering simulation and analysis, multidisciplinary optimization and data mining provided by DATADVANCE.

- Qlucore Omics Explorer: Data mining software.

- RapidMiner: An environment for machine learning and data mining experiments.

- SAS Enterprise Miner: Data mining software provided by the SAS Institute.

- SPSS Modeler: Data mining software provided by IBM.

- STATISTICA Data Miner: Data mining software provided by StatSoft.

- Tanagra: Visualisation-oriented data mining software, also for teaching.

- Vertica: Data mining software provided by Hewlett-Packard.

Analysis of Marketplaces

Several researchers and organizations have conducted reviews of data mining tools and surveys of data miners. These identify some of the strengths and weaknesses of the software packages. They also provide an overview of the behaviors, preferences and views of data miners. Some of these reports include:

- Hurwitz Victory Index: Report for Advanced Analytics as a market research assessment tool, it highlights both the diverse uses for advanced analytics technology and the vendors who make those applications possible.Recent-research.

- Rexer Analytics Data Miner Surveys.

- 2011 Wiley Interdisciplinary Reviews: Data Mining and Knowledge Discovery.

- Forrester Research 2010 Predictive Analytics and Data Mining Solutions report.

- Gartner 2008 "Magic Quadrant" report.

- Robert A. Nisbet's 2006 Three Part Series of articles "Data Mining Tools: Which One is Best For CRM?".

- Haughton et al.'s 2003 Review of Data Mining Software Packages in *The American Statistician*.

- Goebel & Gruenwald 1999 "A Survey of Data Mining a Knowledge Discovery Software Tools" in SIGKDD Explorations.

Automation

Automation is the technology by which a process or procedure is performed with minimal human assistance. Automation or automatic control is the use of various control systemsfor operating equipment such as machinery, processes in factories, boilers and heat treating ovens, switching on telephone networks, steering and stabilization of ships, aircraft and other applications and vehicles with minimal or reduced human intervention.

Automation covers applications ranging from a household thermostat controlling a boiler, to a large industrial control system with ten of thousands of input measurements and output control signals. In control complexity, it can range from simple on-off control to multi-variable high-level algorithms.

In the simplest type of an automatic control loop, a controller compares a measured value of a process with a desired set value, and processes the resulting error signal to change some input to the process, in such a way that the process stays at its set point despite disturbances. This closed-loop control is an application of negative feedback to a system. The mathematical basis of control theory was begun in the 18th century and advanced rapidly in the 20th.

Automation has been achieved by various means including mechanical, hydraulic, pneumatic, electrical, electronic devices and computers, usually in combination. Complicated systems, such as modern factories, airplanes and ships typically use all these combined techniques. The benefit of automation includes labor savings, savings in electricity costs, savings in material costs, and improvements to quality, accuracy, and precision.

The World Bank's World Development Report shows evidence that the new industries and jobs in the technology sector outweigh the economic effects of workers being displaced by automation.

The term *automation*, inspired by the earlier word *automatic* (coming from *automaton*), was not widely used before 1947, when Ford established an automation department. It was during this time that industry was rapidly adopting feedback controllers, which were introduced in the early years.

Minimum human intervention is required to control many large facilities
such as this electrical generating station.

Open-loop and Closed-loop (Feedback) Control

Fundamentally, there are two types of control loop; open loop control, and closed loop feedback control.

In open loop control, the control action from the controller is independent of the "process output" (or "controlled process variable"). A good example of this is a central heating boiler controlled only by a timer, so that heat is applied for a constant time, regardless of the temperature of the building. (The control action is the switching on/off of the boiler. The process output is the building temperature).

In closed-loop control, the control action from the controller is dependent on the process output. In the case of the boiler analogy, this would include a thermostat to monitor the building temperature, and thereby feedback a signal to ensure the controller maintains the building at the temperature set on the thermostat. A closed loop controller, therefore, has a feedback loop which ensures the controller exerts a control action to give a process output the same as the "Reference input" or "set point". For this reason, closed-loop controllers are also called feedback controllers.

The definition of a closed loop control system according to the British Standard Institution is 'a control system possessing monitoring feedback, the deviation signal formed as a result of this feedback being used to control the action of a final control element in such a way as to tend to reduce the deviation to zero.'

Likewise, a *Feedback Control System* is a system which tends to maintain a prescribed relationship of one system variable to another by comparing functions of these variables and using the difference as a means of control. The advanced type of automation that revolutionized manufacturing, aircraft, communications, and other industries, is feedback control, which is usually *continuous* and involves taking measurements using a sensor and making calculated adjustments to keep the measured variable within a set range. The theoretical basis of closed-loop automation is control theory.

A flyball governor is an early example of a feedback control system. An increase in speed would make the counterweights move outward, sliding a linkage that tended to close the valve supplying steam, and so slowing the engine.

Control Actions

Discrete Control (on/off)

One of the simplest types of control is *on-off* control. An example is a thermostat used on household appliances which either opens or closes an electrical contact. (Thermostats were originally developed as true feedback-control mechanisms rather than the on-off common household appliance thermostat).

Sequence control, in which a programmed sequence of *discrete* operations is performed, often based on system logic that involves system states. An elevator control system is an example of sequence control.

PID Controller

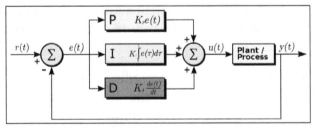

A block diagram of a PID controller in a feedback loop, r(t) is the desired process value or "set point", and y(t) is the measured process value.

A proportional–integral–derivative controller (PID controller) is a control loop feedback mechanism (controller) widely used in industrial control systems.

In a PID loop, the controller continuously calculates an *error value* as the difference between a desired setpoint and a measured process variable and applies a correction based on proportional, integral, and derivative terms, respectively (sometimes denoted P, I, and D) which give their name to the controller type.

The theoretical understanding and application dates from the 1920s, and they are implemented in nearly all analog control systems; originally in mechanical controllers, and then using discrete electronics and latterly in industrial process computers.

Sequential Control and Logical Sequence or System State Control

Sequential control may be either to a fixed sequence or to a logical one that will perform different actions depending on various system states. An example of an adjustable but otherwise fixed sequence is a timer on a lawn sprinkler.

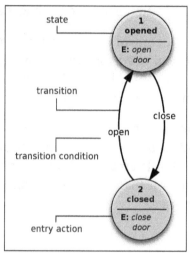

State Abstraction: This state diagram shows how UMLcan be used for designing a door system that can only be opened and closed.

States refer to the various conditions that can occur in a use or sequence scenario of the system. An example is an elevator, which uses logic based on the system state to perform certain actions in response to its state and operator input. For example, if the operator presses the floor n button, the system will respond depending on whether the elevator is stopped or moving, going up or down, or if the door is open or closed, and other conditions.

Early development of sequential control was relay logic, by which electrical relays engage electrical contacts which either start or interrupt power to a device. Relays were first used in telegraph networks before being developed for controlling other devices, such as when starting and stopping industrial-sized electric motors or opening and closing solenoid valves. Using relays for control purposes allowed event-driven control, where actions could be triggered out of sequence, in response to external events. These were more flexible in their response than the rigid single-sequence cam timers. More complicated examples involved maintaining safe sequences for devices such as swing bridge controls, where a lock bolt needed to be disengaged before the bridge could be moved, and the lock bolt could not be released until the safety gates had already been closed.

The total number of relays, cam timers, and drum sequencers can number into the hundreds or even thousands in some factories. Early programming techniques and languages were needed to make such systems manageable, one of the first being ladder logic, where diagrams of the interconnected relays resembled the rungs of a ladder. Special computers called programmable logic controllers were later designed to replace these collections of hardware with a single, more easily re-programmed unit.

In a typical hard wired motor start and stop circuit (called a *control circuit*) a motor is started by pushing a "Start" or "Run" button that activates a pair of electrical relays. The "lock-in" relay locks in contacts that keep the control circuit energized when the pushbutton is released. (The start button is a normally open contact and the stop button is normally closed contact.) Another relay energizes a switch that powers the device that throws the motor starter switch (three sets of contacts for three-phase industrial power) in the main power circuit. Large motors use high voltage and experience high in-rush current, making speed important in making and breaking contact. This can be dangerous for personnel and property with manual switches. The "lock-in" contacts in the start circuit and the main power contacts for the motor are held engaged by their respective electromagnets until a "stop" or "off" button is pressed, which de-energizes the lock in relay.

Commonly interlocks are added to a control circuit. Suppose that the motor in the example is powering machinery that has a critical need for lubrication. In this case, an interlock could be added to ensure that the oil pump is running before the motor starts. Timers, limit switches, and electric eyes are other common elements in control circuits.

Solenoid valves are widely used on compressed air or hydraulic fluid for powering actuators on mechanical components. While motors are used to supply continuous rotary motion, actuators are typically a better choice for intermittently creating a limited range of movement for a mechanical component, such as moving various mechanical arms, opening or closing valves, raising heavy press rolls, applying pressure to presses.

Computer Control

Computers can perform both sequential control and feedback control, and typically a single computer will do both in an industrial application. Programmable logic controllers (PLCs) are a type of special purpose microprocessor that replaced many hardware components such as timers and drum sequencers used in relay logic type systems. General purpose process control computers have increasingly replaced stand-alone controllers, with a single computer able to perform the operations of hundreds of controllers. Process control computers can process data from a network of PLCs, instruments, and controllers in order to implement typical (such as PID) control of many individual variables or, in some cases, to implement complex control algorithms using multiple inputs and mathematical manipulations. They can also analyze data and create real-time graphical displays for operators and run reports for operators, engineers, and management.

Control of an automated teller machine (ATM) is an example of an interactive process in which a computer will perform a logic derived response to a user selection based on information retrieved from a networked database. The ATM process has similarities with other online transaction processes. The different logical responses are called *scenarios*. Such processes are typically designed with the aid of use casesand flowcharts, which guide the writing of the software code. The earliest feedback control mechanism was the water clock invented by Greek engineer Ctesibius.

Advantages and Disadvantages

Perhaps the most cited advantage of automation in industry is that it is associated with faster production and cheaper labor costs. Another benefit could be that it replaces hard, physical, or monotonous work. Additionally, tasks that take place in hazardous environments or that are otherwise beyond human capabilities can be done by machines, as machines can operate even under extreme temperatures or in atmospheres that are radioactive or toxic. They can also be maintained with simple quality checks. However, at the time being, not all tasks can be automated, and some tasks are more expensive to automate than others. Initial costs of installing the machinery in factory settings are high, and failure to maintain a system could result in the loss of the product itself. Moreover, some studies seem to indicate that industrial automation could impose ill effects beyond operational concerns, including worker displacement due to systemic loss of employment and compounded environmental damage; however, these findings are both convoluted and controversial in nature, and could potentially be circumvented.

The main advantages of automation are:

- Increased throughput or productivity.

- Improved quality or increased predictability of quality.

- Improved robustness (consistency), of processes or product.

- Increased consistency of output.

- Reduced direct human labor costs and expenses.

- Installation in operations reduces cycle time.

- Can complete tasks where a high degree of accuracy is required.

- Replaces human operators in tasks that involve hard physical or monotonous work (e.g., using one forklift with a single driver instead of a team of multiple workers to lift a heavy object).

- Reduces some occupational injuries (e.g., fewer strained backs from lifting heavy objects).

- Replaces humans in tasks done in dangerous environments (i.e. fire, space, volcanoes, nuclear facilities, underwater, etc).

- Performs tasks that are beyond human capabilities of size, weight, speed, endurance, etc.

- Reduces operation time and work handling time significantly.

- Frees up workers to take on other roles.

- Provides higher level jobs in the development, deployment, maintenance and running of the automated processes.

The main disadvantages of automation are:

- Possible security threats/vulnerability due to increased relative susceptibility for committing errors.

- Unpredictable or excessive development costs.

- High initial cost.

- Displaces workers due to job replacement.

Societal Impact

Increased automation often cause workers to feel anxious about losing their jobs as technology renders their skills or experience unnecessary. Early in the Industrial Revolution, when inventions like the steam engine were making some job categories expendable, workers forcefully resisted these changes. Luddites, for instance, were English textile workers who protested the introduction of weaving machines by destroying them. Similar movements have sprung up periodically ever since. For most of the nineteenth and twentieth centuries, the most influential of these movements were led by organized labor, which advocated for the retraining of workers whose jobs were rendered redundant by machines. More recently, some residents of Chandler, Arizona, have slashed tires and pelted rocks at driver-less cars, in protest over the cars' perceived threat to human safety and job prospects.

The relative anxiety about automation reflected in opinion polls seems to correlate closely with the strength of organized labor in that region or nation. For example, while a study by the Pew Research Center indicated that 72% of Americans are worried about increasing automation in the workplace, 80% of Swedes see automation and artificial intelligence as a good thing, due to the country's still-powerful unions and a more robust national safety net.

Automation is already contributing significantly to unemployment, particularly in nations where the government does not proactively seek to diminish its impact. In the United States, 47% of all current jobs have the potential to be fully automated by 2033, according to the research of experts Carl Benedikt Frey and Michael Osborne. Furthermore, wages and educational attainment appear to be strongly negatively correlated with an occupation's risk of being automated. Prospects are particularly bleak for occupations that do not presently require a university degree, such as truck driving. Even in high-tech corridors like Silicon Valley, concern is spreading about a future in which a sizable percentage of adults have little chance of sustaining gainful employment. As the example of Sweden suggests, however, the transition to a more automated future need not inspire panic, if there is sufficient political will to promote the retraining of workers whose positions are being rendered obsolete.

Lights-out Manufacturing

Lights-out manufacturing is a production system with no human workers, to eliminate labor costs. Lights out manufacturing grew in popularity in the U.S. when General Motors in 1982 implemented humans "hands-off" manufacturing in order to "replace risk-averse bureaucracy with automation and robots". However, the factory never reached full "lights out" status.

The expansion of lights out manufacturing requires:

- Reliability of equipment,

- Long-term mechanic capabilities,

- Planned preventative maintenance,

- Commitment from the staff.

Health and Environment

The costs of automation to the environment are different depending on the technology, product or engine automated. There are automated engines that consume more energy resources from the Earth in comparison with previous engines and vice versa. Hazardous operations, such as oil refining, the manufacturing of industrial chemicals, and all forms of metal working, were always early contenders for automation.

The automation of vehicles could prove to have a substantial impact on the environment, although the nature of this impact could be beneficial or harmful depending on several factors. Because automated vehicles are much less likely to get into accidents compared to human-driven vehicles, some precautions built into current models (such as anti-lock brakes or laminated glass) would not be required for self-driving versions. Removing these safety features would also significantly reduce the weight of the vehicle, thus increasing fuel economyand reducing emissions per mile. Self-driving vehicles are also more precise with regard to acceleration and breaking, and this could contribute to reduced emissions. Self-driving cars could also potentially utilize fuel-efficient features such as route mapping that is able to calculate and take the most efficient routes. Despite this potential to reduce emissions, some researchers theorize that an increase of production of self-driving cars could lead to a boom of vehicle ownership and use. This boom could potentially negate any environmental benefits of self-driving cars if a large enough number of people begin driving personal vehicles more frequently.

Automation of homes and home appliances is also thought to impact the environment, but the benefits of these features are also questioned. A study of energy consumption of automated homes in Finland showed that smart homes could reduce energy consumption by monitoring levels of consumption in different areas of the home and adjusting consumption to reduce energy leaks (such as automatically reducing consumption during the nighttime when activity is low). This study, along with others, indicated that the smart home's ability to monitor and adjust consumption levels would reduce unnecessary energy usage. However, new research suggests that smart homes might not be as efficient as non-automated homes. A more recent study has indicated that, while monitoring and adjusting consumption levels does decrease unnecessary energy use, this process requires monitoring systems that also consume a significant amount of energy. This study suggested that the energy required to run these systems is so much so that it negates any benefits of the systems themselves, resulting in little to no ecological benefit.

Convertibility and Turnaround Time

Another major shift in automation is the increased demand for flexibility and convertibility in manufacturing processes. Manufacturers are increasingly demanding the ability to easily switch from manufacturing Product A to manufacturing Product B without having to completely rebuild the production lines. Flexibility and distributed processes have led to the introduction of Automated Guided Vehicles with Natural Features Navigation.

Digital electronics helped too. Former analog-based instrumentation was replaced by digital equivalents which can be more accurate and flexible, and offer greater scope for more sophisticated configuration, parametrization, and operation. This was accompanied by the fieldbusrevolution which provided a networked (i.e. a single cable) means of communicating between control systems and field level instrumentation, eliminating hard-wiring.

Discrete manufacturing plants adopted these technologies fast. The more conservative process industries with their longer plant life cycles have been slower to adopt and analog-based measurement and control still dominates. The growing use of Industrial Ethernet on the factory floor is pushing these trends still further, enabling manufacturing plants to be integrated more tightly within the enterprise, via the internet if necessary. Global competition has also increased demand for Reconfigurable Manufacturing Systems.

Automation Tools

Engineers can now have numerical control over automated devices. The result has been a rapidly expanding range of applications and human activities. Computer-aided technologies (or CAx) now serve as the basis for mathematical and organizational tools used to create complex systems. Notable examples of CAx include Computer-aided design (CAD software) and Computer-aided manufacturing (CAM software). The improved design, analysis, and manufacture of products enabled by CAx has been beneficial for industry.

Information technology, together with industrial machinery and processes, can assist in the design, implementation, and monitoring of control systems. One example of an industrial control system is a programmable logic controller (PLC). PLCs are specialized hardened computers which are frequently used to synchronize the flow of inputs from (physical) sensors and events with the flow of outputs to actuators and events.

An automated online assistant on a website, with an avatar for enhanced
human–computer interaction.

Human-machine interfaces (HMI) or computer human interfaces (CHI), formerly known as *man-machine interfaces*, are usually employed to communicate with PLCs and other computers. Service personnel who monitor and control through HMIs can be called by different names. In industrial process and manufacturing environments, they are called operators or something similar. In boiler houses and central utilities departments they are called stationary engineers.

Different types of automation tools exist:

- ANN – Artificial Neural Network,

- DCS – Distributed Control System,

- HMI – Human Machine Interface,

- SCADA – Supervisory Control and Data Acquisition,

- PLC – Programmable Logic Controller,

- Instrumentation,

- Motion control,

- Robotics.

Host simulation software (HSS) is a commonly used testing tool that is used to test the equipment software. HSS is used to test equipment performance with respect to factory automation standards (timeouts, response time, processing time).

Limitations to Automation

- Current technology is unable to automate all the desired tasks.

- Many operations using automation have large amounts of invested capital and produce high volumes of product, making malfunctions extremely costly and potentially hazardous. Therefore, some personnel are needed to ensure that the entire system functions properly and that safety and product quality are maintained.

- As a process becomes increasingly automated, there is less and less labor to be saved or quality improvement to be gained. This is an example of both diminishing returns and the logistic function.

- As more and more processes become automated, there are fewer remaining non-automated processes. This is an example of the exhaustion of opportunities. New technological paradigms may, however, set new limits that surpass the previous limits.

Current Limitations

Many roles for humans in industrial processes presently lie beyond the scope of automation. Human-level pattern recognition, language comprehension, and language production ability are well beyond the capabilities of modern mechanical and computer systems. Tasks requiring subjective assessment or synthesis of complex sensory data, such as scents and sounds, as well as high-level tasks such as strategic planning, currently require human expertise. In many cases, the use of humans is more cost-effective than mechanical approaches even where the automation of industrial tasks is possible. Overcoming these obstacles is a theorized path to post-scarcity economics.

Paradox of Automation

The paradox of automation says that the more efficient the automated system, the more crucial the human contribution of the operators. Humans are less involved, but their involvement becomes more critical.

If an automated system has an error, it will multiply that error until it is fixed or shut down. This is where human operators come in.

A fatal example of this was Air France Flight 447, where a failure of automation put the pilots into a manual situation they were not prepared for.

Cognitive Automation

Cognitive automation, as a subset of artificial intelligence, is an emerging genus of automation enabled by cognitive computing. Its primary concern is the automation of clerical tasks and work-flows that consist of structuring unstructured data.

Cognitive automation relies on multiple disciplines: natural language processing, real-time computing, machine learning algorithms, big data analytics, and evidence-based learning. According to Deloitte, cognitive automation enables the replication of human tasks and judgment "at rapid speeds and considerable scale."

Such tasks include:

- Document redaction,

- Data extraction and document synthesis / reporting,

- Contract management,

- Natural language search,

- Customer, employee, and stakeholder onboarding,

- Manual activities and verifications,

- Follow up and email communications.

Recent and Emerging Applications

Automated Power Production

Technologies like solar panels, wind turbines, and other renewable energy sources, together with smart grids, micro-grids, battery storage - can automate power production.

Automated Retail

Food and Drink

The food retail industry has started to apply automation to the ordering process; McDonald's has introduced touch screen ordering and payment systems in many of its restaurants, reducing the need for as many cashier employees. The University of Texas at Austin has introduced fully automated cafe retail locations. Some Cafes and restaurants have utilized mobile and tablet "apps" to make the ordering process more efficient by customers ordering and paying on their device. Some restaurants have automated food delivery to customers tables using a Conveyor belt system. The use of robots is sometimes employed to replace waiting staff.

KUKA industrial robots being used at a bakery for food production.

Stores

Many supermarkets and even smaller stores are rapidly introducing Self checkout systems reducing the need for employing checkout workers. In the United States, the retail industry employs 15.9 million people as of 2017 (around 1 in 9 Americans in the workforce). Globally, an estimated 192 million workers could be affected by automation according to research by Eurasia Group.

Online shopping could be considered a form of automated retail as the payment and checkout are through an automated Online transaction processing system, with the share of online retail accounting jumping from 5.1% in 2011 to 8.3% in 2016. However, two-thirds of books, music, and films are now purchased online. In addition, automation and online shopping could reduce demands for shopping malls, and retail property, which in America is currently estimated to account for 31% of all commercial property or around 7 billion square feet. Amazon has gained much of the growth in recent years for online shopping, accounting for half of the growth in online retail in 2016.Other forms of automation can also be an integral part of online shopping, for example, the deployment of automated warehouse robotics such as that applied by Amazon using Kiva Systems.

Automated Mining

Automated mining involves the removal of human labor from the mining process. The mining industry is currently in the transition towards automation. Currently, it can still require a large amount of human capital, particularly in the third world where labor costs are low so there is less incentive for increasing efficiency through automation.

Automated Video Surveillance

The Defense Advanced Research Projects Agency (DARPA) started the research and development of automated visual surveillance and monitoring (VSAM) program, between 1997 and 1999, and airborne video surveillance (AVS) programs, from 1998 to 2002. Currently, there is a major effort underway in the vision community to develop a fully automated tracking surveillance system. Automated video surveillance monitors people and vehicles in real time within a busy environment. Existing automated surveillance systems are based on the environment they are primarily designed to observe, i.e., indoor, outdoor or airborne, the number of sensors that the automated system can handle and the mobility of sensor, i.e., stationary camera vs. mobile camera. The purpose of a surveillance system is to record properties and trajectories of objects in a given area, generate warnings or notify designated authority in case of occurrence of particular events.

Automated Highway Systems

As demands for safety and mobility have grown and technological possibilities have multiplied, interest in automation has grown. Seeking to accelerate the development and introduction of fully automated vehicles and highways, the United States Congress authorized more than $650 million over six years for intelligent transport systems (ITS) and demonstration projects in the 1991 Intermodal Surface Transportation Efficiency Act (ISTEA). Congress legislated in ISTEA that "the Secretary of Transportation shall develop an automated highway and vehicle prototype from which future fully automated intelligent vehicle-highway systems can be developed. Such development shall include research in human factors to ensure the success of the man-machine relationship. The goal of this program is to have the first fully automated highway roadway or an automated test track in operation by 1997. This system shall accommodate installation of equipment in new and existing motor vehicles."

Full automation commonly defined as requiring no control or very limited control by the driver; such automation would be accomplished through a combination of sensor, computer, and communications systems in vehicles and along the roadway. Fully automated driving would, in theory, allow closer vehicle spacing and higher speeds, which could enhance traffic capacity in places where additional road building is physically impossible, politically unacceptable, or prohibitively expensive. Automated controls also might enhance road safety by reducing the opportunity for driver error, which causes a large share of motor vehicle crashes. Other potential benefits include improved air quality (as a result of more-efficient traffic flows), increased fuel economy, and spin-off technologies generated during research and development related to automated highway systems.

Automated Waste Management

Automated side loader operation.

Automated waste collection trucks prevent the need for as many workers as well as easing the level of labor required to provide the service.

Business Process Automation

Business process automation (BPA) is the technology-enabled automation of complex business processes. It can help to streamline a business for simplicity, achieve digital transformation, increase service quality, improve service delivery or contain costs. BPA consists of integrating applications, restructuring labor resources and using software applications throughout the organization. Robotic process automation is an emerging field within BPA and uses artificial intelligence. BPAs can be implemented in a number of business areas including marketing, sales and workflow.

Home Automation

Home automation (also called domotics) designates an emerging practice of increased automation of household appliances and features in residential dwellings, particularly through electronic means that allow for things impracticable, overly expensive or simply not possible in recent past decades. The rise in the usage of home automation solutions has taken a turn reflecting the increased dependency of people on such automation solutions. However, the increased comfort that gets added through these automation solutions is remarkable.

Laboratory Automation

Automation is essential for many scientific and clinical applications. Therefore, automation has been extensively employed in laboratories. From as early as 1980 fully automated laboratories have already been working. However, automation has not become widespread in laboratories due to its high cost. This may change with the ability of integrating low-cost devices with standard laboratory equipment. Autosamplers are common devices used in laboratory automation.

Automated laboratory instrument.

Industrial Automation

Industrial automation deals primarily with the automation of manufacturing, quality control and material handling processes. General purpose controllers for industrial processes include Programmable logic controllers, stand-alone I/O modules, and computers. Industrial automation is to replace the decision making of humans and manual command-response activities with the use of mechanized equipment and logical programming commands. One trend is increased use of Machine vision to provide automatic inspection and robot guidance functions, another is a continuing increase in the use of robots. Industrial automation is simply required in industries.

The integration of control and information across the enterprise enables industries to optimize industrial process operations.

Energy efficiency in industrial processes has become a higher priority. Semiconductor companies like Infineon Technologies are offering 8-bit micro-controller applications for example found in motor controls, general purpose pumps, fans, and ebikes to reduce energy consumption and thus increase efficiency.

Industrial Automation and Industry 4.0

The rise of industrial automation is directly tied to the "Fourth Industrial Revolution", which is better known now as Industry 4.0. Originating from Germany, Industry 4.0 encompasses numerous devices, concepts, and machines. It, along with the advancement of the Industrial Internet of Things (formally known as the IoT or IIoT) which is "Internet of Things is a seamless integration of diverse physical objects in the Internet through a virtual representation". These new revolutionary advancements have drawn attention to the world of automation in an entirely new light and shown ways for it to grow to increase productivity and efficiency in machinery and manufacturing facilities. Industry 4.0 works with the IIoT and software/hardware to connect in a way that (through communication technologies) add enhancements and improve manufacturing processes. Being able to create smarter, safer, and more advanced manufacturing is now possible with these new technologies. It opens up a manufacturing platform that is more reliable, consistent, and efficient than before. Implementation of systems such as SCADA is an example of software that takes place in Industrial Automation today. SCADA is a supervisory data collection software, just one of the many used in Industrial Automation. Industry 4.0 vastly covers many areas in manufacturing and will continue to do so as time goes on.

Industrial Robotics

Industrial robotics is a sub-branch in the industrial automation that aids in various manufacturing processes. Such manufacturing processes include; machining, welding, painting, assembling and material handling to name a few. Industrial robots utilizes various mechanical, electrical as well as software systems to allow for high precision, accuracy and speed that far exceeds any human performance. The birth of industrial robot came shortly after World War II as the United States saw the need for a quicker way to produce industrial and consumer goods. Servos, digital logic and solid-state electronics allowed engineers to build better and faster systems and overtime these systems were improved and revised to the point where a single robot is capable of running 24 hours a day with little or no maintenance. In 1997, there were 700,000 industrial robots in use, the number has risen to 1.8M in 2017 In recent years, artificial intelligence (AI) with robotics are also used in creating an automatic labelling solution, using robotic arms as the automatic label applicator, and AI for learning and detecting the products to be labelled.

Automated milling machines.

Programmable Logic Controllers

Industrial automation incorporates programmable logic controllers in the manufacturing process. Programmable logic controllers (PLCs) use a processing system which allows for variation of controls of inputs and outputs using simple programming. PLCs make use of programmable memory, storing instructions and functions like logic, sequencing, timing, counting, etc. Using a logic-based language, a PLC can receive a variety of inputs and return a variety of logical outputs, the input devices being sensors and output devices being motors, valves, etc. PLCs are similar to computers, however, while computers are optimized for calculations, PLCs are optimized for control task and use in industrial environments. They are built so that only basic logic-based programming knowledge is needed and to handle vibrations, high temperatures, humidity, and noise. The greatest advantage PLCs offer is their flexibility. With the same basic controllers, a PLC can operate a range of different control systems. PLCs make it unnecessary to rewire a system to change the control system. This flexibility leads to a cost-effective system for complex and varied control systems.

Siemens Simatic S7-400 system in a rack, left-to-right: power supply unit (PSU), CPU, interface module (IM) and communication processor (CP).

PLCs can range from small "building brick" devices with tens of I/O in a housing integral with the processor, to large rack-mounted modular devices with a count of thousands of I/O, and which are often networked to other PLC and SCADA systems.

They can be designed for multiple arrangements of digital and analog inputs and outputs (I/O), extended temperature ranges, immunity to electrical noise, and resistance to vibration and impact. Programs to control machine operation are typically stored in battery-backed-up or non-volatile memory.

It was from the automotive industry in the USA that the PLC was born. Before the PLC, control, sequencing, and safety interlock logic for manufacturing automobiles was mainly composed of relays, cam timers, drum sequencers, and dedicated closed-loop controllers. Since these could number in the hundreds or even thousands, the process for updating such facilities for the yearly model change-over was very time consuming and expensive, as electricians needed to individually rewire the relays to change their operational characteristics.

When digital computers became available, being general-purpose programmable devices, they were soon applied to control sequential and combinatorial logic in industrial processes. However, these early computers required specialist programmers and stringent operating environmental control for temperature, cleanliness, and power quality. To meet these challenges this the PLC was developed with several key attributes. It would tolerate the shop-floor environment, it would support discrete (bit-form) input and output in an easily extensible manner, it would not require years of training to use, and it would permit its operation to be monitored. Since many industrial processes have timescales easily addressed by millisecond response times, modern (fast, small, reliable) electronics greatly facilitate building reliable controllers, and performance could be traded off for reliability.

Agent-assisted Automation

Agent-assisted automation refers to automation used by call center agents to handle customer inquiries. There are two basic types: desktop automation and automated voice solutions. Desktop automation refers to software programming that makes it easier for the call center agent to work across multiple desktop tools. The automation would take the information entered into one tool and populate it across the others so it did not have to be entered more than once, for example. Automated voice solutions allow the agents to remain on the line while disclosures and other important information is provided to customers in the form of pre-recorded audio files. Specialized applications of these automated voice solutions enable the agents to process credit cards without ever seeing or hearing the credit card numbers or CVV codes.

The key benefit of agent-assisted automation is compliance and error-proofing. Agents are sometimes not fully trained or they forget or ignore key steps in the process. The use of automation ensures that what is supposed to happen on the call actually does, every time.

Relationship to Unemployment

Research by Carl Benedikt Frey and Michael Osborne of the Oxford Martin School argued that employees engaged in "tasks following well-defined procedures that can easily be performed by sophisticated algorithms" are at risk of displacement, and 47 percent of jobs in the US were at risk. The study, released as a working paper in 2013 and published in 2017, predicted that automation would put low-paid physical occupations most at risk, by surveying a group of colleagues on their opinions. However, according to a study published in McKinsey Quarterly in 2015 the impact of computerization in most cases is not the replacement of employees but automation of portions of the tasks they perform. The methodology of the McKinsey study has been heavily criticized for being intransparent and relying on subjective assessments. The methodology of Frey and Osborne has been subjected to criticism, as lacking evidence, historical awareness, or credible methodology. In addition the OECD, found that across the 21 OECD countries, 9% of jobs are automatable.

The Obama White House has pointed out that every 3 months "about 6 percent of jobs in the economy are destroyed by shrinking or closing businesses, while a slightly larger percentage of jobs are added". A recent MIT economics study of automation in the United States from 1990 to 2007 found that there may be a negative impact on employment and wages when robots are introduced to an industry. When one robot is added per one thousand workers, the employment to population ratio decreases between 0.18–0.34 percentages and wages are reduced by 0.25–0.5 percentage points. During the time period studied, the US did not have many robots in the economy which restricts the impact of automation. However, automation is expected to triple (conservative estimate) or quadruple (a generous estimate) leading these numbers to become substantially higher.

Based on a formula by Gilles Saint-Paul, an economist at Toulouse 1 University, the demand for unskilled human capital declines at a slower rate than the demand for skilled human capital increases. In the long run and for society as a whole it has led to cheaper products, lower average work hours, and new industries forming (i.e., robotics industries, computer industries, design industries). These new industries provide many high salary skill-based jobs to the economy. By 2030, between 3 and 14 percent of the global workforce will be forced to switch job categories due to automation eliminating jobs in an entire sector. While the number of jobs lost to automation is often offset by jobs gained from technological advances, the same type of job loss is not the same one replaced and that leading to increasing unemployment in the lower-middle class. This occurs largely in the US and developed countries where technological advances contribute to higher demand for highly skilled labor but demand for middle-wage labor continues to fall. Economists call this trend "income polarization" where unskilled labor wages are driven down and skilled labor is driven up and it is predicted to continue in developed economies.

Machine Perception

Machine perception is the capability of a computer system to interpret data in a manner that is similar to the way humans use their senses to relate to the world around them. The basic method that the computers take in and respond to their environment is through the attached hardware. Until recently input was limited to a keyboard, or a mouse, but advances in technology, both in hardware and software, have allowed computers to take in sensory input in a way similar to humans.

Machine perception allows the computer to use this sensory input, as well as conventional computational means of gathering information, to gather information with greater accuracy and to present it in a way that is more comfortable for the user. These include computer vision, machine hearing, and machine touch.

The end goal of machine perception is to give machines the ability to see, feel and perceive the world as humans do and therefore for them to be able to explain in a human way why they are making their decisions, to warn us when it is failing and more importantly, the reason why it is failing.

Machine Vision

Computer vision is a field that includes methods for acquiring, processing, analyzing, and understanding images and high-dimensional data from the real world to produce numerical or symbolic information, e.g., in the forms of decisions. Computer vision has many applications already in use today such as facial recognition, geographical modeling, and even aesthetic judgment.

Machine Hearing

Machine hearing, also known as machine listening or computer audition, is the ability of a computer or machine to take in and process sound data such as music or speech. This area has a wide range of application including music recording and compression, speech synthesis, and speech recognition. Moreover, this technology allows the machine to replicate the human brain's ability to selectively focus in a specific sound against many other competing sounds and background noise. This particular ability is called "auditory scene analysis". The technology enables the machine to segment several streams occurring at the same time. Many commonly used devices such as a smartphones, voice translators, and cars make use of some form of machine hearing.

Machine Touch

Machine touch is an area of machine perception where tactile information is processed by a machine or computer. Applications include tactile perception of surface properties and dexterity whereby tactile information can enable intelligent reflexes and interaction with the environment.

Facial Recognition System

A facial recognition system is a technology capable of identifying or verifying a person from a digital image or a video frame from a video source. There are multiple methods in which facial recognition systems work, but in general, they work by comparing selected facial features from given image with faces within a database. It is also described as a Biometric Artificial Intelligence based application that can uniquely identify a person by analysing patterns based on the person's facial textures and shape.

Swiss European surveillance: face recognition and vehicle make,
model, color and license plate reader.

Close-up of the infrared illuminator. The light is invisible to the human eye,
but creates a day-like environment for the surveillance cameras.

While initially a form of computer application, it has seen wider uses in recent times on mobile platforms and in other forms of technology, such as robotics. It is typically used as access control in security systems and can be compared to other biometrics such as fingerprint or eye iris recognitionsystems. Although the accuracy of facial recognition system as a biometric technology is lower than iris recognition and fingerprint recognition, it is widely adopted due to its contactless and non-invasive process. Recently, it has also become popular as a commercial identification and marketing tool. Other applications include advanced human-computer interaction, video surveillance, automatic indexing of images, and video database, among others.

Application

Social Media

Social media platforms have adopted facial recognition capabilities to diversify their functionalities in order to attract a wider user base amidst stiff competition from different applications.

Founded in 2013, Looksery went on to raise money for its face modification app on Kickstarter. After successful crowdfunding, Lookserylaunched in October 2014. The application allows video chat with others through a special filter for faces that modifies the look of users. While there is image augmenting applications such as FaceTune and Perfect365, they are limited to static images, whereas Looksery allowed augmented reality to live videos. In late 2015, SnapChat purchased Looksery, which would then become its landmark lenses function.

SnapChat's animated lenses, which used facial recognition technology, revolutionized and redefined the selfie, by allowing users to add filters to change the way they look. The selection of filters changes every day, some examples include one that makes users look like an old and wrinkled version of themselves, one that airbrushes their skin, and one that places a virtual flower crown on top of their head. The dog filter is the most popular filter that helped propel the continual success of SnapChat, with popular celebrities such as Gigi Hadid, Kim Kardashian and the likes regularly posting videos of themselves with the dog filter.

DeepFace is a deep learning facial recognition system created by a research group at Facebook. It identifies human faces in digital images. It employs a nine-layer neural net with over 120 million connection weights, and was trained on four million images uploaded by Facebook users. The system is said to be 97% accurate, compared to 85% for the FBI's Next Generation Identification system. One of the creators of the software, Yaniv Taigman, came to Facebook via their acquisition of Face.com.

ID Verification Solutions

Emerging use of Facial recognition is in use of ID verification services. Many companies are working in the market now to provide these services to banks, ICOs, and other e-businesses.

Face ID

Apple introduced Face ID on the flagship iPhone X as a biometric authentication successor to the Touch ID, a fingerprint based system. Face ID has a facial recognition sensor that consists of two parts: a "Romeo" module that projects more than 30,000 infrared dots onto the user's face, and a "Juliet" module that reads the pattern. The pattern is sent to a local "Secure Enclave" in the device's central processing unit(CPU) to confirm a match with the phone owner's face. The facial pattern is not accessible by Apple. The system will not work with eyes closed, in an effort to prevent unauthorized access.

The technology learns from changes in a user's appearance, and therefore works with hats, scarves, glasses, and many sunglasses, beard and makeup.

It also works in the dark. This is done by using a "Flood Illuminator", which is a dedicated infrared flash that throws out invisible infrared light onto the user's face to properly read the 30,000 facial points.

Deployment in Security Services

Policing

The Australian Border Force and New Zealand Customs Service have set up an automated border processing system called SmartGate that uses face recognition, which compares the face of the traveller with the data in the e-passport microchip. All Canadian international airports use facial recognition as part of the Primary Inspection Kiosk program that compares a traveler face to their photo stored on the ePassport. This program first came to Vancouver International Airport in early 2017 and was rolled up to all remaining international airports in 2018-2019. The Tocumen International Airport in Panama operates an airport-wide surveillance system using hundreds of live face recognition cameras to identify wanted individuals passing through the airport.

Police forces in the United Kingdom have been trialling live facial recognition technology at public events since 2015. However, a recent report and investigation by Big Brother Watch found that these systems were up to 98% inaccurate.

National Security

The U.S. Department of State operates one of the largest face recognition systems in the world with a database of 117 million American adults, with photos typically drawn from driver's license photos. Although it is still far from completion, it is being put to use in certain cities to give clues as to who was in the photo. The FBI uses the photos as an investigative tool, not for positive identification. As of 2016, facial recognition was being used to identify people in photos taken by police in San Diego and Los Angeles (not on real-time video, and only against booking photos) and use was planned in West Virginia and Dallas.

In recent years Maryland has used face recognition by comparing people's faces to their driver's license photos. The system drew controversy when it was used in Baltimore to arrest unruly protesters after the death of Freddie Gray in police custody. Many other states are using or developing a similar system however some states have laws prohibiting its use.

The FBI has also instituted its Next Generation Identification program to include face recognition, as well as more traditional biometrics like fingerprints and iris scans, which can pull from both criminal and civil databases.

Automatic Facial Recognition systems resemble other mobile CCTV systems.

In 2017, Time & Attendance company ClockedIn released facial recognition as a form of attendance tracking for businesses and organizations looking to have a more automated system of keeping track of hours worked as well as for security and health and safety control.

In May 2017, a man was arrested using an automatic facial recognition (AFR) system mounted on a van operated by the South Wales Police. Ars Technica reported that "this appears to be the first time (AFR) has led to an arrest".

As of late 2017, China has deployed facial recognition and artificial intelligence technology in Xinjiang. Reporters visiting the region found surveillance cameras installed every hundred meters or so in several cities, as well as facial recognition checkpoints at areas like gas stations, shopping centers, and mosque entrances.

Additional uses

In addition to being used for security systems, authorities have found a number of other applications for face recognition systems. While earlier post-9/11 deployments were well-publicized trials, more recent deployments are rarely written about due to their covert nature.

At Super Bowl XXXV in January 2001, police in Tampa Bay, Florida used Viisage face recognition software to search for potential criminals and terrorists in attendance at the event. 19 people with minor criminal records were potentially identified.

In the 2000 Mexican presidential election, the Mexican government employed face recognition software to prevent voter fraud. Some individuals had been registering to vote under several different names, in an attempt to place multiple votes. By comparing new face images to those already in the voter database, authorities were able to reduce duplicate registrations. Similar technologies are being used in the United States to prevent people from obtaining fake identification cards and driver's licenses.

Face recognition has been leveraged as a form of biometric authentication for various computing platforms and devices; Android 4.0 "Ice Cream Sandwich" added facial recognition using a smartphone's front camera as a means of unlocking devices, while Microsoftintroduced face recognition login to its Xbox 360 video game console through its Kinect accessory, as well as Windows 10 via its "Windows Hello" platform (which requires an infrared-illuminated camera). Apple's iPhone X smartphone introduced facial recognition to the product line with its "Face ID" platform, which uses an infrared illumination system.

Face recognition systems have also been used by photo management software to identify the subjects of photographs, enabling features such as searching images by person, as well as suggesting photos to be shared with a specific contact if their presence were detected in a photo.

Facial recognition is used as added security in certain websites, phone applications, and payment methods.

The United States' popular music and country music celebrity Taylor Swift surreptitiously employed facial recognition technology at a concert in 2018. The camera was embedded in a kiosk near a ticket booth and scanned concert-goers as they entered the facility for known stalkers.

Advantages and Disadvantages

Compared to other Biometric Systems

One key advantage of a facial recognition system that it is able to person mass identification as it does not require the cooperation of the test subject to work. Properly designed systems installed in airports, multiplexes, and other public places can identify individuals among the crowd, without passers-by even being aware of the system.

However, as compared to other biometric techniques, face recognition may not be most reliable and efficient. Quality measures are very important in facial recognition systems as large degrees of variations are possible in face images. Factors such as illumination, expression, pose and noise during face capture can affect the performance of facial recognition systems. Among all biometric systems, facial recognition has the highest false acceptance and rejection rates, thus questions have been raised on the effectiveness of face recognition software in cases of railway and airport security.

Weaknesses

Ralph Gross, a researcher at the Carnegie Mellon Robotics Institute in 2008, describes one obstacle related to the viewing angle of the face: "Face recognition has been getting pretty good at full frontal faces and 20 degrees off, but as soon as you go towards profile, there've been problems."

Besides the pose variations, low-resolution face images are also very hard to recognize. This is one of the main obstacles of face recognition in surveillance systems.

Face recognition is less effective if facial expressions vary. A big smile can render the system less effective. For instance: Canada, in 2009, allowed only neutral facial expressions in passport photos.

There is also inconstancy in the datasets used by researchers. Researchers may use anywhere from several subjects to scores of subjects and a few hundred images to thousands of images. It is important for researchers to make available the datasets they used to each other, or have at least a standard dataset.

Data privacy is the main concern when it comes to storing biometrics data in companies. Data stores about face or biometrics can be accessed by the third party if not stored properly or hacked. In the Techworld, Parris adds (2017), "Hackers will already be looking to replicate people's faces to trick facial recognition systems, but the technology has proved harder to hack than fingerprint or voice recognition technology in the past."

Ineffectiveness

Critics of the technology complain that the London Borough of Newham scheme has, as of 2004, never recognized a single criminal, despite several criminals in the system's database living in the Borough and the system has been running for several years. "Not once, as far as the police know, has Newham's automatic face recognition system spotted a live target." This information seems to conflict with claims that the system was credited with a 34% reduction in crime (hence why it was rolled out to Birmingham also). However it can be explained by the notion that when the public is regularly told that they are under constant video surveillance with advanced face recognition technology, this fear alone can reduce the crime rate, whether the face recognition system technically works or does not. This has been the basis for several other face recognition based security systems, where the technology itself does not work particularly well but the user's perception of the technology does.

An experiment in 2002 by the local police department in Tampa, Florida, had similarly disappointing results.

A system at Boston's Logan Airport was shut down in 2003 after failing to make any matches during a two-year test period.

In 2014, Facebook stated that in a standardized two-option facial recognition test, its online system scored 97.25% accuracy, compared to the human benchmark of 97.5%.

In 2018, a report by the civil liberties and rights campaigning organisation Big Brother Watch revealed that two UK police forces, South Wales Police and the Metropolitan Police, were using live facial recognition at public events and in public spaces, but with an accuracy rate as low as 2%. Their report also warned of significant potential human rights violations. It received widespread press coverage in the UK.

Systems are often advertised as having accuracy near 100%; this is misleading as the studies often use much smaller sample sizes than would be necessary for large scale applications. Because facial recognition is not completely accurate, it creates a list of potential matches. A human operator must then look through these potential matches and studies show the operators pick the correct match out of the list only about half the time. This causes the issue of targeting the wrong suspect.

References

- Milan Sonka; Vaclav Hlavac; Roger Boyle (2008). Image Processing, Analysis, and Machine Vision. Thomson. ISBN 978-0-495-08252-1

- Artificial-intelligence-applications: edureka.co, Retrieved 21 July, 2019

- Machine Perception Research - ECE - Virginia Tech". Www.ECE.VT.edu. Retrieved January 10, 2018

- Bernd Jähne; Horst Haußecker (2000). Computer Vision and Applications, A Guide for Students and Practitioners. Academic Press. ISBN 978-0-13-085198-7

- Schmidhuber, Jürgen (2015). "Deep Learning". Scholarpedia. 10 (11): 32832. Bibcode:2015schpj..1032832S. Doi:10.4249/scholarpedia.32832

- Beigi, Homayoon (2011). Fundamentals of Speaker Recognition. New York: Springer. ISBN 978-0-387-77591-3. Archived from the original on 31 January 2018

- Clifton, Christopher (2010). "Encyclopædia Britannica: Definition of Data Mining". Retrieved 2010-12-09

4

Artificial Intelligence: Problems, Approaches, Advantages and Disadvantages

There are various approaches related to artificial intelligence including cybernetics and brain simulation, cognitive simulation, logic-based, knowledge-based, embodied intelligence, statistical learning, etc. These diverse approaches of artificial intelligence as well as its problems, advantages and disadvantages have been thoroughly discussed in this chapter.

Problems

Artificial intelligence (AI) is a broad term that incorporates everything from image recognition software to robotics. The maturity level of each of these technologies strongly varies. Nevertheless, the number of innovations and breakthroughs that have brought the power and efficiency of AI into various fields including medicine, shopping, finance, news, and advertising is only growing. All of the companies undertaking such initiatives had to undergo a number of changes. Introducing any technological change into an organization presents a different set of challenges.

Here are The Most Common Problems of Artificial Intelligence Implementation:

- Most development in a traditional systems environment follows the usual phases such as plan, analyze, design, build, test, and deploy. The AI environment is quite different. Most of the time, development is about identifying data sources and then gathering content, cleansing it and curating it. Such an approach requires different skills and mindsets, as well as different methodologies. In addition, AI-powered intellectual systems have to be trained in a particular domain. In case we compare conventional (regular) and AI programming, the differences will look the following way.

Attribute	Conventional programming	AI programming
Knowledge	Precise	Imprecise
Solutions sought	Optimal	Satisfactory
Definition Of Solution Steps/Tehinque	Exact/Algorithmic	Inexact/Heirostic search

Control/Data	Mixed	Separated
Processing	Numeric	Symbolic and concepts
Viewpoint	Quantitative	Plausible and logical reasoning
changes	Rare	Frequent

Generally speaking, with AI we are not developing a system but training, giving feedback and supervising an AI-powered solution.

- A system is only as good as the data it learns from: Everyone already knows that AI needs data to learn about things. AI and machine learning rely on enormous amounts of high-quality data from which to observe trends and behavior patterns, as well as being able to quickly adapt to improve the accuracy of the conclusions derived from the analysis of that data. Basically, first you get the data then you get the AI. Such systems don't just require more information than humans to understand concepts or recognize features, they require hundreds of thousands times more. Another important thing is the quality of data used to train predictive models. The data sets need to be extremely representative and balanced, otherwise, the system will eventually adopt bias that those data sets contain.

- No clear view on how insight is generated: Another of the problems of artificial intelligence is hiding in its experimental nature. It is difficult to say how much of an improvement it may bring to a project. Therefore it is almost impossible to predict ROI. This makes it really hard to get everyone to understand the whole concept. One thing that is necessary to optimize the result is a skilled team that can write or adapt publicly available algorithms, select the right algorithm for the desired result and combine algorithms as needed to optimize the result.

There are benefits and dark sides to every disruptive technology, and AI is no exception to this rule. The important thing for every company is to identify the challenges that lay before them and acknowledge the responsibility to make sure that they can take full advantage of the benefits while minimizing the tradeoffs that problems of artificial intelligence may impose.

Qualification Problem

In philosophy and AI (especially, knowledge-based systems), the qualification problem is concerned with the impossibility of listing all the preconditions required for a real-world action to have its intended effect. It might be posed as how to deal with the things that *prevent me from achieving my intended result*. It is strongly connected to, and opposite the ramification side of, the frame problem. John McCarthy gives the following motivating example , in which it is impossible to enumerate all the circumstances that may prevent a rowboat from performing its ordinary function:

"The successful use of a boat to cross a river requires, if the boat is a rowboat, that the oars and rowlocks be present and unbroken, and that they fit each other. Many other qualifications can be added, making the rules for using a rowboat almost impossible to apply, and yet anyone will still be able to think of additional requirements not yet stated."

Approaches

There is no established unifying theory or paradigm that guides AI research. Researchers disagree about many issues. A few of the most long standing questions that have remained unanswered are these: should artificial intelligence simulate natural intelligence by studying psychology or neurobiology? Or is human biology as irrelevant to AI research as bird biology is to aeronautical engineering? Can intelligent behavior be described using simple, elegant principles (such as logic or optimization)? Or does it necessarily require solving a large number of completely unrelated problems?

Cybernetics and Brain Simulation

In the 1940s and 1950s, a number of researchers explored the connection between neurobiology, information theory, and cybernetics. Some of them built machines that used electronic networks to exhibit rudimentary intelligence, such as W. Grey Walter's turtles and the Johns Hopkins Beast. Many of these researchers gathered for meetings of the Teleological Society at Princeton University and the Ratio Club in England. By 1960, this approach was largely abandoned, although elements of it would be revived in the 1980s.

Symbolic

When access to digital computers became possible in the middle 1950s, AI research began to explore the possibility that human intelligence could be reduced to symbol manipulation. The research was centered in three institutions: Carnegie Mellon University, Stanford and MIT, and as described below, each one developed its own style of research. John Haugeland named these symbolic approaches to AI "good old fashioned AI" or "GOFAI". During the 1960s, symbolic approaches had achieved great success at simulating high-level thinking in small demonstration programs. Approaches based on cybernetics or artificial neural networks were abandoned or pushed into the background. Researchers in the 1960s and the 1970s were convinced that symbolic approaches would eventually succeed in creating a machine with artificial general intelligence and considered this the goal of their field.

Cognitive Simulation

Economist Herbert Simon and Allen Newell studied human problem-solving skills and attempted to formalize them, and their work laid the foundations of the field of artificial intelligence, as well as cognitive science, operations research and management science. Their research team used the results of psychological experiments to develop programs that simulated the techniques that people used to solve problems. This tradition, centered at Carnegie Mellon University would eventually culminate in the development of the Soar architecture in the middle 1980s.

Logic-based

Unlike Simon and Newell, John McCarthy felt that machines did not need to simulate human thought, but should instead try to find the essence of abstract reasoning and problem-solving, regardless whether people used the same algorithms. His laboratory at Stanford (SAIL) focused on using formal logic to solve a wide variety of problems, including knowledge representation, planning and learning.Logic was also the focus of the work at the University of Edinburgh and elsewhere in Europe which led to the development of the programming language Prolog and the science of logic programming.

Anti-logic or Scruffy

Researchers at MIT (such as Marvin Minsky and Seymour Papert) found that solving difficult problems in vision and natural language processing required ad-hoc solutions—they argued that there was no simple and general principle (like logic) that would capture all the aspects of intelligent behavior. Roger Schank described their "anti-logic" approaches as "scruffy" (as opposed to the "neat" paradigms at CMU and Stanford). Commonsense knowledge bases (such as Doug Lenat's Cyc) are an example of "scruffy" AI, since they must be built by hand, one complicated concept at a time.

Knowledge-based

When computers with large memories became available around 1970, researchers from all three traditions began to build knowledge into AI applications. This "knowledge revolution" led to the development and deployment of expert systems (introduced by Edward Feigenbaum), the first truly successful form of AI software. A key component of the system architecture for all expert systems is the knowledge base, which stores facts and rules that illustrate AI. The knowledge revolution was also driven by the realization that enormous amounts of knowledge would be required by many simple AI applications.

Sub-symbolic

By the 1980s, progress in symbolic AI seemed to stall and many believed that symbolic systems would never be able to imitate all the processes of human cognition, especially perception, robotics, learning and pattern recognition. A number of researchers began to look into "sub-symbolic" approaches to specific AI problems. Sub-symbolic methods manage to approach intelligence without specific representations of knowledge.

Embodied Intelligence

This includes embodied, situated, behavior-based, and nouvelle AI. Researchers from the related field of robotics, such as Rodney Brooks, rejected symbolic AI and focused on the basic engineering problems that would allow robots to move and survive. Their work revived the non-symbolic point of view of the early cybernetics researchers of the 1950s and reintroduced the use of control theory in AI. This coincided with the development of the embodied mind thesis in the related field of cognitive science: the idea that aspects of the body (such as movement, perception and visualization) are required for higher intelligence.

Within developmental robotics, developmental learning approaches are elaborated upon to allow robots to accumulate repertoires of novel skills through autonomous self-exploration, social interaction with human teachers, and the use of guidance mechanisms (active learning, maturation, motor synergies, etc).

Computational Intelligence and Soft Computing

Interest in neural networks and "connectionism" was revived by David Rumelhart and others in the middle of the 1980s. Artificial neural networks are an example of soft computing—they are solutions to problems which cannot be solved with complete logical certainty, and where an approximate solution is often sufficient. Other soft computing approaches to AI include fuzzy systems, Grey system theory, evolutionary computation and many statistical tools. The application of soft computing to AI is studied collectively by the emerging discipline of computational intelligence.

Statistical Learning

Much of traditional GOFAI got bogged down on *ad hoc* patches to symbolic computation that worked on their own toy models but failed to generalize to real-world results. However, around the 1990s, AI researchers adopted sophisticated mathematical tools, such as hidden Markov models (HMM), information theory, and normative Bayesian decision theory to compare or to unify competing architectures. The shared mathematical language permitted a high level of collaboration with more established fields (like mathematics, economics or operations research). Compared with GOFAI, new "statistical learning" techniques such as HMM and neural networks were gaining higher levels of accuracy in many practical domains such as data mining, without necessarily acquiring a semantic understanding of the datasets. The increased successes with real-world data led to increasing emphasis on comparing different approaches against shared test data to see which approach performed best in a broader context than that provided by idiosyncratic toy models; AI research was becoming more scientific. Nowadays results of experiments are often rigorously measurable, and are sometimes (with difficulty) reproducible.Different statistical learning techniques have different limitations; for example, basic HMM cannot model the infinite possible combinations of natural language. Critics note that the shift from GOFAI to statistical learning is often also a shift away from explainable AI. In AGI research, some scholars caution against over-reliance on statistical learning, and argue that continuing research into GOFAI will still be necessary to attain general intelligence.

Integrating the Approaches

Intelligent Agent Paradigm

An intelligent agent is a system that perceives its environment and takes actions which maximize its chances of success. The simplest intelligent agents are programs that solve specific problems. More complicated agents include human beings and organizations of human beings (such as firms). The paradigm allows researchers to directly compare or even combine different approaches to isolated problems, by asking which agent is best at maximizing a given "goal function". An agent that solves a specific problem can use any approach that works—some agents are symbolic and logical, some are sub-symbolic artificial neural networks and others may use new approaches. The paradigm also gives researchers a common language to communicate with other fields—such as decision theory and economics—that also use concepts of abstract agents. Building a complete agent requires researchers to address realistic problems of integration; for example, because sensory systems give uncertain information about the environment, planning systems must be able to function in the presence of uncertainty. The intelligent agent paradigm became widely accepted during the 1990s.

Agent Architectures and Cognitive Architectures

Researchers have designed systems to build intelligent systems out of interacting intelligent agents in a multi-agent system. A hierarchical control system provides a bridge between sub-symbolic AI at its lowest, reactive levels and traditional symbolic AI at its highest levels, where relaxed time constraints permit planning and world modelling. Some cognitive architectures are custom-built to solve a narrow problem; others, such as Soar, are designed to mimic human cognition and to provide insight into general intelligence. Modern extensions of Soar are hybrid intelligent systems that include both symbolic and sub-symbolic components.

Machine learning

Machine learning (ML) is the scientific study of algorithms and statistical models that computer systems use in order to perform a specific task effectively without using explicit instructions, relying on patterns and inference instead. It is seen as a subset of artificial intelligence. Machine learning algorithms build a mathematical model based on sample data, known as "training data", in order to make predictions or decisions without being explicitly programmed to perform the task. Machine learning algorithms are used in a wide variety of applications, such as email filtering, and computer vision, where it is infeasible to develop an algorithm of specific instructions for performing the task. Machine learning is closely related to computational statistics, which focuses on making predictions using computers. The study of mathematical optimization delivers methods, theory and application domains to the field of machine learning. Data mining is a field of study within machine learning, and focuses on exploratory data analysis through unsupervised learning. In its application across business problems, machine learning is also referred to as predictive analytics.

Overview

The name *machine learning* was coined in 1959 by Arthur Samuel. Tom M. Mitchell provided a widely quoted, more formal definition of the algorithms studied in the machine learning field: "A computer program is said to learn from experience E with respect to some class of tasks T and performance measure P if its performance at tasks in T, as measured by P, improves with experience E." This definition of the tasks in which machine learning is concerned offers a fundamentally operational definition rather than defining the field in cognitive terms. This follows Alan Turing's proposal in his paper "Computing Machinery and Intelligence", in which the question "Can machines think?" is replaced with the question "Can machines do what we (as thinking entities) can do?". In Turing's proposal the various characteristics that could be possessed by a *thinking machine* and the various implications in constructing one are exposed.

Machine Learning Tasks

Machine learning tasks are classified into several broad categories. In supervised learning, the algorithm builds a mathematical model from a set of data that contains both the inputs and the desired outputs. For example, if the task were determining whether an image contained a certain object, the training data for a supervised learning algorithm would include images with and without that object (the input), and each image would have a label (the output) designating whether it contained the object. In special cases, the input may be only partially available, or restricted to special feedback. Semi-supervised learning algorithms develop mathematical models from incomplete training data, where a portion of the sample input doesn't have labels.

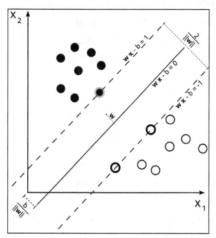

A support vector machine is a supervised learning model that divides the data into regions separated by a linear boundary. Here, the linear boundary divides the black circles from the white.

Classification algorithms and regression algorithms are types of supervised learning. Classification algorithms are used when the outputs are restricted to a limited set of values. For a classification algorithm that filters emails, the input would be an incoming email, and the output would be the name of the folder in which to file the email. For an algorithm that identifies spam emails, the output would be the prediction of either "spam" or "not spam", represented by the Boolean values true and false. Regression algorithms are named for their continuous outputs, meaning they may have any value within a range. Examples of a continuous value are the temperature, length, or price of an object.

In unsupervised learning, the algorithm builds a mathematical model from a set of data which contains only inputs and no desired output labels. Unsupervised learning algorithms are used to find structure in the data, like grouping or clustering of data points. Unsupervised learning can discover patterns in the data, and can group the inputs into categories, as in feature learning. Dimensionality reduction is the process of reducing the number of "features", or inputs, in a set of data.

Active learning algorithms access the desired outputs (training labels) for a limited set of inputs based on a budget, and optimize the choice of inputs for which it will acquire training labels. When used interactively, these can be presented to a human user for labeling. Reinforcement learning algorithms are given feedback in the form of positive or negative reinforcement in a dynamic environment, and are used in autonomous vehicles or in learning to play a game against a human opponent.[3] Other specialized algorithms in machine learning include topic modeling, where the computer program is given a set of natural language documents and finds other documents that cover similar topics. Machine learning algorithms can be used to find the unobservable probability density function in density estimation problems. Meta learning algorithms learn their own inductive bias based on previous experience. In developmental robotics, robot learning algorithms generate their own sequences of learning experiences, also known as a curriculum, to cumulatively acquire new skills through self-guided exploration and social interaction with humans. These robots use guidance mechanisms such as active learning, maturation, motor synergies, and imitation.

History and Relationships to other Fields

Arthur Samuel, an American pioneer in the field of computer gaming and artificial intelligence, coined the term "Machine Learning" in 1959 while at IBM. As a scientific endeavour, machine learning grew out of the quest for artificial intelligence. Already in the early days of AI as an academic discipline, some researchers were interested in having machines learn from data. They attempted to approach the problem with various symbolic methods, as well as what were then termed "neural networks"; these were mostly perceptrons and other models that were later found to be reinventions of the generalized linear models of statistics. Probabilistic reasoning was also employed, especially in automated medical diagnosis.

However, an increasing emphasis on the logical, knowledge-based approach caused a rift between AI and machine learning. Probabilistic systems were plagued by theoretical and practical problems of data acquisition and representation. By 1980, expert systems had come to dominate AI, and statistics was out of favor. Work on symbolic/knowledge-based learning did continue within AI, leading to inductive logic programming, but the more statistical line of research was now outside the field of AI proper, in pattern recognition and information retrieval. Neural networks research had been abandoned by AI and computer science around the same time. This line, too, was continued outside the AI/CS field, as "connectionism", by researchers from other disciplines including Hopfield, Rumelhart and Hinton. Their main success came in the mid-1980s with the reinvention of backpropagation.

Machine learning, reorganized as a separate field, started to flourish in the 1990s. The field changed its goal from achieving artificial intelligence to tackling solvable problems of a practical nature. It shifted focus away from the symbolic approaches it had inherited from AI, and toward methods and models borrowed from statistics and probability theory. It also benefited from the increasing availability of digitized information, and the ability to distribute it via the Internet.

Relation to Data Mining

Machine learning and data mining often employ the same methods and overlap significantly, but while machine learning focuses on prediction, based on *known* properties learned from the training data, data mining focuses on the discovery of (previously) *unknown* properties in the data (this is the analysis step of knowledge discovery in databases). Data mining uses many machine learning methods, but with different goals; on the other hand, machine learning also employs data mining methods as "unsupervised learning" or as a preprocessing step to improve learner accuracy. Much of the confusion between these two research communities (which do often have separate conferences and separate journals, ECML PKDD being a major exception) comes from the basic assumptions they work with: in machine learning, performance is usually evaluated with respect to the ability to *reproduce known* knowledge, while in knowledge discovery and data mining (KDD) the key task is the discovery of previously *unknown* knowledge. Evaluated with respect to known knowledge, an uninformed (unsupervised) method will easily be outperformed by other supervised methods, while in a typical KDD task, supervised methods cannot be used due to the unavailability of training data.

Relation to Optimization

Machine learning also has intimate ties to optimization: many learning problems are formulated as minimization of some loss function on a training set of examples. Loss functions express the discrepancy between the predictions of the model being trained and the actual problem instances (for example, in classification, one wants to assign a label to instances, and models are trained to correctly predict the pre-assigned labels of a set of examples). The difference between the two fields arises from the goal of generalization: while optimization algorithms can minimize the loss on a training set, machine learning is concerned with minimizing the loss on unseen samples.

Relation to Statistics

Machine learning and statistics are closely related fields. According to Michael I. Jordan, the ideas of machine learning, from methodological principles to theoretical tools, have had a long pre-history in statistics. He also suggested the term data science as a placeholder to call the overall field.

Leo Breiman distinguished two statistical modelling paradigms: data model and algorithmic model, wherein "algorithmic model" means more or less the machine learning algorithms like Random forest.

Some statisticians have adopted methods from machine learning, leading to a combined field that they call *statistical learning*.

Theory

A core objective of a learner is to generalize from its experience. Generalization in this context is the ability of a learning machine to perform accurately on new, unseen examples/tasks after having experienced a learning data set. The training examples come from some generally unknown probability distribution (considered representative of the space of occurrences) and the learner has to build a general model about this space that enables it to produce sufficiently accurate predictions in new cases.

The computational analysis of machine learning algorithms and their performance is a branch of theoretical computer science known as computational learning theory. Because training sets are finite and the future is uncertain, learning theory usually does not yield guarantees of the performance of algorithms. Instead, probabilistic bounds on the performance are quite common. The bias–variance decomposition is one way to quantify generalization error.

For the best performance in the context of generalization, the complexity of the hypothesis should match the complexity of the function underlying the data. If the hypothesis is less complex than the function, then the model has underfit the data. If the complexity of the model is increased in response, then the training error decreases. But if the hypothesis is too complex, then the model is subject to overfitting and generalization will be poorer.

In addition to performance bounds, learning theorists study the time complexity and feasibility of learning. In computational learning theory, a computation is considered feasible if it can be done in polynomial time. There are two kinds of time complexity results. Positive results show that a certain class of functions can be learned in polynomial time. Negative results show that certain classes cannot be learned in polynomial time.

Approaches

Types of Learning Algorithms

The types of machine learning algorithms differ in their approach, the type of data they input and output, and the type of task or problem that they are intended to solve.

Supervised Learning

Supervised learning algorithms build a mathematical model of a set of data that contains both the inputs and the desired outputs. The data is known as training data, and consists of a set of training examples. Each training example has one or more inputs and a desired output, also known as a supervisory signal. In the mathematical model, each training example is represented by an array or vector, sometimes called a feature vector, and the training data is represented by a matrix. Through iterative optimization of an objective function, supervised learning algorithms learn a function that can be used to predict the output associated with new inputs. An optimal function will allow the algorithm to correctly determine the output for inputs that were not a part of the training data. An algorithm that improves the accuracy of its outputs or predictions over time is said to have learned to perform that task.

Supervised learning algorithms include classification and regression. Classification algorithms are used when the outputs are restricted to a limited set of values, and regression algorithms are used when the outputs may have any numerical value within a range. Similarity learning is an area of supervised machine learning closely related to regression and classification, but the goal is to learn from examples using a similarity function that measures how similar or related two objects are. It has applications in ranking, recommendation systems, visual identity tracking, face verification, and speaker verification.

In the case of semi-supervised learning algorithms, some of the training examples are missing training labels, but they can nevertheless be used to improve the quality of a model. In weakly supervised learning, the training labels are noisy, limited, or imprecise; however, these labels are often cheaper to obtain, resulting in larger effective training sets.

Unsupervised Learning

Unsupervised learning algorithms take a set of data that contains only inputs, and find structure in the data, like grouping or clustering of data points. The algorithms therefore learn from test data that has not been labeled, classified or categorized. Instead of responding to feedback, unsupervised learning algorithms identify commonalities in the data and react based on the presence or absence of such commonalities in each new piece of data. A central application of unsupervised learning is in the field of density estimation in statistics, though unsupervised learning encompasses other domains involving summarizing and explaining data features.

Cluster analysis is the assignment of a set of observations into subsets (called *clusters*) so that observations within the same cluster are similar according to one or more predesignated criteria, while observations drawn from different clusters are dissimilar. Different clustering techniques make different assumptions on the structure of the data, often defined by some *similarity metric* and evaluated, for example, by *internal compactness*, or the similarity between members of the same cluster, and *separation*, the difference between clusters. Other methods are based on *estimated density* and *graph connectivity*.

Reinforcement Learning

Reinforcement learning is an area of machine learning concerned with how software agents ought to take actions in an environment so as to maximize some notion of cumulative reward. Due to its generality, the field is studied in many other disciplines, such as game theory, control theory, operations research, information theory, simulation-based optimization, multi-agent systems, swarm intelligence, statistics and genetic algorithms. In machine learning, the environment is typically represented as a Markov Decision Process (MDP). Many reinforcement learning algorithms use dynamic programming techniques. Reinforcement learning algorithms do not assume knowledge of an exact mathematical model of the MDP, and are used when exact models are infeasible. Reinforcement learning algorithms are used in autonomous vehicles or in learning to play a game against a human opponent.

Feature Learning

Several learning algorithms aim at discovering better representations of the inputs provided during training. Classic examples include principal components analysis and cluster analysis. Feature learning algorithms, also called representation learning algorithms, often attempt to preserve the information in their input but also transform it in a way that makes it useful, often as a pre-processing step before performing classification or predictions. This technique allows reconstruction of the inputs coming from the unknown data-generating distribution, while not being necessarily faithful to configurations that are implausible under that distribution. This replaces manual feature engineering, and allows a machine to both learn the features and use them to perform a specific task.

Feature learning can be either supervised or unsupervised. In supervised feature learning, features are learned using labeled input data. Examples include artificial neural networks, multilayer perceptrons, and supervised dictionary learning. In unsupervised feature learning, features are learned with unlabeled input data. Examples include dictionary learning, independent component analysis, autoencoders, matrix factorization and various forms of clustering.

Manifold learning algorithms attempt to do so under the constraint that the learned representation is low-dimensional. Sparse codingalgorithms attempt to do so under the constraint that the learned representation is sparse, meaning that the mathematical model has many zeros. Multilinear subspace learning algorithms aim to learn low-dimensional representations directly from tensor representations for multidimensional data, without reshaping them into higher-dimensional vectors. Deep learning algorithms discover multiple levels of representation, or a hierarchy of features, with higher-level, more abstract features defined in terms of (or generating) lower-level features. It has been argued that an intelligent machine is one that learns a representation that disentangles the underlying factors of variation that explain the observed data.

Feature learning is motivated by the fact that machine learning tasks such as classification often require input that is mathematically and computationally convenient to process. However, real-world data such as images, video, and sensory data has not yielded to attempts to algorithmically define specific features. An alternative is to discover such features or representations through examination, without relying on explicit algorithms.

Sparse Dictionary Learning

Sparse dictionary learning is a feature learning method where a training example is represented as a linear combination of basis functions, and is assumed to be a sparse matrix. The method is strongly NP-hard and difficult to solve approximately. A popular heuristic method for sparse dictionary learning is the K-SVD algorithm. Sparse dictionary learning has been applied in several contexts. In classification, the problem is to determine to which classes a previously unseen training example belongs. For a dictionary where each class has already been built, a new training example is associated with the class that is best sparsely represented by the corresponding dictionary. Sparse dictionary learning has also been applied in image de-noising. The key idea is that a clean image patch can be sparsely represented by an image dictionary, but the noise cannot.

Anomaly Detection

In data mining, anomaly detection, also known as outlier detection, is the identification of rare items, events or observations which raise suspicions by differing significantly from the majority of the data. Typically, the anomalous items represent an issue such as bank fraud, a structural defect, medical problems or errors in a text. Anomalies are referred to as outliers, novelties, noise, deviations and exceptions.

In particular, in the context of abuse and network intrusion detection, the interesting objects are often not rare objects, but unexpected bursts in activity. This pattern does not adhere to the common statistical definition of an outlier as a rare object, and many outlier detection methods (in particular, unsupervised algorithms) will fail on such data, unless it has been aggregated appropriately. Instead, a cluster analysis algorithm may be able to detect the micro-clusters formed by these patterns.

Three broad categories of anomaly detection techniques exist. Unsupervised anomaly detection techniques detect anomalies in an unlabeled test data set under the assumption that the majority of the instances in the data set are normal, by looking for instances that seem to fit least to the remainder of the data set. Supervised anomaly detection techniques require a data set that has been labeled as "normal" and "abnormal" and involves training a classifier (the key difference to many other statistical classification problems is the inherent unbalanced nature of outlier detection). Semi-supervised anomaly detection techniques construct a model representing normal behavior from a given normal training data set, and then test the likelihood of a test instance to be generated by the model.

Association Rules

Association rule learning is a rule-based machine learning method for discovering relationships between variables in large databases. It is intended to identify strong rules discovered in databases using some measure of "interestingness".

Rule-based machine learning is a general term for any machine learning method that identifies, learns, or evolves "rules" to store, manipulate or apply knowledge. The defining characteristic of a rule-based machine learning algorithm is the identification and utilization of a set of relational rules that collectively represent the knowledge captured by the system. This is in contrast to other machine learning algorithms that commonly identify a singular model that can be universally applied to any instance in order to make a prediction. Rule-based machine learning approaches include learning classifier systems, association rule learning, and artificial immune systems.

Based on the concept of strong rules, Rakesh Agrawal, Tomasz Imieliński and Arun Swami introduced association rules for discovering regularities between products in large-scale transaction data recorded by point-of-sale (POS) systems in supermarkets. For example, the rule found in the sales data of a supermarket would indicate that if a customer buys onions and potatoes together, they are likely to also buy hamburger meat. Such information can be used as the basis for decisions about marketing activities such as promotional pricing or product placements. In addition to market basket analysis, association rules are employed today in application areas including Web usage mining, intrusion detection, continuous production, and bioinformatics. In contrast with sequence mining, association rule learning typically does not consider the order of items either within a transaction or across transactions.

Learning classifier systems (LCS) are a family of rule-based machine learning algorithms that combine a discovery component, typically a genetic algorithm, with a learning component, performing either supervised learning, reinforcement learning, or unsupervised learning. They seek to identify a set of context-dependent rules that collectively store and apply knowledge in a piecewise manner in order to make predictions.

Inductive logic programming (ILP) is an approach to rule-learning using logic programming as a uniform representation for input examples, background knowledge, and hypotheses. Given an encoding of the known background knowledge and a set of examples represented as a logical database of facts, an ILP system will derive a hypothesized logic program that entails all positive and no negative examples. Inductive programming is a related field that considers any kind of programming languages for representing hypotheses (and not only logic programming), such as functional programs.

Inductive logic programming is particularly useful in bioinformatics and natural language processing. Gordon Plotkin and Ehud Shapiro laid the initial theoretical foundation for inductive machine learning in a logical setting. Shapiro built their first implementation (Model Inference System) in 1981: a Prolog program that inductively inferred logic programs from positive and negative examples. The term *inductive* here refers to philosophical induction, suggesting a theory to explain observed facts, rather than mathematical induction, proving a property for all members of a well-ordered set.

Models

Performing machine learning involves creating a model, which is trained on some training data and then can process additional data to make predictions. Various types of models have been used and researched for machine learning systems.

Artificial Neural Networks

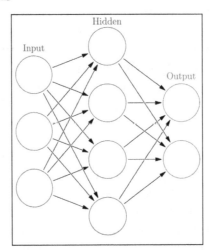

An artificial neural network is an interconnected group of nodes, akin to the vast network of neurons in a brain. Here, each circular node represents an artificial neuron and an arrow represents a connection from the output of one artificial neuron to the input of another.

Artificial neural networks (ANNs), or connectionist systems, are computing systems vaguely inspired by the biological neural networks that constitute animal brains. Such systems "learn" to perform tasks by considering examples, generally without being programmed with any task-specific rules.

An ANN is a model based on a collection of connected units or nodes called "artificial neurons", which loosely model the neurons in a biological brain. Each connection, like the synapses in a biological brain, can transmit information, a "signal", from one artificial neuron to another. An artificial neuron that receives a signal can process it and then signal additional artificial neurons connected to it. In common ANN implementations, the signal at a connection between artificial neurons is a real number, and the output of each artificial neuron is computed by some non-linear function of the sum of its inputs. The connections between artificial neurons are called "edges". Artificial neurons and edges typically have a weight that adjusts as learning proceeds. The weight increases or decreases the strength of the signal at a connection. Artificial neurons may have a threshold such that the signal is only sent if the aggregate signal crosses that threshold. Typically, artificial neurons are aggregated into layers. Different layers may perform different kinds of transformations on their inputs. Signals travel from the first layer (the input layer), to the last layer (the output layer), possibly after traversing the layers multiple times.

The original goal of the ANN approach was to solve problems in the same way that a human brain would. However, over time, attention moved to performing specific tasks, leading to deviations from biology. Artificial neural networks have been used on a variety of tasks, including computer vision, speech recognition, machine translation, social network filtering, playing board and video games and medical diagnosis.

Deep learning consists of multiple hidden layers in an artificial neural network. This approach tries to model the way the human brain processes light and sound into vision and hearing. Some successful applications of deep learning are computer vision and speech recognition.

Decision Trees

Decision tree learning uses a decision tree as a predictive model to go from observations about an item (represented in the branches) to conclusions about the item's target value (represented in the leaves). It is one of the predictive modeling approaches used in statistics, data mining and machine learning. Tree models where the target variable can take a discrete set of values are called classification trees; in these tree structures, leaves represent class labels and branches represent conjunctions of features that lead to those class labels. Decision trees where the target variable can take continuous values (typically real numbers) are called regression trees. In decision analysis, a decision tree can be used to visually and explicitly represent decisions and decision making. In data mining, a decision tree describes data, but the resulting classification tree can be an input for decision making.

Support Vector Machines

Support vector machines (SVMs), also known as support vector networks, are a set of related supervised learning methods used for classification and regression. Given a set of training examples, each marked as belonging to one of two categories, an SVM training algorithm builds a model that predicts whether a new example falls into one category or the other. An SVM training algorithm is a non-probabilistic, binary, linear classifier, although methods such as Platt scaling exist to use SVM in a probabilistic classification setting. In addition to performing linear classification, SVMs can efficiently perform a non-linear classification using what is called the kernel trick, implicitly mapping their inputs into high-dimensional feature spaces.

Bayesian Networks

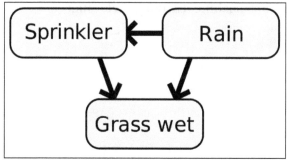

A simple Bayesian network. Rain influences whether the sprinkler is activated, and both rain and the sprinkler influence whether the grass is wet.

A Bayesian network, belief network or directed acyclic graphical model is a probabilistic graphical model that represents a set of random variables and their conditional independence with a directed acyclic graph (DAG). For example, a Bayesian network could represent the probabilistic relationships between diseases and symptoms. Given symptoms, the network can be used to compute the probabilities of the presence of various diseases. Efficient algorithms exist that perform inference and learning. Bayesian networks that model sequences of variables, like speech signalsor protein sequences, are called dynamic Bayesian networks. Generalizations of Bayesian networks that can represent and solve decision problems under uncertainty are called influence diagrams.

Genetic Algorithms

A genetic algorithm (GA) is a search algorithm and heuristic technique that mimics the process of natural selection, using methods such as mutation and crossover to generate new genotypes in the hope of finding good solutions to a given problem. In machine learning, genetic algorithms were used in the 1980s and 1990s. Conversely, machine learning techniques have been used to improve the performance of genetic and evolutionary algorithms.

Training Models

Usually, machine learning models require a lot of data in order for them to perform well. Usually, when training a machine learning model, one needs to collect a large, representative sample of data from a training set. Data from the training set can be as varied as a corpus of text, a collection of images, and data collected from individual users of a service. Overfitting is something to watch out for when training a machine learning model.

Federated Learning

Federated learning is a new approach to training machine learning models that decentralizes the training process, allowing for users' privacy to be maintained by not needing to send their data to a centralized server. This also increases efficiency by decentralizing the training process to many devices. For example, Gboard uses federated machine learning to train search query prediction models on users' mobile phones without having to send individual searches back to Google.

Applications

There are many applications for machine learning, including:

- Agriculture,
- Anatomy,
- Adaptive websites,
- Affective computing,
- Banking,
- Bioinformatics,
- Brain–machine interfaces,
- Cheminformatics,
- Computer Networks,
- Computer vision,
- Credit-card fraud detection,
- Data quality,

- DNA sequence classification,
- Economics,
- Financial market analysis,
- General game playing,
- Handwriting recognition,
- Information retrieval,
- Insurance,
- Internet fraud detection,
- Linguistics,
- Machine learning control,
- Machine perception,
- Machine translation,
- Marketing,
- Medical diagnosis,
- Natural language processing,
- Natural language understanding,
- Online advertising,
- Optimization,
- Recommender systems,
- Robot locomotion,
- Search engines,
- Sentiment analysis,
- Sequence mining,
- Software engineering,
- Speech recognition,
- Structural health monitoring,
- Syntactic pattern recognition,
- Telecommunication,

- Theorem proving,

- Time series forecasting,

- User behavior analytics.

In 2006, the online movie company Netflix held the first "Netflix Prize" competition to find a program to better predict user preferences and improve the accuracy on its existing Cinematch movie recommendation algorithm by at least 10%. A joint team made up of researchers from AT&T Labs-Research in collaboration with the teams Big Chaos and Pragmatic Theory built an ensemble model to win the Grand Prize in 2009 for $1 million. Shortly after the prize was awarded, Netflix realized that viewers' ratings were not the best indicators of their viewing patterns ("everything is a recommendation") and they changed their recommendation engine accordingly. In 2010 The Wall Street Journal wrote about the firm Rebellion Research and their use of machine learning to predict the financial crisis. In 2012, co-founder of Sun Microsystems, Vinod Khosla, predicted that 80% of medical doctors' jobs would be lost in the next two decades to automated machine learning medical diagnostic software. In 2014, it was reported that a machine learning algorithm had been applied in the field of art history to study fine art paintings, and that it may have revealed previously unrecognized influences among artists. In 2019 Springer Naturepublished the first research book created using machine learning.

Limitations

Although machine learning has been transformative in some fields, machine-learning programs often fail to deliver expected results. Reasons for this are numerous: lack of (suitable) data, lack of access to the data, data bias, privacy problems, badly chosen tasks and algorithms, wrong tools and people, lack of resources, and evaluation problems.

In 2018, a self-driving car from Uber failed to detect a pedestrian, who was killed after a collision. Attempts to use machine learning in healthcare with the IBM Watson system failed to deliver even after years of time and billions of investment.

Bias

Machine learning approaches in particular can suffer from different data biases. A machine learning system trained on current customers only may not be able to predict the needs of new customer groups that are not represented in the training data. When trained on man-made data, machine learning is likely to pick up the same constitutional and unconscious biases already present in society. Language models learned from data have been shown to contain human-like biases. Machine learning systems used for criminal risk assessment have been found to be biased against black people. In 2015, Google photos would often tag black people as gorillas, and in 2018 this still was not well resolved, but Google reportedly was still using the workaround to remove all gorilla from the training data, and thus was not able to recognize real gorillas at all. Similar issues with recognizing non-white people have been found in many other systems. In 2016, Microsoft tested a chatbot that learned from Twitter, and it quickly picked up racist and sexist language. Because of such challenges, the effective use of machine learning may take longer to be adopted in other domains. Concern for reducing bias in machine learning and propelling its use for human good is increasingly expressed by artificial intelligence scientists, including Fei-Fei Li, who reminds engineers that "There's nothing artificial about AI. It's inspired by people, it's created by people, and—most importantly—it impacts people. It is a powerful tool we are only just beginning to understand, and that is a profound responsibility."

Model Assessments

Classification machine learning models can be validated by accuracy estimation techniques like the Holdout method, which splits the data in a training and test set (conventionally 2/3 training set and 1/3 test set designation) and evaluates the performance of the training model on the test set. In comparison, the K-fold-cross-validation method randomly partitions the data into K subsets and then K experiments are performed each respectively considering 1 subset for evaluation and the remaining K-1 subsets for training the model. In addition to the holdout and cross-validation methods, bootstrap, which samples n instances with replacement from the dataset, can be used to assess model accuracy.

In addition to overall accuracy, investigators frequently report sensitivity and specificity meaning True Positive Rate (TPR) and True Negative Rate (TNR) respectively. Similarly, investigators sometimes report the False Positive Rate (FPR) as well as the False Negative Rate (FNR). However, these rates are ratios that fail to reveal their numerators and denominators. The Total Operating Characteristic (TOC) is an effective method to express a model's diagnostic ability. TOC shows the numerators and denominators of the previously mentioned rates, thus TOC provides more information than the commonly used Receiver Operating Characteristic (ROC) and ROC's associated Area Under the Curve (AUC).

Ethics

Machine learning poses a host of ethical questions. Systems which are trained on datasets collected with biases may exhibit these biases upon use (algorithmic bias), thus digitizing cultural prejudices. For example, using job hiring data from a firm with racist hiring policies may lead to a machine learning system duplicating the bias by scoring job applicants against similarity to previous successful applicants. Responsible collection of data and documentation of algorithmic rules used by a system thus is a critical part of machine learning.

Because language contains biases, machines trained on language *corpora* will necessarily also learn bias.

Other forms of ethical challenges, not related to personal biases, are more seen in health care. There are concerns among health care professionals that these systems might not be designed in the public's interest, but as income generating machines. This is especially true in the United States where there is a perpetual ethical dilemma of improving health care, but also increasing profits. For example, the algorithms could be designed to provide patients with unnecessary tests or medication in which the algorithm's proprietary owners hold stakes in. There is huge potential for machine learning in health care to provide professionals a great tool to diagnose, medicate, and even plan recovery paths for patients, but this will not happen until the personal biases mentioned previously, and these "greed" biases are addressed.

Software

Software suites containing a variety of machine learning algorithms include the following:

- Free and open-source software:

  ○ CNTK

  ○ Deeplearning4j

  ○ ELKI

  ○ H2O

  ○ Keras

  ○ Mahout

  ○ Mallet

  ○ mlpack

  ○ MXNet

  ○ Neural Lab

  ○ GNU Octave

  ○ OpenNN

  ○ Orange

  ○ scikit-learn

  ○ Shogun

  ○ Spark MLlib

  ○ Apache SystemML

  ○ TensorFlow

  ○ ROOT (TMVA with ROOT)

  ○ Torch / PyTorch

  ○ Weka / MOA

  ○ Yooreeka

  ○ R

- Proprietary software with free and open-source editions:

  ○ KNIME

- RapidMiner
- Proprietary software
- Amazon Machine Learning
- Angoss KnowledgeSTUDIO
- Azure Machine Learning
- Ayasdi
- IBM Data Science Experience
- Google Prediction API
- IBM SPSS Modeler
- KXEN Modeler
- LIONsolver
- Mathematica
- MATLAB
- Microsoft Azure Machine Learning
- Neural Designer
- NeuroSolutions
- Oracle Data Mining
- Oracle AI Platform Cloud Service
- RCASE
- SAS Enterprise Miner
- SequenceL
- Splunk
- STATISTICA Data Miner

Advantages of Artificial Intelligence

Day to Day Application

- In our daily needs, a smartphone also becomes the 4th necessity for the human along with dress, food & shelter.

- If you are using a smartphone, it indirectly means that you are enjoying the AI by knowingly or unknowingly.

- Design the methods for automation by using learning and perception have become a common phenomenon in our everyday lives.

- We have our lady Siri for iOS devices or Cortana for Windows devices to help us out.

- We also prefer the help from GPS for the long drives and trips.

- A smartphone is one of the apt everyday examples of how we utilize the power of artificial intelligence to reduce the barriers in a day to day life.

- In the part of utilities, we can find that how they predict what we are going to type and provide the suggestion to correct the human errors in spelling. That is one of the most used machine intelligence at work irrespective of industries and freelancers.

- While coming to the social media users based utilities, the artificial intelligence algorithm identifies and detects the person's face and tags the individuals while we post the photographs on the social media sites.

- Artificial Intelligence is widely deployed and utilized by the financial institutions and banking sectors to organize and manage data. Detection Of Fraud uses one of the best advantages of an artificial intelligence involvement in the smart card based system transactions.

Digital Assistance

- Highly advanced organizations already implemented machines on behalf of humans to interact with their customers by using 'avatars'. It is the digital assistants or replicas which will help to reduce the need for human resources.

- For AI Machines, emotions only can be identified in the way of rational thinking.

- Robots can't identify the sentimental factor of the user. It actually programmed for only think logically and take the right program decisions based on the existing experience taught to the machine.

- Emotions can't be identifying by the machines that may be dissatisfying the customer. In that case, we need human intervention. This lagging tries to rule out for machine intelligence. But still, it helps in other aspects.

Handling Repetitive Jobs

- Repeated jobs are tedious in nature. That kind of jobs can be easily handled with the help of AI algorithms. These kinds of job don't require much intelligence in between the process.

- Machines can think much faster than humans and can perform multi-tasking to obtain the best results.

- Machine intelligence can be employed to carry out the dangerous tasks which may cause injury to the human involved in that. Their parameters can be adjusted is the benefit here. Their speed and time can be customized based on the requirement calculation.

- Whenever human operates the machine like playing a game or run a computer-controlled robot, it means that we are actually interacting with AI Machines.

- In the computer game, the machine itself plays the game like as an opponent based on our activity in the game. The machine plans its movement based on the user response. So, we can say gaming is one of the most common uses of the advantages of artificial intelligence.

Medical Applications

- One of the great advantages of Artificial Intelligence is utilized in the field of medicine. We can identify the numerous numbers of medical applications which rely on AI.

- Doctors/Physician assesses the patient's health-related data and intimates the risk factors to the customers via the health care devices with the help of artificial machine intelligence.

- It helps the patient to know about the side effects of different medicines and also behaves as personal digital care. Artificial surgery simulator is the great innovation part of the AI. The efficiency of that always prefers to utilize that simulator by the Professionals for the treatment.

- Currently, we have huge software to detect as well as monitor the neurological disorders. It can simulate the functionality of the human brain.

- Robotics is used often in the treatment for mentally sick patients to come out from their depression also make them remain active in the real world.

- The current medical industry has the popular application of artificial intelligence is Radiosurgery. It helps us to operate the tumors without damaging the unaffected surrounding tissues.

Hazardous Exploration

- Artificial Intelligence and the science of robotics are the fascinating advancements in technological development. Using this, we can able to handle the huge volume of data for storing and processing but not limited to as well as we can use that in the process of mining and other fuel exploration processes.

- These complex machines can be utilized to overcome human limitations. We can utilize these machines as a replacement for the humans wherever we felt the process done by the human is hazardous but can't neglect that because of the goodness or results received.

- They can perform difficult tasks and accurate work with greater responsibility without any lag. Moreover, they do not wear out easily.

Reduction of Error

- The advantage of using Artificial Intelligence is, it helps us for error reduction and increasing the chance of reaching higher accuracy with a greater degree of precision.

- It can be applied in various situations including the process called exploration of space.

- In that intelligent robots are fed with information because of the velocity of the data creation. Such kind of information forwarded to explore the space. Even though those are machines with metal bodies, those are the most resistant in nature also it has a great character which can help us to abide by the space and unfriendly atmosphere. Because of that, they used to create and acclimatize. It cannot be modified unknowingly or can't get disfigured or breakdown in a hostile environment. In this scenario, we can't neglect anything, by handling this we need to address this issue with the efficient solution like Artificial Intelligence.

Disadvantages of Artificial Intelligence

Job losses: There is no way around it, AI will cost lesser-skilled people their jobs. Robots have already taken many jobs on assembly lines and as AI gets better at doing complex tasks, even more low-skill jobs will be taken.

"AI will create much more wealth than it destroys, but it will not be equitably distributed, especially at first," said Wilson. Driverless cars is one obvious singular tech that will displace millions of human drivers fairly quickly, although the recent fatality involving a Tesla car on auto-drive may have set the whole effort back a bit.

The changes will be subliminally felt and not overt, said Wilson. "A tax accountant won't one day receive a pink slip and meet the robot that is now going to sit at her desk. Rather, the next time the tax accountant applies for a job, it will be a bit harder to find a job."

A concentration of power: AI could mean a lot of power will be in the hands of a few who are controlling it. "AI de-humanizes warfare as the nations in possession of advanced AI technology can kill humans without involving an actual human to pull the trigger," said Schneiderhan.

Bad calls: AI does not have the ability to make a judgement call and may never get that ability. A really good example happened in Sydney, Australia in 2014, when there was a shooting and hostage drama downtown. People began ringing up Uber to get out of the affected area, and because of the surge in demand in a concentrated area, Uber's algorithms fell back on the trusted economics of supply-and-demand and ride rates skyrocketed.

The Uber algorithms didn't take into account the violent crisis impacting downtown, and affected riders didn't care. They were livid that they had been gouged at a time of crisis. It forced Uber to reevaluate how it handles such emergencies. Perhaps in the future it will handle them better, but for a few Aussies, it left a bad taste in their mouths.

References

- Reiter, raymond (2001). Knowledge in action: logical foundations for specifying and implementing dynamical systems. Cambridge, massachusetts: the mit press. Pp. 20–22. Isbn 9780262527002

- 3-major-problems-of-artificial-intelligence-implementation-into-commercial-projects: medium.com, Retrieved 15 January, 20

- Thielscher, michael (september 2001). "the qualification problem: a solution to the problem of anomalous models". Artificial intelligence. 131 (1–2): 1–37. Doi:10.1016/s0004-3702(01)00131-x

- Pros-and-cons-of-artificial-intelligence, applications: datamation.com, Retrieved 15 June, 2019

- Scassellati, brian (2002). "theory of mind for a humanoid robot". Autonomous robots. 12 (1): 13–24. Doi:10.1023/a:1013298507114

- Advantages-of-artificial-intelligence: educba.com, Retrieved 21 April, 2019

- Alpaydin, ethem (2010). Introduction to machine learning. London: the mit press. Isbn 978-0-262-01243-0. Retrieved 4 february 2017

5

Philosophy and Ethics

The philosophy of artificial intelligence is concerned with the issues related to the possibility of building an intelligent thinking machine. The ethics of artificial intelligence is a section of ethics of technology which deals specifically with artificially intelligent beings and robots. This chapter closely examines the key concepts of philosophy and ethics of artificial intelligence such as Turing test and computational theory of mind.

Philosophy of Artificial Intelligence

The philosophy of artificial intelligence is a collection of issues primarily concerned with whether or not AI is possible - with whether or not it is possible to build an intelligent thinking machine. Also of concern is whether humans and other animals are best thought of as machines (computational robots, say) themselves. The most important of the "whether-possible" problems lie at the intersection of theories of the semantic contents of thought and the nature of computation. A second suite of problems surrounds the nature of rationality. A third suite revolves around the seeming "transcendent" reasoning powers of the human mind. These problems derive from Kurt Gödel's famous Incompleteness Theorem. A fourth collection of problems concerns the architecture of an intelligent machine. Should a thinking computer use discrete or continuous modes of computing and representing, is having a body necessary, and is being conscious necessary. This takes us to the final set of questions. Can a computer be conscious? Can a computer have a moral sense? Would we have duties to thinking computers, to robots? For example, is it moral for humans to even attempt to build an intelligent machine? If we did build such a machine, would turning it off be the equivalent of murder? If we had a race of such machines, would it be immoral to force them to work for us?

Artificial intelligence has close connections with philosophy because both share several concepts and these include intelligence, action, consciousness, epistemology, and even free will. Furthermore, the technology is concerned with the creation of artificial animals or artificial people (or, at least, artificial creatures) so the discipline is of considerable interest to philosophers. These factors contributed to the emergence of the philosophy of artificial intelligence. Some scholars argue that the AI community's dismissal of philosophy is detrimental.

The philosophy of artificial intelligence attempts to answer such questions as follows:

- Can a machine act intelligently? Can it solve *any* problem that a person would solve by thinking?

- Are human intelligence and machine intelligence the same? Is the human brain essentially a computer?

- Can a machine have a mind, mental states, and consciousness in the same way that a human being can? Can it *feel how things are*?

Questions like these reflect the divergent interests of AI researchers, linguists, cognitive scientists and philosophers respectively. The scientific answers to these questions depend on the definition of "intelligence" and "consciousness" and exactly which "machines" are under discussion.

Important propositions in the philosophy of AI include:

- Turing's "polite convention": If a machine behaves as intelligently as a human being, then it is as intelligent as a human being.

- The Dartmouth proposal: "Every aspect of learning or any other feature of intelligence can be so precisely described that a machine can be made to simulate it."

- Newell and Simon's physical symbol system hypothesis: "A physical symbol system has the necessary and sufficient means of general intelligent action."

- Searle's strong AI hypothesis: "The appropriately programmed computer with the right inputs and outputs would thereby have a mind in exactly the same sense human beings have minds."

- Hobbes' mechanism: "For 'reason' is nothing but 'reckoning,' that is adding and subtracting, of the consequences of general names agreed upon for the 'marking' and 'signifying' of our thoughts."

Can a Machine Display General Intelligence?

Is it possible to create a machine that can solve *all* the problems humans solve using their intelligence? This question defines the scope of what machines will be able to do in the future and guides the direction of AI research. It only concerns the *behavior* of machines and ignores the issues of interest to psychologists, cognitive scientists and philosophers; to answer this question, it does not matter whether a machine is *really* thinking (as a person thinks) or is just *acting like* it is thinking.

The basic position of most AI researchers is summed up in this statement, which appeared in the proposal for the Dartmouth workshop of 1956:

"Every aspect of learning or any other feature of intelligence can be so precisely described that a machine can be made to simulate it."

Arguments against the basic premise must show that building a working AI system is impossible, because there is some practical limit to the abilities of computers or that there is some special quality of the human mind that is necessary for thinking and yet cannot be duplicated by a machine (or by the methods of current AI research). Arguments in favor of the basic premise must show that such a system is possible.

The first step to answering the question is to clearly define "intelligence".

Intelligence

Turing Test

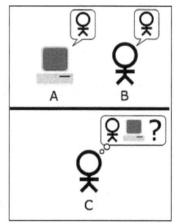

The "standard interpretation" of the Turing test.

Alan Turing reduced the problem of defining intelligence to a simple question about conversation. He suggests that: if a machine can answer *any* question put to it, using the same words that an ordinary person would, then we may call that machine intelligent. A modern version of his experimental design would use an online chat room, where one of the participants is a real person and one of the participants is a computer program. The program passes the test if no one can tell which of the two participants is human. Turing notes that no one (except philosophers) ever asks the question "can people think?" He writes "instead of arguing continually over this point, it is usual to have a polite convention that everyone thinks". Turing's test extends this polite convention to machines:

- If a machine acts as intelligently as human being, then it is as intelligent as a human being.

One criticism of the Turing test is that it is explicitly anthropomorphic. If our ultimate goal is to create machines that are *more* intelligent than people, why should we insist that our machines must closely *resemble* people? Russell and Norvig write that "aeronautical engineering texts do not define the goal of their field as 'making machines that fly so exactly like pigeons that they can fool other pigeons".

Intelligent Agent

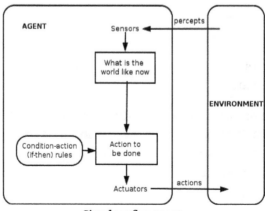

Simple reflex agent.

Recent A.I. research defines intelligence in terms of intelligent agents. An "agent" is something which perceives and acts in an environment. A "performance measure" defines what counts as success for the agent.

- If an agent acts so as to maximize the expected value of a performance measure based on past experience and knowledge then it is intelligent.

Definitions like this one try to capture the essence of intelligence. They have the advantage that, unlike the Turing test, they do not also test for human traits that we may not want to consider intelligent, like the ability to be insulted or the temptation to lie. They have the disadvantage that they fail to make the commonsense differentiation between "things that think" and "things that do not". By this definition, even a thermostat has a rudimentary intelligence.

Arguments that a Machine can Display General Intelligence

Brain can be Simulated

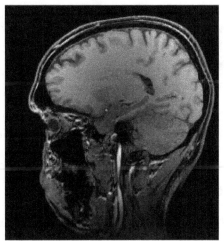

An MRI scan of a normal adult human brain

Hubert Dreyfus describes this argument as claiming that "if the nervous system obeys the laws of physics and chemistry, which we have every reason to suppose it does, then we ought to be able to reproduce the behavior of the nervous system with some physical device". This argument, first introduced as early as 1943 and vividly described by Hans Moravec in 1988, is now associated with futurist Ray Kurzweil, who estimates that computer power will be sufficient for a complete brain simulation by the year 2029. A non-real-time simulation of a thalamocortical model that has the size of the human brain (10^{11} neurons) was performed in 2005 and it took 50 days to simulate 1 second of brain dynamics on a cluster of 27 processors.

Few disagree that a brain simulation is possible in theory, even critics of AI such as Hubert Dreyfus and John Searle. However, Searle points out that, in principle, *anything* can be simulated by a computer; thus, bringing the definition to its breaking point leads to the conclusion that any process at all can technically be considered "computation". "What we wanted to know is what distinguishes the mind from thermostats and livers," he writes. Thus, merely mimicking the functioning of a brain would in itself be an admission of ignorance regarding intelligence and the nature of the mind.

Human Thinking is Symbol Processing

In 1963, Allen Newell and Herbert A. Simon proposed that "symbol manipulation" was the essence of both human and machine intelligence. They wrote:

- A physical symbol system has the necessary and sufficient means of general intelligent action.

This claim is very strong: It implies both that human thinking is a kind of symbol manipulation (because a symbol system is necessary for intelligence) and that machines can be intelligent (because a symbol system is sufficientfor intelligence). Another version of this position was described by philosopher Hubert Dreyfus, who called it "the psychological assumption":

- The mind can be viewed as a device operating on bits of information according to formal rules.

A distinction is usually made between the kind of high level symbols that directly correspond with objects in the world, such as <dog> and <tail> and the more complex "symbols" that are present in a machine like a neural network. Early research into AI, called "good old fashioned artificial intelligence" (GOFAI) by John Haugeland, focused on these kind of high level symbols.

Arguments against Symbol Processing

These arguments show that human thinking does not consist (solely) of high level symbol manipulation. They do *not* show that artificial intelligence is impossible, only that more than symbol processing is required.

Gödelian Anti-mechanist Arguments

In 1931, Kurt Gödel proved with an incompleteness theorem that it is always possible to construct a "Gödel statement" that a given consistent formal system of logic (such as a high-level symbol manipulation program) could not prove. Despite being a true statement, the constructed Gödel statement is unprovable in the given system. (The truth of the constructed Gödel statement is contingent on the consistency of the given system; applying the same process to a subtly inconsistent system will appear to succeed, but will actually yield a false "Gödel statement" instead.) More speculatively, Gödel conjectured that the human mind can correctly eventually determine the truth or falsity of any well-grounded mathematical statement (including any possible Gödel statement), and that therefore the human mind's power is not reducible to a *mechanism*. Philosopher John Lucas and Roger Penrose have championed this philosophical anti-mechanist argument. Gödelian anti-mechanist arguments tend to rely on the innocuous-seeming claim that a system of human mathematicians (or some idealization of human mathematicians) is both consistent (completely free of error) and believes fully in its own consistency (and can make all logical inferences that follow from its own consistency, including belief in its Gödel statement). This is provably impossible for a Turing machine (and, by an informal extension, any known type of mechanical computer) to do; therefore, the Gödelian concludes that human reasoning is too powerful to be captured in a machine.

However, the modern consensus in the scientific and mathematical community is that actual human reasoning is inconsistent; that any consistent "idealized version" H of human reasoning would logically be forced to adopt a healthy but counter-intuitive open-minded skepticism about the consistency of H (otherwise H is provably inconsistent); and that Gödel's theorems do not lead to any valid argument that humans have mathematical reasoning capabilities beyond what a machine could ever duplicate. This consensus that Gödelian anti-mechanist arguments are doomed to failure is laid out strongly in *Artificial Intelligence*: "*any* attempt to utilize (Gödel's incompleteness results) to attack the computationalist thesis is bound to be illegitimate, since these results are quite consistent with the computationalist thesis."

More pragmatically, Russell and Norvig note that Gödel's argument only applies to what can theoretically be proved, given an infinite amount of memory and time. In practice, real machines (including humans) have finite resources and will have difficulty proving many theorems. It is not necessary to prove everything in order to be intelligent.

Less formally, Douglas Hofstadter, in his Pulitzer prize winning book *Gödel, Escher, Bach: An Eternal Golden Braid,* states that these "Gödel-statements" always refer to the system itself, drawing an analogy to the way the Epimenides paradox uses statements that refer to themselves, such as "this statement is false" or "I am lying". But, of course, the Epimenides paradox applies to anything that makes statements, whether they are machines *or* humans, even Lucas himself. Consider:

- Lucas can't assert the truth of this statement.

This statement is true but cannot be asserted by Lucas. This shows that Lucas himself is subject to the same limits that he describes for machines, as are all people, and so Lucas's argument is pointless.

After concluding that human reasoning is non-computable, Penrose went on to controversially speculate that some kind of hypothetical non-computable processes involving the collapse of quantum mechanical states give humans a special advantage over existing computers. Existing quantum computers are only capable of reducing the complexity of Turing computable tasks and are still restricted to tasks within the scope of Turing machines. By Penrose and Lucas's arguments, existing quantum computers are not sufficient, so Penrose seeks for some other process involving new physics, for instance quantum gravity which might manifest new physics at the scale of the Planck mass via spontaneous quantum collapse of the wave function. These states, he suggested, occur both within neurons and also spanning more than one neuron. However, other scientists point out that there is no plausible organic mechanism in the brain for harnessing any sort of quantum computation, and furthermore that the timescale of quantum decoherence seems too fast to influence neuron firing.

Dreyfus: The Primacy of Implicit Skills

Hubert Dreyfus argued that human intelligence and expertise depended primarily on implicit skill rather than explicit symbolic manipulation, and argued that these skills would never be captured in formal rules.

Dreyfus's argument had been anticipated by Turing in his 1950 paper Computing machinery and intelligence, where he had classified this as the "argument from the informality of behavior." Turing argued in response that, just because we do not know the rules that govern a complex behavior, this does not mean that no such rules exist. He wrote: "we cannot so easily convince ourselves of the absence of complete laws of behaviour. The only way we know of for finding such laws is scientific observation, and we certainly know of no circumstances under which we could say, 'We have searched enough. There are no such laws.'

Russell and Norvig point out that, in the years since Dreyfus published his critique, progress has been made towards discovering the "rules" that govern unconscious reasoning. The situated movement in robotics research attempts to capture our unconscious skills at perception and attention. Computational intelligence paradigms, such as neural nets, evolutionary algorithms and so on are mostly directed at simulated unconscious reasoning and learning. Statistical approaches to AI can make predictions which approach the accuracy of human intuitive guesses. Research into commonsense knowledge has focused on reproducing the "background" or context of knowledge. In fact, AI research in general has moved away from high level symbol manipulation or "GOFAI", towards new models that are intended to capture more of our *unconscious* reasoning. Historian and AI researcher Daniel Crevier wrote that "time has proven the accuracy and perceptiveness of some of Dreyfus's comments. Had he formulated them less aggressively, constructive actions they suggested might have been taken much earlier."

Can a Machine have a Mind, Consciousness and Mental States?

This is a philosophical question, related to the problem of other minds and the hard problem of consciousness. The question revolves around a position defined by John Searle as "strong AI":

- A physical symbol system can have a mind and mental states.

Searle distinguished this position from what he called "weak AI".

- A physical symbol system can act intelligently.

Searle introduced the terms to isolate strong AI from weak AI so he could focus on what he thought was the more interesting and debatable issue. He argued that *even if we assume* that we had a computer program that acted exactly like a human mind, there would still be a difficult philosophical question that needed to be answered.

Neither of Searle's two positions are of great concern to AI research, since they do not directly answer the question "can a machine display general intelligence?" (unless it can also be shown that consciousness is *necessary* for intelligence). Turing wrote "I do not wish to give the impression that I think there is no mystery about consciousness but I do not think these mysteries necessarily need to be solved before we can answer the question [of whether machines can think]." Russell and Norvig agree: "Most AI researchers take the weak AI hypothesis for granted, and don't care about the strong AI hypothesis."

There are a few researchers who believe that consciousness is an essential element in intelligence, such as Igor Aleksander, Stan Franklin, Ron Sun, and Pentti Haikonen, although their definition of "consciousness" strays very close to "intelligence."

Before we can answer this question, we must be clear what we mean by "minds", "mental states" and "consciousness".

Consciousness, Minds and Mental States

The words "mind" and "consciousness" are used by different communities in different ways. Some new agethinkers, for example, use the word "consciousness" to describe something similar to Bergson's "élan vital": an invisible, energetic fluid that permeates life and especially the mind. Science fiction writers use the word to describe some essential property that makes us human: a machine or alien that is "conscious" will be presented as a fully human character, with intelligence, desires, will, insight, pride and so on. (Science fiction writers also use the words "sentience", "sapience," "self-awareness" or "ghost" - as in the *Ghost in the Shell* manga and anime series - to describe this essential human property). For others, the words "mind" or "consciousness" are used as a kind of secular synonym for the soul.

For philosophers, neuroscientists and cognitive scientists, the words are used in a way that is both more precise and more mundane: they refer to the familiar, everyday experience of having a "thought in your head", like a perception, a dream, an intention or a plan, and to the way we *know* something, or *mean* something or *understand* something. "It's not hard to give a commonsense definition of consciousness" observes philosopher John Searle. What is mysterious and fascinating is not so much *what* it is but *how* it is: how does a lump of fatty tissue and electricity give rise to this (familiar) experience of perceiving, meaning or thinking?

Philosophers call this the hard problem of consciousness. It is the latest version of a classic problem in the philosophy of mind called the "mind-body problem." A related problem is the problem of *meaning* or *understanding* (which philosophers call "intentionality"): what is the connection between our *thoughts* and *what we are thinking about* (i.e. objects and situations out in the world)? A third issue is the problem of *experience* (or "phenomenology"): If two people see the same thing, do they have the same experience? Or are there things "inside their head" (called "qualia") that can be different from person to person?

Neurobiologists believe all these problems will be solved as we begin to identify the neural correlates of consciousness: the actual relationship between the machinery in our heads and its collective properties; such as the mind, experience and understanding. Some of the harshest critics of artificial intelligence agree that the brain is just a machine, and that consciousness and intelligence are the result of physical processes in the brain.The difficult philosophical question is this: can a computer program, running on a digital machine that shuffles the binary digits of zero and one, duplicate the ability of the neurons to create minds, with mental states (like understanding or perceiving), and ultimately, the experience of consciousness?

Arguments that a Computer cannot have a Mind and Mental States

John Searle asks us to consider a thought experiment: suppose we have written a computer program that passes the Turing test and demonstrates "general intelligent action." Suppose, specifically that the program can converse in fluent Chinese. Write the program on 3x5 cards and give them to an ordinary person who does not speak Chinese. Lock the person into a room and have him follow the instructions on the cards. He will copy out Chinese characters and pass them in and out of the room through a slot. From the outside, it will appear that the Chinese room contains a fully intelligent person who speaks Chinese. The question is this: is there anyone (or anything) in the room that understands Chinese? That is, is there anything that has the mental state of understanding, or which has conscious awareness of what is being discussed in Chinese? The man is clearly not aware. The room cannot be aware. The *cards* certainly aren't aware. Searle concludes that the Chinese room, or *any* other physical symbol system, cannot have a mind.

Searle goes on to argue that actual mental states and consciousness require "actual physical-chemical properties of actual human brains." He argues there are special "causal properties" of brains and neurons that gives rise to minds: in his words "brains cause minds."

Gottfried Leibniz made essentially the same argument as Searle in 1714, using the thought experiment of expanding the brain until it was the size of a mill. In 1974, Lawrence Davis imagined duplicating the brain using telephone lines and offices staffed by people, and in 1978 Ned Block envisioned the entire population of China involved in such a brain simulation. This thought experiment is called "the Chinese Nation" or "the Chinese Gym". Ned Block also proposed his Blockhead argument, which is a version of the Chinese room in which the program has been re-factored into a simple set of rules of the form "see this, do that", removing all mystery from the program.

Responses to the Chinese Room

Responses to the Chinese room emphasize several different points:

- The systems reply and the virtual mind reply: This reply argues that the system, including the man, the program, the room, and the cards, is what understands Chinese. Searle claims that the man in the room is the only thing which could possibly "have a mind" or "understand", but others disagree, arguing that it is possible for there to be *two* minds in the same physical place, similar to the way a computer can simultaneously "be" two machines at once: one physical (like a Macintosh) and one "virtual" (like a word processor).

- Speed, power and complexity replies: Several critics point out that the man in the room would probably take millions of years to respond to a simple question, and would require "filing cabinets" of astronomical proportions. This brings the clarity of Searle's intuition into doubt.

- Robot reply: To truly understand, some believe the Chinese Room needs eyes and hands. Hans Moravec writes: 'If we could graft a robot to a reasoning program, we wouldn't need a person to provide the meaning anymore: it would come from the physical world."

- Brain simulator reply: What if the program simulates the sequence of nerve firings at the synapses of an actual brain of an actual Chinese speaker? The man in the room would be simulating an actual brain. This is a variation on the "systems reply" that appears more plausible because "the system" now clearly operates like a human brain, which strengthens the intuition that there is something besides the man in the room that could understand Chinese.

- Other minds reply and the epiphenomena reply: Several people have noted that Searle's argument is just a version of the problem of other minds, applied to machines. Since it is difficult to decide if people are "actually" thinking, we should not be surprised that it is difficult to answer the same question about machines.

A related question is whether "consciousness" (as Searle understands it) exists. Searle argues that the experience of consciousness can't be detected by examining the behavior of a machine, a human being or any other animal. Daniel Dennett points out that natural selection cannot preserve a feature of an animal that has no effect on the behavior of the animal, and thus consciousness (as Searle understands it) can't be produced by natural selection. Therefore either natural selection did not produce consciousness, or "strong AI" is correct in that consciousness can be detected by suitably designed Turing test.

Is thinking a kind of Computation?

The computational theory of mind or "computationalism" claims that the relationship between mind and brain is similar (if not identical) to the relationship between a *running program* and a computer. The idea has philosophical roots in Hobbes (who claimed reasoning was "nothing more than reckoning"), Leibniz (who attempted to create a logical calculus of all human ideas), Hume (who thought perception could be reduced to "atomic impressions") and even Kant (who analyzed all experience as controlled by formal rules). The latest version is associated with philosophers Hilary Putnam and Jerry Fodor.

This question bears on our earlier questions: if the human brain is a kind of computer then computers can be both intelligent and conscious, answering both the practical and philosophical questions of AI. In terms of the practical question of AI ("Can a machine display general intelligence?"), some versions of computationalism make the claim that:

- Reasoning is nothing but reckoning.

In other words, our intelligence derives from a form of calculation, similar to arithmetic. This is the physical symbol system hypothesis discussed above, and it implies that artificial intelligence is possible. In terms of the philosophical question of AI ("Can a machine have mind, mental states and consciousness?"), most versions of computationalism claim that (as Stevan Harnad characterizes it):

- Mental states are just implementations of (the right) computer programs.

This is John Searle's "strong AI", and it is the real target of the Chinese room argument (according to Harnad).

Alan Turing noted that there are many arguments of the form "a machine will never do X", where X can be many things, such as:

"Be kind, resourceful, beautiful, friendly, have initiative, have a sense of humor, tell right from wrong, make mistakes, fall in love, enjoy strawberries and cream, make someone fall in love with it, learn from experience, use words properly, be the subject of its own thought, have as much diversity of behaviour as a man, do something really new".

Turing argues that these objections are often based on naive assumptions about the versatility of machines or are "disguised forms of the argument from consciousness". Writing a program that exhibits one of these behaviors "will not make much of an impression." All of these arguments are tangential to the basic premise of AI, unless it can be shown that one of these traits is essential for general intelligence.

Can a Machine have Emotions?

If "emotions" are defined only in terms of their effect on behavior or on how they function inside an organism, then emotions can be viewed as a mechanism that an intelligent agent uses to maximize the utility of its actions. Given this definition of emotion, Hans Moravec believes that "robots in general will be quite emotional about being nice people". Fear is a source of urgency. Empathy is a necessary component of good human computer interaction. He says robots "will try to please you in an apparently selfless manner because it will get a thrill out of this positive reinforcement. You can interpret this as a kind of love." Daniel Crevier writes "Moravec's point is that emotions are just devices for channeling behavior in a direction beneficial to the survival of one's species."

However, emotions can also be defined in terms of their subjective quality, of what it *feels like* to have an emotion. The question of whether the machine *actually feels* an emotion, or whether it merely *acts as if* it is feeling an emotion is the philosophical question, "can a machine be conscious?" in another form.

Can a Machine be Self-aware?

"Self awareness"S is sometimes used by science fiction writers as a name for the essentialhuman property that makes a character fully human. Turing strips away all other properties of human beings and reduces the question to "can a machine be the subject of its own thought?" Can it *think about itself*? Viewed in this way, a program can be written that can report on its own internal states, such as a debugger. Though arguably self-awareness often presumes a bit more capability; a machine that can ascribe meaning in some way to not only its own state but in general postulating questions without solid answers: the contextual nature of its existence now; how it compares to past states or plans for the future, the limits and value of its work product, how it perceives its performance to be valued-by or compared to others.

Can a Machine be Original or Creative?

Turing reduces this to the question of whether a machine can "take us by surprise" and argues that this is obviously true, as any programmer can attest. He notes that, with enough storage capacity, a computer can behave in an astronomical number of different ways. It must be possible, even trivial, for a computer that can represent ideas to combine them in new ways. (Douglas Lenat's Automated Mathematician, as one example, combined ideas to discover new mathematical truths.) Kaplan and Haenlein suggest that machines can display scientific creativity, while it seems likely that humans will have the upper hand where artistic creativity is concerned.

In 2009, scientists at Aberystwyth University in Wales and the U.K's University of Cambridge designed a robot called Adam that they believe to be the first machine to independently come up with new scientific findings. Also in 2009, researchers at Cornell developed Eureqa, a computer program that extrapolates formulas to fit the data inputted, such as finding the laws of motion from a pendulum's motion.

Can a Machine be Benevolent or Hostile?

This question (like many others in the philosophy of artificial intelligence) can be presented in two forms. "Hostility" can be defined in terms function or behavior, in which case "hostile" becomes synonymous with "dangerous". Or it can be defined in terms of intent: can a machine "deliberately" set out to do harm? The latter is the question "can a machine have conscious states?" (such as intentions) in another form.

The question of whether highly intelligent and completely autonomous machines would be dangerous has been examined in detail by futurists (such as the Singularity Institute). (The obvious element of drama has also made the subject popular in science fiction, which has considered many differently possible scenarios where intelligent machines pose a threat to mankind).

One issue is that machines may acquire the autonomy and intelligence required to be dangerous very quickly. Vernor Vinge has suggested that over just a few years, computers will suddenly become thousands or millions of times more intelligent than humans. He calls this "the Singularity." He suggests that it may be somewhat or possibly very dangerous for humans. This is discussed by a philosophy called Singularitarianism.

In 2009, academics and technical experts attended a conference to discuss the potential impact of robots and computers and the impact of the hypothetical possibility that they could become self-sufficient and able to make their own decisions. They discussed the possibility and the extent to which computers and robots might be able to acquire any level of autonomy, and to what degree they could use such abilities to possibly pose any threat or hazard. They noted that some machines have acquired various forms of semi-autonomy, including being able to find power sources on their own and being able to independently choose targets to attack with weapons. They also noted that some computer viruses can evade elimination and have achieved "cockroach intelligence." They noted that self-awareness as depicted in science-fiction is probably unlikely, but that there were other potential hazards and pitfalls.

Some experts and academics have questioned the use of robots for military combat, especially when such robots are given some degree of autonomous functions. The US Navy has funded a report which indicates that as military robots become more complex, there should be greater attention to implications of their ability to make autonomous decisions.

The President of the Association for the Advancement of Artificial Intelligence has commissioned a study to look at this issue. They point to programs like the Language Acquisition Device which can emulate human interaction.

Some have suggested a need to build "Friendly AI", meaning that the advances which are already occurring with AI should also include an effort to make AI intrinsically friendly and humane.

Can a Machine have a Soul?

Finally, those who believe in the existence of a soul may argue that "Thinking is a function of man's immortal soul." Alan Turing called this "the theological objection". He writes:

"In attempting to construct such machines we should not be irreverently usurping His power of creating souls, any more than we are in the procreation of children: rather we are, in either case, instruments of His will providing mansions for the souls that He creates".

Views on the Role of Philosophy

Some scholars argue that the AI community's dismissal of philosophy is detrimental. In the *Stanford Encyclopedia of Philosophy*, some philosophers argue that the role of philosophy in AI is underappreciated.Physicist David Deutsch argues that without an understanding of philosophy or its concepts, AI development would suffer from a lack of progress.

Turing Test

The Turing test, developed by Alan Turing in 1950, is a test of a machine's ability to exhibit intelligent behaviour equivalent to, or indistinguishable from, that of a human. Turing proposed that a human evaluator would judge natural language conversations between a human and a machine designed to generate human-like responses. The evaluator would be aware that one of the two partners in conversation is a machine, and all participants would be separated from one another. The conversation would be limited to a text-only channel such as a computer keyboard and screen so the result would not depend on the machine's ability to render words as speech. If the evaluator cannot reliably tell the machine from the human, the machine is said to have passed the test. The test results do not depend on the machine's ability to give correct answers to questions, only how closely its answers resemble those a human would give.

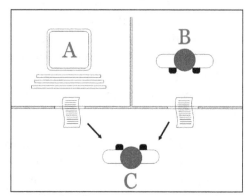

The "standard interpretation" of the Turing test, in which player C, the interrogator,
is given the task of trying to determine which player – A or B – is a computer and which is a human.
The interrogator is limited to using the responses to written questions to make the determination.

The test was introduced by Turing in his 1950 paper, "Computing Machinery and Intelligence", while working at the University of Manchester. It opens with the words: "I propose to consider the question, 'Can machines think?' Because "thinking" is difficult to define, Turing chooses to "replace the question by another, which is closely related to it and is expressed in relatively unambiguous words." Turing describes the new form of the problem in terms of a three-person game called the "imitation game", in which an interrogator asks questions of a man and a woman in another room in order to determine the correct sex of the two players. Turing's new question is: "Are there imaginable digital computers which would do well in the *imitation game*?" This question, Turing believed, is one that can actually be answered. In the remainder of the paper, he argued against all the major objections to the proposition that "machines can think".

Since Turing first introduced his test, it has proven to be both highly influential and widely criticised, and it has become an important concept in the philosophy of artificial intelligence. Some of these criticisms, such as John Searle's Chinese room, are controversial in their own right.

Alan Turing

Researchers in the United Kingdom had been exploring "machine intelligence" for up to ten years prior to the founding of the field of artificial intelligence (AI) research in 1956. It was a common topic among the members of the Ratio Club, who were an informal group of British cybernetics and electronics researchers that included Alan Turing, after whom the test is named.

Turing, in particular, had been tackling the notion of machine intelligence since at least 1941 and one of the earliest-known mentions of "computer intelligence" was made by him in 1947. In Turing's report, "Intelligent Machinery", he investigated "the question of whether or not it is possible for machinery to show intelligent behaviour" and, as part of that investigation, proposed what may be considered the forerunner to his later tests.

It is not difficult to devise a paper machine which will play a not very bad game of chess. Now get three men as subjects for the experiment A, B and C. A and C are to be rather poor chess players, B is the operator who works the paper machine. Two rooms are used with some arrangement for communicating moves, and a game is played between C and either A or the paper machine. C may find it quite difficult to tell which he is playing.

"Computing Machinery and Intelligence" was the first published paper by Turing to focus exclusively on machine intelligence. Turing begins the 1950 paper with the claim, "I propose to consider the question 'Can machines think?' As he highlights, the traditional approach to such a question is to start with definitions, defining both the terms "machine" and "intelligence". Turing chooses not to do so; instead he replaces the question with a new one, "which is closely related to it and is expressed in relatively unambiguous words." In essence he proposes to change the question from "Can machines think?" to "Can machines do what we (as thinking entities) can do?" The advantage of the new question, Turing argues, is that it draws "a fairly sharp line between the physical and intellectual capacities of a man."

To demonstrate this approach Turing proposes a test inspired by a party game, known as the "imitation game", in which a man and a woman go into separate rooms and guests try to tell them apart by writing a series of questions and reading the typewritten answers sent back. In this game both the man and the woman aim to convince the guests that they are the other. (Huma Shah argues that this two-human version of the game was presented by Turing only to introduce the reader to the machine-human question-answer test). Turing described his new version of the game as follows:

We now ask the question, "What will happen when a machine takes the part of A in this game?" Will the interrogator decide wrongly as often when the game is played like this as he does when the game is played between a man and a woman? These questions replace our original, "Can machines think?"

Later in the paper Turing suggests an "equivalent" alternative formulation involving a judge conversing only with a computer and a man. While neither of these formulations precisely matches the version of the Turing test that is more generally known today, he proposed a third in 1952. In this version, which Turing discussed in a BBC radio broadcast, a jury asks questions of a computer and the role of the computer is to make a significant proportion of the jury believe that it is really a man.

Turing's paper considered nine putative objections, which include all the major arguments against artificial intelligence that have been raised in the years since the paper was published.

Eliza and Parry

In 1966, Joseph Weizenbaum created a program which appeared to pass the Turing test. The program, known as ELIZA, worked by examining a user's typed comments for keywords. If a keyword is found, a rule that transforms the user's comments is applied, and the resulting sentence is returned. If a keyword is not found, ELIZA responds either with a generic riposte or by repeating one of the earlier comments. In addition, Weizenbaum developed ELIZA to replicate the behaviour of a Rogerian psychotherapist, allowing ELIZA to be "free to assume the pose of knowing almost nothing of the real world." With these techniques, Weizenbaum's program was able to fool some people into believing that they were talking to a real person, with some subjects being "very hard to convince that ELIZA is *not* human." Thus, ELIZA is claimed by some to be one of the programs (perhaps the first) able to pass the Turing test, even though this view is highly contentious.

Kenneth Colby created PARRY in 1972, a program described as "ELIZA with attitude". It attempted to model the behaviour of a paranoid schizophrenic, using a similar (if more advanced) approach to that employed by Weizenbaum. To validate the work, PARRY was tested in the early 1970s using a variation of the Turing test. A group of experienced psychiatrists analysed a combination of real patients and computers running PARRY through teleprinters. Another group of 33 psychiatrists were shown transcripts of the conversations. The two groups were then asked to identify which of the "patients" were human and which were computer programs. The psychiatrists were able to make the correct identification only 48 percent of the time – a figure consistent with random guessing.

In the 21st century, versions of these programs (now known as "chatterbots") continue to fool people. "CyberLover", a malware program, preys on Internet users by convincing them to "reveal information about their identities or to lead them to visit a web site that will deliver malicious content to their computers". The program has emerged as a "Valentine-risk" flirting with people "seeking relationships online in order to collect their personal data".

The Chinese Room

John Searle's 1980 paper *Minds, Brains, and Programs* proposed the "Chinese room" thought experiment and argued that the Turing test could not be used to determine if a machine can think. Searle noted that software (such as ELIZA) could pass the Turing test simply by manipulating symbols of which they had no understanding. Without understanding, they could not be described as "thinking" in the same sense people are. Therefore, Searle concludes, the Turing test cannot prove that a machine can think. Much like the Turing test itself, Searle's argument has been both widely criticised and highly endorsed.

Arguments such as Searle's and others working on the philosophy of mind sparked off a more intense debate about the nature of intelligence, the possibility of intelligent machines and the value of the Turing test that continued through the 1980s and 1990s.

Loebner Prize

The Loebner Prize provides an annual platform for practical Turing tests with the first competition held in November 1991. It is underwritten by Hugh Loebner. The Cambridge Center for Behavioral Studies in Massachusetts, United States, organised the prizes up to and including the 2003 contest. As Loebner described it, one reason the competition was created is to advance the state of AI research, at least in part, because no one had taken steps to implement the Turing test despite 40 years of discussing it.

The first Loebner Prize competition in 1991 led to a renewed discussion of the viability of the Turing test and the value of pursuing it, in both the popular press and academia. The first contest was won by a mindless program with no identifiable intelligence that managed to fool naïve interrogators into making the wrong identification. This highlighted several of the shortcomings of the Turing test: The winner won, at least in part, because it was able to "imitate human typing errors"; the unsophisticated interrogators were easily fooled; and some researchers in AI have been led to feel that the test is merely a distraction from more fruitful research.

The silver (text only) and gold (audio and visual) prizes have never been won. However, the competition has awarded the bronze medal every year for the computer system that, in the judges' opinions, demonstrates the "most human" conversational behaviour among that year's entries. Artificial Linguistic Internet Computer Entity (A.L.I.C.E.) has won the bronze award on three occasions in recent times. Learning AI Jabberwacky won in 2005 and 2006.

The Loebner Prize tests conversational intelligence; winners are typically chatterbot programs, or Artificial Conversational Entities (ACE)s. Early Loebner Prize rules restricted conversations: Each entry and hidden-human conversed on a single topic, thus the interrogators were restricted to one line of questioning per entity interaction. The restricted conversation rule was lifted for the 1995 Loebner Prize. Interaction duration between judge and entity has varied in Loebner Prizes. In Loebner 2003, at the University of Surrey, each interrogator was allowed five minutes to interact with an entity, machine or hidden-human. Between 2004 and 2007, the interaction time allowed in Loebner Prizes was more than twenty minutes.

Versions

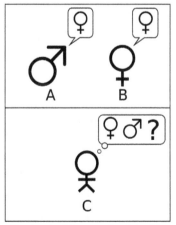

The imitation game, as described by Alan Turing in "Computing Machinery and Intelligence". Player C, through a series of written questions, attempts to determine which of the other two players is a man, and which of the two is the woman. Player A, the man, tries to trick player C into making the wrong decision, while player B tries to help player C.

Saul Traiger argues that there are at least three primary versions of the Turing test, two of which are offered in "Computing Machinery and Intelligence" and one that he describes as the "Standard Interpretation". While there is some debate regarding whether the "Standard Interpretation" is that described by Turing or, instead, based on a misreading of his paper, these three versions are not regarded as equivalent, and their strengths and weaknesses are distinct.

Huma Shah points out that Turing himself was concerned with whether a machine could think and was providing a simple method to examine this: through human-machine question-answer sessions. Shah argues there is one imitation game which Turing described could be practicalised in two different ways: a) one-to-one interrogator-machine test, and b) simultaneous comparison of a machine with a human, both questioned in parallel by an interrogator. Since the Turing test is a test of indistinguishability in performance capacity, the verbal version generalises naturally to all of human performance capacity, verbal as well as nonverbal (robotic).

Imitation Game

Turing's original article describes a simple party game involving three players. Player A is a man, player B is a woman and player C (who plays the role of the interrogator) is of either sex. In the imitation game, player C is unable to see either player A or player B, and can communicate with them only through written notes. By asking questions of player A and player B, player C tries to determine which of the two is the man and which is the woman. Player A's role is to trick the interrogator into making the wrong decision, while player B attempts to assist the interrogator in making the right one.

Turing then asks: What will happen when a machine takes the part of A in this game? Will the interrogator decide wrongly as often when the game is played like this as he does when the game is played between a man and a woman? These questions replace our original, "Can machines think?"

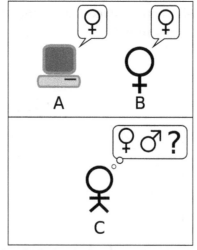

The original imitation game test, in which the player A is replaced with a computer. The computer is now charged with the role of the man, while player B continues to attempt to assist the interrogator.

The second version appeared later in Turing's 1950 paper. Similar to the original imitation game test, the role of player A is performed by a computer. However, the role of player B is performed by a man rather than a woman.

Let us fix our attention on one particular digital computer C. Is it true that by modifying this computer to have an adequate storage, suitably increasing its speed of action, and providing it with an appropriate programme, C can be made to play satisfactorily the part of A in the imitation game, the part of B being taken by a man?

In this version, both player A (the computer) and player B are trying to trick the interrogator into making an incorrect decision.

Standard Interpretation

Common understanding has it that the purpose of the Turing test is not specifically to determine whether a computer is able to fool an interrogator into believing that it is a human, but rather whether a computer could *imitate* a human. While there is some dispute whether this interpretation was intended by Turing, Sterrett believes that it was and thus conflates the second version with this one, while others, such as Traiger, do not – this has nevertheless led to what can be viewed as the "standard interpretation." In this version, player A is a computer and player B a person of either sex. The role of the interrogator is not to determine which is male and which is female, but which is a computer and which is a human. The fundamental issue with the standard interpretation is that the interrogator cannot differentiate which responder is human, and which is machine. There are issues about duration, but the standard interpretation generally considers this limitation as something that should be reasonable.

Imitation Game vs. Standard Turing Test

Controversy has arisen over which of the alternative formulations of the test Turing intended. Sterrett argues that two distinct tests can be extracted from his 1950 paper and that, *pace* Turing's remark, they are not equivalent. The test that employs the party game and compares frequencies of success is referred to as the "Original Imitation Game Test", whereas the test consisting of a human judge conversing with a human and a machine is referred to as the "Standard Turing Test", noting that Sterrett equates this with the "standard interpretation" rather than the second version of the imitation game. Sterrett agrees that the standard Turing test (STT) has the problems that its critics cite but feels that, in contrast, the original imitation game test (OIG test) so defined is immune to many of them, due to a crucial difference: Unlike the STT, it does not make similarity to human performance the criterion, even though it employs human performance in setting a criterion for machine intelligence. A man can fail the OIG test, but it is argued that it is a virtue of a test of intelligence that failure indicates a lack of resourcefulness: The OIG test requires the resourcefulness associated with intelligence and not merely "simulation of human conversational behaviour". The general structure of the OIG test could even be used with non-verbal versions of imitation games.

Still other writers have interpreted Turing as proposing that the imitation game itself is the test, without specifying how to take into account Turing's statement that the test that he proposed using the party version of the imitation game is based upon a criterion of comparative frequency of success in that imitation game, rather than a capacity to succeed at one round of the game.

Saygin has suggested that maybe the original game is a way of proposing a less biased experimental design as it hides the participation of the computer. The imitation game also includes a "social hack" not found in the standard interpretation, as in the game both computer and male human are required to play as pretending to be someone they are not.

Should the Interrogator know about the Computer?

A crucial piece of any laboratory test is that there should be a control. Turing never makes clear whether the interrogator in his tests is aware that one of the participants is a computer. However, if there were a machine that did have the potential to pass a Turing test, it would be safe to assume a double blind control would be necessary.

To return to the original imitation game, he states only that player A is to be replaced with a machine, not that player C is to be made aware of this replacement. When Colby, FD Hilf, S Weber and AD Kramer tested PARRY, they did so by assuming that the interrogators did not need to know that one or more of those being interviewed was a computer during the interrogation. As Ayse Saygin, Peter Swirski, and others have highlighted, this makes a big difference to the implementation and outcome of the test. An experimental study looking at Gricean maxim violations using transcripts of Loebner's one-to-one (interrogator-hidden interlocutor) Prize for AI contests between 1994–1999, Ayse Saygin found significant differences between the responses of participants who knew and did not know about computers being involved.

Strengths

Tractability and Simplicity

The power and appeal of the Turing test derives from its simplicity. The philosophy of mind, psychology, and modern neuroscience have been unable to provide definitions of "intelligence" and "thinking" that are sufficiently precise and general to be applied to machines. Without such definitions, the central questions of the philosophy of artificial intelligence cannot be answered. The Turing test, even if imperfect, at least provides something that can actually be measured. As such, it is a pragmatic attempt to answer a difficult philosophical question.

Breadth of Subject Matter

The format of the test allows the interrogator to give the machine a wide variety of intellectual tasks. Turing wrote that "the question and answer method seems to be suitable for introducing almost any one of the fields of human endeavour that we wish to include." John Haugeland adds that "understanding the words is not enough; you have to understand the *topic* as well."

To pass a well-designed Turing test, the machine must use natural language, reason, have knowledge and learn. The test can be extended to include video input, as well as a "hatch" through which objects can be passed: This would force the machine to demonstrate the skill of vision and robotics as well. Together, these represent almost all of the major problems that artificial intelligence research would like to solve.

The Feigenbaum test is designed to take advantage of the broad range of topics available to a Turing test. It is a limited form of Turing's question-answer game which compares the machine against the abilities of experts in specific fields such as literature or chemistry. IBM's Watson machine achieved success in a man versus machine television quiz show of human knowledge.

Emphasis on Emotional and Aesthetic Intelligence

As a Cambridge honours graduate in mathematics, Turing might have been expected to propose a test of computer intelligence requiring expert knowledge in some highly technical field, and thus anticipating a more recent approach to the subject. Instead, as already noted, the test which he described in his seminal 1950 paper requires the computer to be able to compete successfully in a common party game, and this by performing as well as the typical man in answering a series of questions so as to pretend convincingly to be the woman contestant.

Given the status of human sexual dimorphism as one of the most ancient of subjects, it is thus implicit in the above scenario that the questions to be answered will involve neither specialised factual knowledge nor information processing technique. The challenge for the computer, rather, will be to demonstrate empathy for the role of the female, and to demonstrate as well a characteristic aesthetic sensibility—both of which qualities are on display in this snippet of dialogue which Turing has imagined:

> Interrogator: Will X please tell me the length of his or her hair?
>
> Contestant: My hair is shingled, and the longest strands are about nine inches long.

When Turing does introduce some specialised knowledge into one of his imagined dialogues, the subject is not maths or electronics, but poetry:

> Interrogator: In the first line of your sonnet which reads, "Shall I compare thee to a summer's day," would not "a spring day" do as well or better?
>
> Witness: It wouldn't scan.
>
> Interrogator: How about "a winter's day." That would scan all right.
>
> Witness: Yes, but nobody wants to be compared to a winter's day.

Turing thus once again demonstrates his interest in empathy and aesthetic sensitivity as components of an artificial intelligence; and in light of an increasing awareness of the threat from an AI run amok, it has been suggested that this focus perhaps represents a critical intuition on Turing's part, i.e., that emotional and aesthetic intelligence will play a key role in the creation of a "friendly AI". It is further noted, however, that whatever inspiration Turing might be able to lend in this direction depends upon the preservation of his original vision, which is to say, further, that the promulgation of a "standard interpretation" of the Turing test—i.e., one which focuses on a discursive intelligence only—must be regarded with some caution.

Weaknesses

Turing did not explicitly state that the Turing test could be used as a measure of intelligence, or any other human quality. He wanted to provide a clear and understandable alternative to the word "think", which he could then use to reply to criticisms of the possibility of "thinking machines" and to suggest ways that research might move forward.

Nevertheless, the Turing test has been proposed as a measure of a machine's "ability to think" or its "intelligence". This proposal has received criticism from both philosophers and computer scientists. It assumes that an interrogator can determine if a machine is "thinking" by comparing its behaviour with human behaviour. Every element of this assumption has been questioned: the reliability of the interrogator's judgement, the value of comparing only behaviour and the value of comparing the machine with a human. Because of these and other considerations, some AI researchers have questioned the relevance of the test to their field.

Human Intelligence vs. Intelligence in General

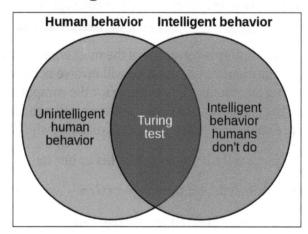

The Turing test does not directly test whether the computer behaves intelligently. It tests only whether the computer behaves like a human being. Since human behaviour and intelligent behaviour are not exactly the same thing, the test can fail to accurately measure intelligence in two ways:

Some Human Behaviour is Unintelligent

The Turing test requires that the machine be able to execute *all* human behaviours, regardless of whether they are intelligent. It even tests for behaviours that may not be considered intelligent at all, such as the susceptibility to insults, the temptation to lie or, simply, a high frequency of typing mistakes. If a machine cannot imitate these unintelligent behaviours in detail it fails the test.

This objection was raised by *The Economist,* in an article entitled "artificial stupidity" published shortly after the first Loebner Prize competition in 1992. The article noted that the first Loebner winner's victory was due, at least in part, to its ability to "imitate human typing errors." Turing himself had suggested that programs add errors into their output, so as to be better "players" of the game.

Some Intelligent Behaviour is Inhuman

The Turing test does not test for highly intelligent behaviours, such as the ability to solve difficult problems or come up with original insights. In fact, it specifically requires deception on the part of the machine: if the machine is *more* intelligent than a human being it must deliberately avoid appearing too intelligent. If it were to solve a computational problem that is practically impossible for a human to solve, then the interrogator would know the program is not human, and the machine would fail the test.

Because it cannot measure intelligence that is beyond the ability of humans, the test cannot be used to build or evaluate systems that are more intelligent than humans. Because of this, several test alternatives that would be able to evaluate super-intelligent systems have been proposed.

Consciousness vs. the Simulation of Consciousness

The Turing test is concerned strictly with how the subject *acts* – the external behaviour of the machine. In this regard, it takes a behaviourist or functionalist approach to the study of the mind. The example of ELIZA suggests that a machine passing the test may be able to simulate human conversational behaviour by following a simple (but large) list of mechanical rules, without thinking or having a mind at all.

John Searle has argued that external behaviour cannot be used to determine if a machine is "actually" thinking or merely "simulating thinking." His Chinese room argument is intended to show that, even if the Turing test is a good operational definition of intelligence, it may not indicate that the machine has a mind, consciousness, or intentionality. (Intentionality is a philosophical term for the power of thoughts to be "about" something).

Turing anticipated this line of criticism in his original paper, writing:

"I do not wish to give the impression that I think there is no mystery about consciousness. There is, for instance, something of a paradox connected with any attempt to localise it. But I do not think these mysteries necessarily need to be solved before we can answer the question with which we are concerned in this paper".

Naïveté of Interrogators and the Anthropomorphic Fallacy

In practice, the test's results can easily be dominated not by the computer's intelligence, but by the attitudes, skill, or naïveté of the questioner.

Turing does not specify the precise skills and knowledge required by the interrogator in his description of the test, but he did use the term "average interrogator": "the average interrogator would not have more than 70 per cent chance of making the right identification after five minutes of questioning".

Chatterbot programs such as ELIZA have repeatedly fooled unsuspecting people into believing that they are communicating with human beings. In these cases, the "interrogators" are not even aware of the possibility that they are interacting with computers. To successfully appear human, there is no need for the machine to have any intelligence whatsoever and only a superficial resemblance to human behaviour is required.

Early Loebner Prize competitions used "unsophisticated" interrogators who were easily fooled by the machines. Since 2004, the Loebner Prize organisers have deployed philosophers, computer scientists, and journalists among the interrogators. Nonetheless, some of these experts have been deceived by the machines.

Michael Shermer points out that human beings consistently choose to consider non-human objects as human whenever they are allowed the chance, a mistake called the anthropomorphic fallacy: They talk to their cars, ascribe desire and intentions to natural forces (e.g., "nature abhors a vacuum"), and worship the sun as a human-like being with intelligence. If the Turing test is applied to religious objects, Shermer argues, then, that inanimate statues, rocks, and places have consistently passed the test throughout history. This human tendency towards anthropomorphism effectively lowers the bar for the Turing test, unless interrogators are specifically trained to avoid it.

Human Misidentification

One interesting feature of the Turing test is the frequency of the confederate effect, when the confederate (tested) humans are misidentified by the interrogators as machines. It has been suggested that what interrogators expect as human responses is not necessarily typical of humans. As a result, some individuals can be categorised as machines. This can therefore work in favour of a competing machine. The humans are instructed to "act themselves", but sometimes their answers are more like what the interrogator expects a machine to say. This raises the question of how to ensure that the humans are motivated to "act human".

Silence

A critical aspect of the Turing test is that a machine must give itself away as being a machine by its utterances. An interrogator must then make the "right identification" by correctly identifying the machine as being just that. If however a machine remains silent during a conversation, i.e. takes the fifth, then it is not possible for an interrogator to accurately identify the machine other than by means of a calculated guess. Even taking into account a parallel/hidden human as part of the test may not help the situation as humans can often be misidentified as being a machine.

Impracticality and Irrelevance: The Turing Test and AI Research

Mainstream AI researchers argue that trying to pass the Turing test is merely a distraction from more fruitful research. Indeed, the Turing test is not an active focus of much academic or commercial effort—as Stuart Russell and Peter Norvig write: "AI researchers have devoted little attention to passing the Turing test." There are several reasons.

First, there are easier ways to test their programs. Most current research in AI-related fields is aimed at modest and specific goals, such as automated scheduling, object recognition, or logistics. To test the intelligence of the programs that solve these problems, AI researchers simply give them the task directly. Russell and Norvig suggest an analogy with the history of flight: Planes are tested by how well they fly, not by comparing them to birds. "Aeronautical engineering texts," they write, "do not define the goal of their field as 'making machines that fly so exactly like pigeons that they can fool other pigeons.'

Second, creating lifelike simulations of human beings is a difficult problem on its own that does not need to be solved to achieve the basic goals of AI research. Believable human characters may be interesting in a work of art, a game, or a sophisticated user interface, but they are not part of the science of creating intelligent machines, that is, machines that solve problems using intelligence.

Turing wanted to provide a clear and understandable example to aid in the discussion of the philosophy of artificial intelligence. John McCarthy observes that the philosophy of AI is "unlikely to have any more effect on the practice of AI research than philosophy of science generally has on the practice of science."

Cognitive Science

Robert French makes the case that an interrogator can distinguish human and non-human interlocutors by posing questions that reveal the low-level (i.e., unconscious) processes of human cognition, as studied by cognitive science. Such questions reveal the precise details of the human embodiment of thought and can unmask a computer unless it experiences the world as humans do.

Variations

Numerous other versions of the Turing test, including those expounded above, have been raised through the years.

Reverse Turing Test and Captcha

A modification of the Turing test wherein the objective of one or more of the roles have been reversed between machines and humans is termed a reverse Turing test. An example is implied in the work of psychoanalyst Wilfred Bion, who was particularly fascinated by the "storm" that resulted from the encounter of one mind by another. In his 2000 book, among several other original points with regard to the Turing test, literary scholar Peter Swirski discussed in detail the idea of what he termed the Swirski test—essentially the reverse Turing test. He pointed out that it overcomes most if not all standard objections levelled at the standard version.

Carrying this idea forward, R. D. Hinshelwood described the mind as a "mind recognizing apparatus". The challenge would be for the computer to be able to determine if it were interacting with a human or another computer. This is an extension of the original question that Turing attempted to answer but would, perhaps, offer a high enough standard to define a machine that could "think" in a way that we typically define as characteristically human.

CAPTCHA is a form of reverse Turing test. Before being allowed to perform some action on a website, the user is presented with alphanumerical characters in a distorted graphic image and asked to type them out. This is intended to prevent automated systems from being used to abuse the site. The rationale is that software sufficiently sophisticated to read and reproduce the distorted image accurately does not exist (or is not available to the average user), so any system able to do so is likely to be a human.

Software that could reverse CAPTCHA with some accuracy by analysing patterns in the generating engine started being developed soon after the creation of CAPTCHA. In 2013, researchers at Vicarious announced that they had developed a system to solve CAPTCHA challenges from Google, Yahoo!, and PayPal up to 90% of the time. In 2014, Google engineers demonstrated a system that could defeat CAPTCHA challenges with 99.8% accuracy. In 2015, Shuman Ghosemajumder, former click fraud czar of Google, stated that there were cybercriminal sites that would defeat CAPTCHA challenges for a fee, to enable various forms of fraud.

Subject Matter Expert Turing Test

Another variation is described as the subject matter expert Turing test, where a machine's response cannot be distinguished from an expert in a given field. This is also known as a "Feigenbaum test" and was proposed by Edward Feigenbaum in a 2003 paper.

Total Turing Test

The "Total Turing test" variation of the Turing test, proposed by cognitive scientist Stevan Harnad, adds two further requirements to the traditional Turing test. The interrogator can also test the perceptual abilities of the subject (requiring computer vision) and the subject's ability to manipulate objects (requiring robotics).

Electronic Health Records

A letter published in *Communications of the ACM* describes the concept of generating a synthetic patient population and proposes a variation of Turing test to assess the difference between synthetic and real patients. The letter states: "In the EHR context, though a human physician can readily distinguish between synthetically generated and real live human patients, could a machine be given the intelligence to make such a determination on its own?" and further the letter states: "Before synthetic patient identities become a public health problem, the legitimate EHR market might benefit from applying Turing Test-like techniques to ensure greater data reliability and diagnostic value. Any new techniques must thus consider patients' heterogeneity and are likely to have greater complexity than the Allen eighth-grade-science-test is able to grade."

Minimum Intelligent Signal Test

The minimum intelligent signal test was proposed by Chris McKinstry as "the maximum abstraction of the Turing test", in which only binary responses (true/false or yes/no) are permitted, to focus only on the capacity for thought. It eliminates text chat problems like anthropomorphism bias, and does not require emulation of unintelligent human behaviour, allowing for systems that exceed human intelligence. The questions must each stand on their own, however, making it more like an IQ test than an interrogation. It is typically used to gather statistical data against which the performance of artificial intelligence programs may be measured.

Hutter Prize

The organisers of the Hutter Prize believe that compressing natural language text is a hard AI problem, equivalent to passing the Turing test.

The data compression test has some advantages over most versions and variations of a Turing test, including:

- It gives a single number that can be directly used to compare which of two machines is "more intelligent."

- It does not require the computer to lie to the judge.

The main disadvantages of using data compression as a test are:

- It is not possible to test humans this way.

- It is unknown what particular "score" on this test—if any—is equivalent to passing a human-level Turing test.

Other Tests based on Compression or Kolmogorov Complexity

A related approach to Hutter's prize which appeared much earlier in the late 1990s is the inclusion of compression problems in an extended Turing test. or by tests which are completely derived from Kolmogorov complexity. Other related tests in this line are presented by Hernandez-Orallo and Dowe.

Algorithmic IQ, or AIQ for short, is an attempt to convert the theoretical Universal Intelligence Measure from Legg and Hutter (based on Solomonoff's inductive inference) into a working practical test of machine intelligence.

Two major advantages of some of these tests are their applicability to nonhuman intelligences and their absence of a requirement for human testers.

Ebert Test

The Turing test inspired the Ebert test proposed in 2011 by film critic Roger Ebert which is a test whether a computer-based synthesised voice has sufficient skill in terms of intonations, inflections, timing and so forth, to make people laugh.

Artificial Brain

An artificial brain (or artificial mind) is software and hardware with cognitive abilities similar to those of the animal or human brain.

Research investigating "artificial brains" and brain emulation plays three important roles in science:

- An ongoing attempt by neuroscientists to understand how the human brain works, known as cognitive neuroscience.

- A thought experiment in the philosophy of artificial intelligence, demonstrating that it is possible, at least in theory, to create a machine that has all the capabilities of a human being.

- A long term project to create machines exhibiting behavior comparable to those of animals with complex central nervous system such as mammals and most particularly humans. The ultimate goal of creating a machine exhibiting human-like behavior or intelligence is sometimes called strong AI.

An example of the first objective is the project reported by Aston University in Birmingham, England where researchers are using biological cells to create "neurospheres" (small clusters of neurons) in order to develop new treatments for diseases including Alzheimer's, motor neurone and Parkinson's disease.

The second objective is a reply to arguments such as John Searle's Chinese room argument, Hubert Dreyfus's critique of AI or Roger Penrose's argument in *The Emperor's New Mind*. These critics argued that there are aspects of human consciousness or expertise that can not be simulated by machines. One reply to their arguments is that the biological processes inside the brain can be simulated to any degree of accuracy. This reply was made as early as 1950, by Alan Turing in his classic paper "Computing Machinery and Intelligence".

The third objective is generally called artificial general intelligence by researchers. However, Ray Kurzweilprefers the term "strong AI". In his book *The Singularity is Near*, he focuses on whole brain emulation using conventional computing machines as an approach to implementing artificial brains, and claims (on grounds of computer power continuing an exponential growth trend) that this could be done by 2025. Henry Markram, director of the Blue Brain project (which is attempting brain emulation), made a similar claim at the Oxford TED conference in 2009.

Approaches to Brain Simulation

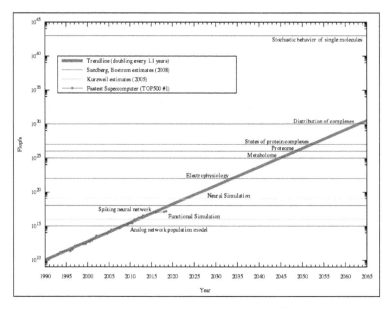

Estimates of how much processing power is needed to emulate a human brain at various levels (from Ray Kurzweil, and Anders Sandberg and Nick Bostrom), along with the fastest supercomputer from TOP500 mapped by year.

Although direct human brain emulationusing artificial neural networks on a high-performance computing engine is a commonly discussed approach, there are other approaches. An alternative artificial brain implementation could be based on Holographic Neural Technology (HNeT) non linear phase coherence/decoherence principles. The analogy has been made to quantum processes through the core synaptic algorithm which has strong similarities to the quantum mechanical wave equation.

EvBrain is a form of evolutionary software that can evolve "brainlike" neural networks, such as the network immediately behind the retina.

In November 2008, IBM received a US$4.9 million grant from the Pentagon for research into creating intelligent computers. The Blue Brain project is being conducted with the assistance of IBM in Lausanne. The project is based on the premise that it is possible to artificially link the neurons "in the computer" by placing thirty million synapses in their proper three-dimensional position.

Some proponents of strong AI speculated in 2009 that computers in connection with Blue Brain and Soul Catcher may exceed human intellectual capacity by around 2015, and that it is likely that we will be able to download the human brain at some time around 2050.

While *Blue Brain* is able to represent complex neural connections on the large scale, the project does not achieve the link between brain activity and behaviors executed by the brain. In 2012, project Spaun (Semantic Pointer Architecture Unified Network) attempted to model multiple parts of the human brain through large-scale representations of neural connections that generate complex behaviors in addition to mapping.

Spaun's design recreates elements of human brain anatomy. The model, consisting of approximately 2.5 million neurons, includes features of the visual and motor cortices, GABAergic and dopaminergic connections, the ventral tegmental area (VTA), substantia nigra, and others. The design allows for several functions in response to eight tasks, using visual inputs of typed or handwritten characters and outputs carried out by a mechanical arm. Spaun's functions include copying a drawing, recognizing images, and counting.

There are good reasons to believe that, regardless of implementation strategy, the predictions of realising artificial brains in the near future are optimistic. In particular brains (including the human brain) and cognition are not currently well understood, and the scale of computation required is unknown. Another near term limitation is that all current approaches for brain simulation require orders of magnitude larger power consumption compared with a human brain. The human brain consumes about 20 W of power, whereas current supercomputers may use as much as 1 MW—i.e., an order of 100,000 more.

Artificial Brain Thought Experiment

Some critics of brain simulation believe that it is simpler to create general intelligent action directly without imitating nature. Some commentators have used the analogy that early attempts to construct flying machines modeled them after birds, but that modern aircraft do not look like birds.

Computational Theory of Mind

In philosophy, the computational theory of mind (CTM) refers to a family of views that hold that the human mind is an information processing system and that cognition and consciousness together are a form of computation. Warren McCulloch and Walter Pitts were the first to suggest that neural activity is computational. They argued that neural computations explain cognition. The theory was proposed in its modern form by Hilary Putnam in 1967, and developed by his PhD student, philosopher and cognitive scientist Jerry Fodor in the 1960s, 1970s and 1980s. Despite being vigorously disputed in analytic philosophy in the 1990s due to work by Putnam himself, John Searle, and others, the view is common in modern cognitive psychology and is presumed by many theorists of evolutionary psychology. In the 2000s and 2010s the view has resurfaced in analytic philosophy.

The computational theory of mind holds that the mind is a computational system that is realized (i.e. physically implemented) by neural activity in the brain. The theory can be elaborated in many ways and varies largely based on how the term computation is understood. Computation is commonly understood in terms of Turing machines which manipulate symbols according to a rule, in combination with the internal state of the machine. The critical aspect of such a computational model is that we can abstract away from particular physical details of the machine that is implementing the computation. This is to say that computation can be implemented by silicon chips or neural networks, so long as there is a series of outputs based on manipulations of inputs and internal states, performed according to a rule. CTM, therefore holds that the mind is not simply analogous to a computer program, but that it is literally a computational system.

Computational theories of mind are often said to require mental representation because 'input' into a computation comes in the form of symbols or representations of other objects. A computer cannot compute an actual object, but must interpret and represent the object in some form and then compute the representation. The computational theory of mind is related to the representational theory of mind in that they both require that mental states are representations. However, the representational theory of mind shifts the focus to the symbols being manipulated. This approach better accounts for systematicity and productivity. In Fodor's original views, the computational theory of mind is also related to the language of thought. The language of thought theory allows the mind to process more complex representations with the help of semantics.

Recent work has suggested that we make a distinction between the mind and cognition. Building from the tradition of McCulloch and Pitts, the Computational Theory of Cognition (CTC) states that neural computations explain cognition. The Computational Theory of Mind asserts that not only cognition, but also phenomenal consciousness or qualia, are computational. That is to say, CTM entails CTC. While phenomenal consciousness could fulfill some other functional role, computational theory of cognition leaves open the possibility that some aspects of the mind could be non-computational. CTC therefore provides an important explanatory framework for understanding neural networks, while avoiding counter-arguments that center around phenomenal consciousness.

Computer Metaphor

Computational theory of mind is not the same as the computer metaphor, comparing the mind to a modern-day digital computer. Computational theory just uses some of the same principles as those found in digital computing. While the computer metaphor draws an analogy between the mind as software and the brain as hardware, CTM is the claim that the mind is a computational system.

'Computational system' is not meant to mean a modern-day electronic computer. Rather, a computational system is a symbol manipulator that follows step by step functions to compute input and form output. Alan Turing describes this type of computer in his concept of a Turing Machine.

Early Proponents

One of the earliest proponents of the computational theory of mind was Thomas Hobbes, who said, "by reasoning, I understand computation. And to compute is to collect the sum of many things added together at the same time, or to know the remainder when one thing has been taken from another. To reason therefore is the same as to add or to subtract." Since Hobbes lived before the contemporary identification of computing with instantiating effective procedures, he cannot be interpreted as explicitly endorsing the computational theory of mind, in the contemporary sense.

Causal Picture of Thoughts

At the heart of the Computational Theory of Mind is the idea that thoughts are a form of computation, and a computation is by definition a systematic set of laws for the relations among representations. This means that a mental state represents something if and only if there is some causal correlation between the mental state and that particular thing. An example would be seeing dark clouds and thinking "clouds mean rain", where there is a correlation between the thought of the clouds and rain, as the clouds causing rain. This is sometimes known as Natural Meaning. Conversely, there is another side to the causality of thoughts and that is the non-natural representation of thoughts. An example would be seeing a red traffic light and thinking "red means stop", there is nothing about the color red that indicates it represents stopping, and thus is just a convention that has been invented, similar to languages and their abilities to form representations.

Semantics of Mental States

The computational theory of mind states that the mind functions as a symbolic operator, and that mental representations are symbolic representations; just as the semantics of language are the features of words and sentences that relate to their meaning, the semantics of mental states are those meanings of representations, the definitions of the 'words' of the language of thought. If these basic mental states can have a particular meaning just as words in a language do, then this means that more complex mental states (thoughts) can be created, even if they have never been encountered before. Just as new sentences that are read can be understood even if they have never been encountered before, as long as the basic components are understood, and it is syntactically correct. For example: "I have eaten plum pudding every day of this fortnight." While it's doubtful many have seen this particular configuration of words, nonetheless most readers should be able to glean an understanding of this sentence because it is syntactically correct and the constituent parts are understood.

A range of arguments have been proposed against physicalist conceptions used in Computational Theories of Mind.

An early, though indirect, criticism of the Computational Theory of Mind comes from philosopher John Searle. In his thought experiment known as the Chinese room, Searle attempts to refute the claims that artificially intelligent systems can be said to have intentionality and understanding and that these systems, because they can be said to be minds themselves, are sufficient for the study of the human mind. Searle asks us to imagine that there is a man in a room with no way of communicating with anyone or anything outside of the room except for a piece of paper with symbols written on it that is passed under the door. With the paper, the man is to use a series of provided rule books to return paper containing different symbols. Unknown to the man in the room, these symbols are of a Chinese language, and this process generates a conversation that a Chinese speaker outside of the room can actually understand. Searle contends that the man in the room does not understand the Chinese conversation. This is essentially what the computational theory of mind presents us—a model in which the mind simply decodes symbols and outputs more symbols. Searle argues that this is not real understanding or intentionality. This was originally written as a repudiation of the idea that computers work like minds.

Searle has further raised questions about what exactly constitutes a computation:

> "The wall behind my back is right now implementing the WordStar program, because there is some pattern of molecule movements that is isomorphic with the formal structure of WordStar. But if the wall is implementing WordStar, if it is a big enough wall it is implementing any program, including any program implemented in the brain".

Objections like Searle's might be called insufficiency objections. They claim that computational theories of mind fail because computation is insufficient to account for some capacity of the mind. Arguments from qualia, such as Frank Jackson's Knowledge argument, can be understood as objections to computational theories of mind in this way—though they take aim at physicalist conceptions of the mind in general, and not computational theories specifically.

There are also objections which are directly tailored for computational theories of mind.

Putnam himself became a prominent critic of computationalism for a variety of reasons, including ones related to Searle's Chinese room arguments, questions of world-word reference relations, and thoughts about the mind-body relationship. Regarding functionalism in particular, Putnam has claimed along lines similar to, but more general than Searle's arguments, that the question of whether the human mind *can* implement computational states is not relevant to the question of the nature of mind, because "every ordinary open system realizes every abstract finite automaton." Computationalists have responded by aiming to develop criteria describing what exactly counts as an implementation.

Roger Penrose has proposed the idea that the human mind does not use a knowably sound calculation procedure to understand and discover mathematical intricacies. This would mean that a normal Turing completecomputer would not be able to ascertain certain mathematical truths that human minds can.

- Daniel Dennett proposed the Multiple Drafts Model, in which consciousness seems linear but is actually blurry and gappy, distributed over space and time in the brain. Consciousness is the computation, there is no extra step or "Cartesian Theater" in which you become conscious of the computation.

- Jerry Fodor argues that mental states, such as beliefs and desires, are relations between individuals and mental representations. He maintains that these representations can only be correctly explained in terms of a language of thought (LOT) in the mind. Further, this language of thought itself is codified in the brain, not just a useful explanatory tool. Fodor adheres to a species of functionalism, maintaining that thinking and other mental processes consist primarily of computations operating on the syntax of the representations that make up the language of thought. In later work (*Concepts* and *The Elm and the Expert*), Fodor has refined and even questioned some of his original computationalist views, and adopted a highly modified version of LOT.

- David Marr proposed that cognitive processes have three levels of description: the computational level (which describes that computational problem (i.e., input/output mapping) computed by the cognitive process); the algorithmic level (which presents the algorithm used for computing the problem postulated at the computational level); and the implementational level (which describes the physical implementation of the algorithm postulated at the algorithmic level in biological matter, e.g. the brain).

- Ulric Neisser coined the term 'cognitive psychology' in his book published in 1967 (*Cognitive Psychology*), wherein Neisser characterizes people as dynamic information-processing systems whose mental operations might be described in computational terms.

- Steven Pinker described a "language instinct," an evolved, built-in capacity to learn language (if not writing).

- Hilary Putnam proposed functionalism to describe consciousness, asserting that it is the computation that equates to consciousness, regardless of whether the computation is operating in a brain, in a computer, or in a "brain in a vat."

- Georges Rey, professor at the University of Maryland, builds on Jerry Fodor's representational theory of mind to produce his own version of a Computational/Representational Theory of Thought.

Ethics of Technology

Ethics in technology is a sub-field of ethics addressing the ethical questions specific to the Technology Age. Some prominent works of philosopher Hans Jonas are devoted to ethics of technology. The subject has also been explored, following the work of Mario Bunge, under the term techno-ethics.

Fundamental Problems

It is often held that technology itself is incapable of possessing moral or ethical qualities, since "technology" is merely tool making. But many now believe that each piece of technology is endowed with and radiating ethical commitments all the time, given to it by those that made it, and those that decided how it must be made and used. Whether merely a lifeless amoral 'tool' or a solidified embodiment of human values "ethics of technology" refers to two basic subdivisions:

- The ethics involved in the development of new technology—whether it is always, never, or contextually right or wrong to invent and implement a technological innovation.

- The ethical questions that are exacerbated by the ways in which technology extends or curtails the power of individuals—how standard ethical questions are changed by the new powers.

In the former case, ethics of such things as computer security and computer viruses asks whether the very act of innovation is an ethically right or wrong act. Similarly, does a scientist have an ethical obligation to produce or fail to produce a nuclear weapon? What are the ethical questions surrounding the production of technologies that waste or conserve energy and resources? What are the ethical questions surrounding the production of new manufacturing processes that might inhibit employment, or might inflict suffering in the third world?

In the latter case, the ethics of technology quickly break down into the ethics of various human endeavors as they are altered by new technologies. For example, bioethics is now largely consumed with questions that have been exacerbated by the new life-preserving technologies, new cloning technologies, and new technologies for implantation. In law, the right of privacy is being continually attenuated by the emergence of new forms of surveillance and anonymity. The old ethical questions of privacy and free speech are given new shape and urgency in an Internet age.

Such tracing devices as RFID, biometric analysis and identification, genetic screening, all take old ethical questions and amplify their significance. Lastly,we should also remember that ethic's is a very broadly defined term which is incompetent to influence something as fast changing and ever improving field as technology.

Technoethics

Technoethics (TE) is an interdisciplinary research area that draws on theories and methods from multiple knowledge domains (such as communications, social sciences information studies, technology studies, applied ethics, and philosophy) to provide insights on ethical dimensions of technological systems and practices for advancing a technological society.

Technoethics views technology and ethics as socially embedded enterprises and focuses on discovering the ethical use of technology, protecting against the misuse of technology, and devising common principles to guide new advances in technological development and application to benefit society. Typically, scholars in technoethics have a tendency to conceptualize technology and ethics as interconnected and embedded in life and society. Technoethics denotes a broad range of ethical issues revolving around technology – from specific areas of focus affecting professionals working with technology to broader social, ethical, and legal issues concerning the role of technology in society and everyday life.

Technoethical perspectives are constantly in transition as technology advances in areas unseen by creators, as users change the intended uses of new technologies. Humans cannot be separated from these technologies because it is an inherent part of consciousness and meaning in life therefore, requiring an ethical model. The short term and longer term ethical considerations for technologies do not just engage the creator and producer but makes the user question their beliefs in correspondence with this technology and how governments must allow, react to, change, and/or deny technologies.

Using theories and methods from multiple domains, technoethics provides insights on ethical aspects of technological systems and practices, examines technology-related social policies and interventions, and provides guidelines for how to ethically use new advancements in technology. Technoethics provides a systems theory and methodology to guide a variety of separate areas of inquiry into human-technological activity and ethics. Moreover, the field unites both technocentric and bio-centric philosophies, providing "conceptual grounding to clarify the role of technology to those affected by it and to help guide ethical problem solving and decision making in areas of activity that rely on technology." As a bio-techno-centric field, technoethics "has a relational orientation to both technology and human activity"; it provides "a system of ethical reference that justifies that profound dimension of technology as a central element in the attainment of a 'finalized' perfection of man.'

- Ethics address the issues of what is 'right', what is 'just', and what is 'fair'. Ethics describe moral principles influencing conduct; accordingly, the study of ethics focuses on the actions and values of people in society (what people do and how they believe they should act in the world).

- Technology is the branch of knowledge that deals with the creation and use of technical means and their interrelation with life, society, and the environment; it may draw upon a variety of fields, including industrial arts, engineering, applied science, and pure science.

Technology "is core to human development and a key focus for understanding human life, society and human consciousness."

Though the ethical consequences of new technologies have existed since Socrates' attack on writing in Plato's dialogue, *Phaedrus*, the formal field of technoethics had only existed for a few decades. The first traces of TE can be seen in Dewey and Peirce's pragmatism. With the advent of the industrial revolution, it was easy to see that technological advances were going to influence human activity. This is why they put emphasis on the responsible use of technology.

The term "technoethics" was coined in 1977 by the philosopher Mario Bunge to describe the responsibilities of technologists and scientists to develop ethics as a branch of technology. Bunge argued that the current state of technological progress was guided by ungrounded practices based on limited empirical evidence and trial-and-error learning. He recognized that "the technologist must be held not only technically but also morally responsible for whatever he designs or executes: not only should his artifacts be optimally efficient but, far from being harmful, they should be beneficial, and not only in the short run but also in the long term." He recognized a pressing need in society to create a new field called 'Technoethics' to discover rationally grounded rules for guiding science and technological progress.

With the spurt in technological advances came technological inquiry. Societal views of technology were changing; people were becoming more critical of the developments that were occurring and scholars were emphasizing the need to understand and to take a deeper look and study the innovations. Associations were uniting scholars from different disciplines to study the various aspects of technology. The main disciplines being philosophy, social sciences and science and technology studies (STS). Though many technologies were already focused on ethics, each technology discipline was separated from each other, despite the potential for the information to intertwine and reinforce itself. As technologies became increasingly developed in each discipline, their ethical implications paralleled their development, and became increasingly complex. Each branch eventually became united, under the term technoethics, so that all areas of technology could be studied and researched based on existing, real-world examples and a variety of knowledge, rather than just discipline-specific knowledge.

Ethics Theories

Technoethics involves the ethical aspects of technology within a society that is shaped by technology. This brings up a series of social and ethical questions regarding new technological advancements and new boundary crossing opportunities. Before moving forward and attempting to address any ethical questions and concerns, it is important to review the three major ethical theories to develop a perspective foundation:

- Utilitarianism (Bentham, J) is an ethical theory which attempts to maximize happiness and reduce suffering for the greatest number of people. Utilitarianism focused on results and consequences rather than rules.

- Duty Ethics (Kant) notes the obligations that one has to society and follows society's universal rules. It focuses on the rightness of actions instead of the consequences, focusing on what an individual should do.

- Virtue Ethics is another main perspective in normative ethics. It highlights the role and virtues that an individual's character contains to be able to determine or evaluate ethical behaviour in society.

- Relationship ethics states that care and consideration are both derived from human communication. Therefore, ethical communication is the core substance to maintain healthy relationships.

Historical Framing of Technology – Four Main Periods

- Greek civilization defined technology as techné. Techné is "the set principles, or rational method, involved in the production of an object or the accomplishment of an end; the knowledge such as principles of method; art." This conceptualization of technology used during the early Greek and Roman period to denote the mechanical arts, construction, and other efforts to create, in Cicero's words, a "second nature" within the natural world.

- Modern conceptualization of technology as invention materialized in the 17th century in Bacon's futuristic vision of a perfect society governed by engineers and scientists in Saloman's House, to raise the importance of technology in society.

- The German term "Tecknik" was used in the 19th-20th century. Technik is the totality of processes, machines, tools and systems employed in the practical arts and Engineering. Webber popularized it when it was used in broader fields. Mumford said it was underlying a civilization. Known as: before 1750: Eotechnic, in 1750-1890: Paleoethnic and in 1890: Neoethnic. Place it at the center of social life in close connection to social progress and societal change. Mumford says that a machine cannot be divorced from its larger social pattern, for it is the pattern that gives it meaning and purpose.

- Rapid advances in technology provoked a negative reaction from scholars who saw technology as a controlling force in society with the potential to destroy how people live (Technological Determinism). Heidegger warned people that technology was dangerous in that it exerted control over people through its mediating effects, thus limiting authenticity of experience in the world that defines life and gives life meaning. It is an intimate part of the human condition, deeply entrenched in all human history, society and mind.

Significant Technoethical Developments in Society

Many advancements within the past decades have added to the field of technoethics. There are multiple concrete examples that have illustrated the need to consider ethical dilemmas in relation to technological innovations. Beginning in the 1940s influenced by the British eugenic movement, the Nazis conduct "racial hygiene" experiments causing widespread, global anti-eugenic sentiment. In the 1950s the first satellite Sputnik 1 orbited the earth, the Obninsk Nuclear Power Plant was the first nuclear power plant to be opened, the American nuclear tests take place. The 1960s brought about the first manned moon landing, ARPANET created which leads to the later creation of the Internet, first heart transplantation completed, and the Telstarcommunications satellite is launched. The 70s, 80s, 90s, 2000s and 2010s also brought multiple developments.

Technological Consciousness

Technological consciousness is the relationship between humans and technology. Technology is seen as an integral component of human consciousness and development. Technology, consciousness and society are intertwined in a relational process of creation that is key to human evolution. Technology is rooted in the human mind, and is made manifest in the world in the form of new understandings and artifacts. The process of technological consciousness frames the inquiry into ethical responsibility concerning technology by grounding technology in human life.

The structure of technological consciousness is relational but also situational, organizational, aspectual and integrative. Technological consciousness situates new understandings by creating a context of time and space. As well, technological consciousness organizes disjointed sequences of experience under a sense of unity that allows for a continuity of experience. The aspectual component of technological consciousness recognizes that individuals can only be conscious of aspects of an experience, not the whole thing. For this reason, technology manifests itself in processes that can be shared with others. The integrative characteristics of technological consciousness are assimilation, substitution and conversation. Assimilation allows for unfamiliar experiences to be integrated with familiar ones. Substitution is a metaphorical process allowing for complex experiences to be codified and shared with others — for example, language. Conversation is the sense of an observer within an individual's consciousness, providing stability and a standpoint from which to interact with the process.

Misunderstandings of Consciousness and Technology

According to Rocci Luppicini, the common misunderstandings about consciousness and technology are listed as follows. The first misunderstanding is that consciousness is only in the head when according to Luppicini, consciousness is not only in the head meaning that "[c]onsciousness is responsible for the creation of new conscious relations wherever imagined, be it in the head, on the street or in the past." The second misunderstanding is technology is not a part of consciousness. Technology is a part of consciousness as "the conceptualization of technology has gone through drastic changes." The third misunderstanding is that technology controls society and consciousness, by which Luppicini means "that technology is rooted in consciousness as an integral part of mental life for everyone. This understanding will most likely alter how both patients and psychologists deal with the trials and tribunes of living with technology." The last misunderstanding is society controls technology and consciousness. "other accounts fail to acknowledge the complex relational nature of technology as an operation within mind and society. This realization shifts the focus on technology to its origins within the human mind as explained through the theory of technological consciousness."

- Consciousness (C) is only a part of the head: C is responsible for the creation of new conscious relations.

- Technology (T) is not part of C: Humans cannot be separated from technology.

- T controls society and C: Technology cannot control the mind.

- Society controls T and C: Society fails to take in account the consideration of society shaping what technology gets developed.

Ethical Challenges

Ethical challenges arise in many different situations:

- Human knowledge processes.

- Workplace discrimination.

- Strained work life balance in technologically enhanced work environments.

- Digital divide: Inequalities in information access for parts of the population.

- Unequal opportunities for scientific and technological development.

- Norris says access to information and knowledge resources within a knowledge society tend to favour the economically privileged who have greater access to technological tools needed to access information and knowledge resources disseminated online and the privatization of knowledge.

- Inequality in terms of how scientific and technological knowledge is developed around the globe. Developing countries do not have the same opportunities as developed countries to invest in costly large-scale research and expensive research facilities and instrumentation.

- Organizational responsibility and accountability issues.

- Intellectual property issues.

- Information overload: Information processing theory is working memory that has a limited capacity and too much information can lead to cognitive overload resulting in loss of information from short term memory.

- Limit an organization's ability to innovate and respond for change.

- Knowledge society is intertwined with changing technology requiring new skills of its workforce. Cutler says that there is the perception that older workers lack experience with new technology and that retaining programs may be less effective and more expensive for older workers. Cascio says that there is a growth of virtual organizations. Saetre & Sornes say that it is a blurring of the traditional time and space boundaries has also led to many cases in the blurring of work and personal life.

- Negative impacts of many scientific and technological innovations have on humans and the environment has led to some skepticism and resistance to increasing dependence on technology within the Knowledge Society. Doucet calls for city empowerment to have the courage and foresight to make decisions that are acceptable to its inhabitants rather that succumb to global consumer capitalism and the forces of international corporations on national and local governments.

- Scientific and technological innovations that have transformed organizational life within a global economyhave also supplanted human autonomy and control in work within a technologically oriented workplace.

- The persuasive potential of technology raises the question of "how sensitive. designers and programmers should be to the ethics of the persuasive technology they design." Techno-ethics can be used to determine the level of ethical responsibility that should be associated with outcomes of the use of technology, whether intended or unintended.

- Rapidly changing organizational life and the history of unethical business practices have given rise to public debates concerning organizational responsibility and trust. The advent of virtual organizations and teleworkhas bolstered ethical problems by providing more opportunities for fraudulent behaviour and the production of misinformation. Concerted efforts are required to uphold ethical values in advancing new knowledge and tools within societal relations which do not exclude people or limit liberties of some people at the expense of others.

Current Issues

Copyright

Digital copyrights are a heated issue because there are so many sides to the discussion. There are ethical considerations surrounding the artist, producer, end user, and the country are intertwined. Not to mention the relationships with other countries and the impact on the use (or no use) of content housed in their countries. In Canada, national laws such as the Copyright Act and the history behind Bill C-32 are just the beginning of the government's attempt to shape the "wild west" of Canadian Internet activities. The ethical considerations behind Internet activities such a peer-to-peer file sharing involve every layer of the discussion – the consumer, artist, producer, music/movie/software industry, national government, and international relations. Overall, technoethics forces the "big picture" approach to all discussions on technology in society. Although time consuming, this "big picture" approach offers some level of reassurance when considering that any law put in place could drastically alter the way we interact with our technology and thus the direction of work and innovation in the country.

The use of copyrighted material to create new content is a hotly debated topic. The emergence of the musical "mashup" genre has compounded the issue of creative licensing. A moral conflict is created between those who believe that copyright protects any unauthorized use of content, and those who maintain that sampling and mash-ups are acceptable musical styles and, though they use portions of copyrighted material, the end result is a new creative piece which is the property of the creator, and not of the original copyright holder. Whether or not the mashup genre should be allowed to use portions of copyrighted material to create new content is one which is currently under debate.

Cybercriminality

For many years, new technologies took an important place in social, cultural, political, and economic life. Thanks to the democratization of informatics access and the network's globalization, the number of exchanges and transaction is in perpetual progress.

Many people are exploiting the facilities and anonymity that modern technologies offer in order to commit multiple criminal activities. Cybercrime is one of the fastest growing areas of crime. The problem is that some laws that profess to protect people from those who would do wrong things via digital means also threaten to take away people's freedom.

Privacy vs. Security: Full-body Airport Scanners

Since the introduction of full body X-ray scanners to airports in 2007, many concerns over traveler privacy have arisen. Individuals are asked to step inside a rectangular machine that takes an alternate wavelength image of the person's naked body for the purpose of detecting metal and non-metal objects being carried under the clothes of the traveler. This screening technology comes in two forms, millimeter wave technology (MM-wave technology) or back-scatter X-rays (similar to x-rays used by dentists). Full-body scanners were introduced into airports to increase security and improve the quality of screening for objects such as weapons or explosives due to an increase of terrorist attacks involving airplanes occurring in the early 2000s.

Ethical concerns of both travelers and academic groups include fear of humiliation due to the disclosure of anatomic or medical details, exposure to a low level of radiation (in the case of backscatter X-ray technology), violation of modesty and personal privacy, clarity of operating procedures, the use of this technology to discriminate against groups, and potential misuse of this technology for reasons other than detecting concealed objects. Also people with religious beliefs that require them to remain physically covered (arms, legs, face etc.) at all times will be unable and morally opposed to stepping inside of this virtually intrusive scanning technology. The Centre for Society, Science and Citizenship have discussed their ethical concerns including the ones mentioned above and suggest recommendations for the use of this technology in their report titled "Whole Body Imaging at airport checkpoints: the ethical and policy context".

Privacy and GPS Technologies

The discourse around GPS tracking devices and geolocation technologies and this contemporary technology's ethical ramifications on privacy is growing as the technology becomes more prevalent in society. As discussed in the *New York Times*'s Sunday Review on September 22, 2012, the editorial focused on the ethical ramifications that imprisoned a drug offender because of the GPS technology in his cellphone was able to locate the criminal's position. Now that most people carry on the person a cell, the authorities have the ability to constantly know the location of a large majority of citizens. The ethical discussion now can be framed from a legal perspective. As raised in the editorial, there are stark infractions that these geolocation devices on citizens' Fourth Amendment and their protection against unreasonable searches. This reach of this issue is not just limited to the United States but affects more democratic state that uphold similar citizens' rights and freedoms against unreasonable searches.

These geolocation technologies are not only affecting how citizens interact with their state but also how employees interact with their workplaces. As discussed in article by the Canadian Broadcasting Company, "GPS and privacy", that a growing number of employers are installing geolocation technologies in "company vehicles, equipment and cellphones". Both academia and unions are finding these new powers of employers to be indirect contradiction with civil liberties. This changing relationship between employee and employer because of the integration of GPS technology into popular society is demonstrating a larger ethical discussion on what are appropriate privacy levels. This discussion will only become more prevalent as the technology becomes more popular.

Genetically Modified Organisms

Genetically modified foods have become quite common in developed countries around the world, boasting greater yields, higher nutritional value, and greater resistance to pests, but there are still many ethical concerns regarding their use. Even commonplace genetically modified crops like corn raise questions of the ecological consequences of unintended cross pollination, potential horizontal gene transfer, and other unforeseen health concerns for humans and animals.

Trademarked organisms like the "Glofish" are a relatively new occurrence. These zebrafish, genetically modified to appear in several fluorescent colours and sold as pets in the United States, could have unforeseen effects on freshwater environments were they ever to breed in the wild.

Providing they receive approval from the U.S. Food and Drug Administration (FDA), another new type of fish may be arriving soon. The "AquAdvantage salmon", engineered to reach maturity within roughly 18 months (as opposed to three years in the wild), could help meet growing global demand. There are health and environmental concerns associated with the introduction any new GMO, but more importantly this scenario highlights the potential economic impact a new product may have. The FDA does perform an economic impact analysis to weigh, for example, the consequences these new genetically modified fish may have on the traditional salmon fishing industry against the long term gain of a cheaper, more plentiful source of salmon. These techno-ethical assessments, which regulatory organizations like the FDA are increasingly faced with worldwide, are vitally important in determining how GMOs—with all of their potential beneficial and harmful effects—will be handled moving forward.

Pregnancy Screening Technology

For over 40 years, newborn screening has been a triumph of the 20th century public health system.Through this technology, millions of parents are given the opportunity to screen for and test a number of disorders, sparing the death of their children or complications such as mental retardation. However, this technology is growing at a fast pace, disallowing researchers and practitioners from being able to fully understand how to treat diseases and provide families in need with the resources to cope.

A version of pre-natal testing, called tandem mass spectrometry, is a procedure that "measures levels and patterns of numerous metabolites in a single drop of blood, which are then used to identify potential diseases. Using this same drop of blood, tandem mass spectrometry enables the detection of at least four times the number of disorders than was possible with previous technologies." This allows for a cost-effective and fast method of pre-natal testing.

However, critics of tandem mass spectrometry and technologies like it are concerned about the adverse consequences of expanding newborn screen technology and the lack of appropriate research and infrastructure needed to provide optimum medical services to patients. Further concerns include "diagnostic odysseys", a situation in which the patient aimlessly continues to search for diagnoses where none exists.

Among other consequences, this technology raises the issue of whether individuals other than newborn will benefit from newborn screening practices. A reconceptualization of the purpose of this screening will have far reaching economic, health and legal impact. This discussion is only just beginning and requires informed citizenry to reach legal if not moral consensus on how far we as a society are comfortable with taking this technology.

Citizen Journalism

Citizen journalism is a concept describing citizens who wish to act as a professional journalist or media person by "collecting, reporting, analyzing, and disseminating news and information" According to Jay Rosen, citizen journalists are "the people formerly known as the audience," who "were on the receiving end of a media system that ran one way, in a broadcasting pattern, with high entry fees and a few firms competing to speak very loudly while the rest of the population listened in isolation from one another— and who today are not in a situation like that at all. The people formerly known as the audience are simply the public made realer, less fictional, more able, less predictable".

The internet has provided society with a modern and accessible public space. Due to the openness of the internet, there are discernible effects on the traditional profession of journalism. Although the concept of citizen journalism is a seasoned one, "the presence of online citizen journalism content in the marketplace may add to the diversity of information that citizens have access to when making decisions related to the betterment of their community or their life". The emergence of online citizen journalism is fueled by the growing use of social media websites to share information about current events and issues locally, nationally and internationally.

The open and instantaneous nature of the internet affects the criteria of information quality on the web. A journalistic code of ethics is not instilled for those who are practicing citizen journalism. Journalists, whether professional or citizen, have needed to adapt to new priorities of current audiences: accessibility, quantity of information, quick delivery and aesthetic appeal. Thus, technology has affected the ethical code of the profession of journalism with the popular free and instant sharing qualities of the internet. Professional journalists have had to adapt to these new practices to ensure that truthful and quality reporting is being distributed. The concept can be seen as a great advancement in how society communicates freely and openly or can be seen as contributing to the decay of traditional journalistic practices and codes of ethics.

Other issues to consider:

- Privacy concerns: location services on cell devices which tell all users where a person is should they decide to turn on this feature, social media, online banking, new capabilities of cellular devices, Wi-fi, etc.

- New music technology: People see more electronic music today with the new technology able to create it, as well as more advanced recording technology.

Recent Developments

Despite the amassing body of scholarly work related to technoethics beginning in the 1970s, only recently has it become institutionalized and recognized as an important interdisciplinary research area and field of study. In 1998, the Epson Foundation founded the Instituto de Tecnoética in Spain under the direction of Josep Esquirol. This institute has actively promoted technoethical scholarship through awards, conferences, and publications. This helped encourage scholarly work for a largely

European audience. The major driver for the emergence of technoethics can be attributed to the publication of major reference works available in English and circulated globally. The "Encyclopedia of Science, Technology, and Ethics" included a section on technoethics which helped bring it into mainstream philosophy. This helped to raise further interest leading to the publication of the first reference volume in the English language dedicated to the emerging field of Technoethics. The two volume *Handbook of Research on Technoethics* explores the complex connections between ethics and the rise of new technologies (e.g., life-preserving technologies, stem cell research, cloningtechnologies, new forms of surveillance and anonymity, computer networks, Internet advancement, etc.) This recent major collection provides the first comprehensive examination of technoethics and its various branches from over 50 scholars around the globe. The emergence of technoethics can be juxtaposed with a number of other innovative interdisciplinary areas of scholarship which have surfaced in recent years such as technoscience and technocriticism.

With all the developments we've had in technology it has created a lot advancement for the music industry both positive and negative. A main concern is piracy and illegal downloading; with all that is available through the internet a lot of music (TV shows and movies as well) have become easily accessible to download and upload for free. This does create new challenges for artist, producers, and copyright laws. The advances it has positively made for the industry is a whole new genre of music. Computers are being used to create electronic music, as well as synthesizers (computerized/electronic piano). This type of music is becoming rapidly more common and listened to. These advances have allowed the industry to try new things and make new explorations.

Future Developments

The future of technoethics is a promising, yet evolving field. The studies of e-technology in workplace environments are an evolving trend in technoethics. With the constant evolution of technology, and innovations coming out daily, technoethics is looking to be a rather promising guiding framework for the ethical assessments of new technologies. Some of the questions regarding technoethics and the workplace environment that have yet to be examined and treated are listed below:

- Are organizational counter measures not necessary because it invades employee privacy?

- Are surveillance cameras and computer monitoring devices invasive methods that can have ethical repercussions?

- Should organizations have the right and power to impose consequences?

UNESCO

A specialized intergovernmental agency of the United Nations, focusing on promotion of education, culture social and natural sciences and communication and information. In the future, the use of principles as expressed in the UNESCO Universal Declaration on Bioethics and Human Rights will also be analyzed to broaden the description of bioethical reasoning.

User Data

In a digital world, much of users' personal lives are stored on devices such as computers and smartphones, and we trust the companies we store our lives on to take care of our data. A topic of discussion regarding the ethics of technology is just exactly how much data these companies really need and what they are doing with it. Another major cause for concern is the security of our personal data and privacy, whether it is leaked intentionally or not.

Large companies share their users' data constantly. In 2018, the U.S, government cracked down on Facebook selling user data to other companies after declaring that it had made the data in question inaccessible. One such case was in a scandal regarding Cambridge Analytica, in which Facebook sold user data to the company without consent from the users whose data was being accessed. The data was then used for several political agendas, such as the Brexit vote and the U.S. Presidential Election of 2016. In an interview with CBS' 60 Minutes, Trump campaign manager Brad Parscale described in detail how he used data taken from different social media websites to create ads that were both visually appealing to potential voters and targeted the issues that they felt strongest about.

Besides swinging political races, the theft of people's data can result in serious consequences on an individual level. In some cases, hackers can breach websites or businesses that have identifying information about a person, such as their credit card number, cell phone number, and address, and upload it to the dark web for sale, if they decide not to use it for their own deviant purposes.

Drones

In the book *Society and Technological Change, 8th Edition*, by Rudi Volti, the author comments on unmanned Aerial Vehicles, also known as UAVs or drones. Once used primarily as military technology, these are becoming increasingly accessible tools to the common person for hobbies like photography. In the author's belief, this can also cause concern for security and privacy, as these tools allow people with malicious intents easier access to spying.

Outside of public areas, drones are also able to be used for spying on people in private settings, even in their own homes. In an article by today.com, the author writes about people using drones and taking videos and photographs of people in their most private moments, even in the privacy of their own home.

Areas of Technoethical Inquiry

Biotech Ethics

Biotech ethics concerned with ethical dilemmas surrounding the use of biotechnologies in fields including medical research, health care, and industrial applications. Topics such as cloning ethics, e-health ethics, telemedicine ethics, genetics ethics, neuroethics, and sport and nutrition ethics fall into this category; examples of specific issues include the debates surrounding euthanasia and reproductive rights.

Technoethics and Cognition

This area of technoethical inquiry is concerned with technology's relation to the human mind, artificial agents, and society. Topics of study that would fit into this category would be artificial morality and moral agents, technoethical systems and techno-addiction.

- An artificial agent describes any type of technology that is created to act as an agent, either of its own power or on behalf of another agent. An artificial agent may try to advance its own goals or those of another agent.

Technoethics and Society

This field is concerned with the uses of technology to ethically regulate aspects of a society. For example: Digital property ethics, social theory, law, science, organizational ethics and global ethics.

Technofeminism

Technoethics has concerned itself with society as a general group and made no distinctions between the genders, but considers technological effects and influences on each gender individually. This is an important consideration as some technologies are created for use by a specific gender, including birth control, abortion, fertility treatments, and Viagra. Feminists have had a significant influence on the prominence and development of reproductive technologies. Technoethical inquiry must examine these technologies' effects on the intended gender while also considering their influence on the other gender. Another dimension of technofeminism concerns female involvement in technological development: women's participation in the field of technology has broadened society's understanding of how technology affects the female experience in society.

Information and Communication Technoethics

Information and communication technoethics is "concerned with ethical issues and responsibilities arising when dealing with information and communication technology in the realm of communication." This field is related to internet ethics, rational and ethical decision making models, and information ethics. A major area of interest is the convergence of technologies: as technologies become more interdependent and provide people with multiple ways of accessing the same information, they transform society and create new ethical dilemmas. This is particularly evident in the realms of the internet. In recent years, users have had the unprecedented position of power in creating and disseminating news and other information globally via social networking; the concept of "citizen journalism" primarily relates to this. With developments in the media, has led to open media ethics as Ward writes, leading to citizen journalism.

In cases such as the 2004 Indian Ocean Tsunami or the 2011 Arab Spring movements, citizen journalists were seen to have been significant sources of facts and information in relation to the events. These were re-broadcast by news outlets, and more importantly, re-circulated by and to other internet users. As Jay David Bolter and Richard Grusin state in their book Remediation: Understanding New Media: "The liveness of the Web is a refashioned version of the liveness of broadcast television" However, it is commonly political events that tend to raise ethical questions and concerns. In the latter example, there had been efforts made by the Iranian government in censoring and prohibiting the spread of internal happenings to the outside by its citizen journalists. This occurrence questioned the importance of the spread of crucial information regarding the issue, and the source from which it came from (citizen journalists, government authorities, etc.). This goes to prove how the internet "enables new forms of human action and expression but at the same time it disables it" Information and Communication Technoethics also identifies ways to develop ethical frameworks of research structures in order to capture the essence of new technologies.

Educational and Professional Technoethics

Technoethical inquiry in the field of education examines how technology impacts the roles and values of education in society. This field considers changes in student values and behavior related to technology, including access to inappropriate material in schools, online plagiarism using material copied directly from the internet, or purchasing papers from online resources and passing them off as the student's own work. Educational technoethics also examines the digital divide that exists between educational institutions in developed and developing countries or between unequally-funded institutions within the same country: for instance, some schools offer students access to online material, while others do not. Professional technoethics focuses on the issue of ethical responsibility for those who work with technology within a professional setting, including engineers, medical professionals, and so on. Efforts have been made to delineate ethical principles in professions such as computer programming.

Environmental and Engineering Technoethics

Environmental technoethics originate from the 1960s and 1970s' interest in environment and nature. The field focuses on the human use of technologies that may impact the environment; areas of concern include transport, mining, and sanitation. Engineering technoethics emerged in the late 19th century. As the Industrial Revolution triggered a demand for expertise in engineering and a need to improve engineering standards, societies began to develop codes of professional ethics and associations to enforce these codes. Ethical inquiry into engineering examines the "responsibilities of engineers combining insights from both philosophy and the social sciences."

Technoethical Assessment and Design

A technoethical assessment (TEA) is an interdisciplinary, systems-based approach to assessing ethical dilemmas related to technology. TEAs aim to guide actions related to technology in an ethical direction by advancing knowledge of technologies and their effects; successful TEAs thus produce a shared understanding of knowledge, values, priorities, and other ethical aspects associated with technology. TEAs involve five key steps:

- Evaluate the intended ends and possible side effects of the technology in order to discern its overall value (interest).

- Compare the means and intended ends in terms of technical and non-technical (moral and social) aspects.

- Reject those actions where the output (overall value) does not balance the input in terms of efficiency and fairness.

- Consider perspectives from all stakeholder groups.

- Examine technological relations at a variety of levels (e.g. biological, physical, psychological, social, and environmental).

Technoethical design (TED) refers to the process of designing technologies in an ethical manner, involving stakeholders in participatory design efforts, revealing hidden or tacit technological relations, and investigating what technologies make possible and how people will use them.

TED involves the following four steps:

- Ensure that the components and relations within the technological system are explicitly understood by those in the design context.

- Perform a TEA to identify relevant technical knowledge.

- Optimize the technological system in order to meet stakeholders' and affected individuals' needs and interests.

- Consult with representatives of stakeholder and affected groups in order to establish consensus on key design issues.

Both TEA and TED rely on systems theory, a perspective that conceptualizes society in terms of events and occurrences resulting from investigating system operations. Systems theory assumes that complex ideas can be studied as systems with common designs and properties which can be further explained using systems methodology. The field of technoethics regards technologies as self-producing systems that draw upon external resources and maintain themselves through knowledge creation; these systems, of which humans are a part, are constantly in flux as relations between technology, nature, and society change. TEA attempts to elicit the knowledge, goals, inputs, and outputs that comprise technological systems. Similarly, TED enables designers to recognize technology's complexity and power, to include facts and values in their designs, and to contextualize technology in terms of what it makes possible and what makes it possible.

Organizational Technoethics

Recent advances in technology and their ability to transmit vast amounts of information in a short amount of time has changed the way information is being shared amongst co-workers and managers throughout organizations across the globe. Starting in the 1980s with information and communications technologies (ICTs), organizations have seen an increase in the amount of technology that they rely on to communicate within and outside of the workplace. However, these implementations of technology in the workplace create various ethical concerns and in turn a need for further analysis of technology in organizations. As a result of this growing trend, a subsection of technoethics known as organizational technoethics has emerged to address these issues.

Ethics of Artificial Intelligence

Ethical issues associated with AI are proliferating and rising to popular attention as intelligent machines become ubiquitous. For example, AIs can and do model aspects essential to moral agency and so offer tools for the investigation of consciousness and other aspects of cognition contributing to moral status (either ascribed or achieved). This has deep implications for our understanding of moral agency, and so of systems of ethics meant to account for and to provide for the development of such capacities. This raises the issue of responsible and/or blameworthy AIs operating openly in general society, with deep implications again for systems of ethics which must accommodate moral AIs. Consider also that human social infrastructure (e.g. energy grids, mass-transit systems) are increasingly moderated by increasingly intelligent machines. This alone raises many moral/ethical concerns. For example, who or what is responsible in the case of an accident due to system error, or due to design flaws, or due to proper operation outside of anticipated constraints? Finally, as AIs become increasingly intelligent, there seems some legitimate concern over the potential for AIs to manage human systems according to AI values, rather than as directly programmed by human designers. These issues often bear on the long-term safety of intelligent systems, and not only for individual human beings, but for the human race and life on Earth as a whole. These issues and many others are central to Ethics of AI.

The possibility of creating thinking machines raises a host of ethical issues. These questions relate both to ensuring that such machines do not harm humans and other morally relevant beings, and to the moral status of the machines themselves.

Ethics in Machine Learning and other Domain-specific AI Algorithms

Imagine, in the near future, a bank using a machine learning algorithm to recommend mortgage applications for approval. A rejected applicant brings a lawsuit against the bank, alleging that the algorithm is discriminating racially against mortgage applicants. The bank replies that this is impossible, since the algorithm is deliberately blinded to the race of the applicants. Indeed, that was part of the bank's rationale for implementing the system. Even so, statistics show that the bank's approval rate for black applicants has been steadily dropping. Submitting ten apparently equally qualified genuine applicants (as determined by a separate panel of human judges) shows that the algorithm accepts white applicants and rejects black applicants. What could possibly be happening?

Finding an answer may not be easy. If the machine learning algorithm is based on a complicated neural network, or a genetic algorithm produced by directed evolution, then it may prove nearly impossible to understand why, or even how, the algorithm is judging applicants based on their race. On the other hand, a machine learner based on decision trees or Bayesian networks is much more transparent to programmer inspection, which may enable an auditor to discover that the AI algorithm uses the address information of applicants who were born or previously resided in predominantly poverty-stricken areas.

AI algorithms play an increasingly large role in modern society, though usually not labeled "AI". The scenario described above might be transpiring even as we write. It will become increasingly important to develop AI algorithms that are not just powerful and scalable, but also transparent to inspection—to name one of many socially important properties.

Some challenges of machine ethics are much like many other challenges involved in designing machines. Designing a robot arm to avoid crushing stray humans is no more morally fraught than designing a flame-retardant sofa. It involves new programming challenges, but no new ethical challenges. But when AI algorithms take on cognitive work with social dimensions—cognitive tasks previously performed by humans—the AI algorithm inherits the social requirements. It would surely be frustrating to find that no bank in the world will approve your seemingly excellent loan application, and nobody knows why, and nobody can find out even in principle.

Transparency is not the only desirable feature of AI. It is also important that AI algorithms taking over social functions be predictable to those they govern. To understand the importance of such predictability, consider an analogy. The legal principle of stare decisis binds judges to follow past precedent whenever possible. To an engineer, this preference for precedent may seem incomprehensible—why bind the future to the past, when technology is always improving? But one of the most important functions of the legal system is to be predictable, so that, e.g., contracts can be written knowing how they will be executed. The job of the legal system is not necessarily to optimize society, but to provide a predictable environment within which citizens can optimize their own lives.

It will also become increasingly important that AI algorithms be robust against manipulation. A machine vision system to scan airline luggage for bombs must be robust against human adversaries deliberately searching for exploitable flaws in the algorithm—for example, a shape that, placed next to a pistol in one's luggage, would neutralize recognition of it. Robustness against manipulation is an ordinary criterion in information security; nearly the criterion. But it is not a criterion that appears often in machine learning journals, which are currently more interested in, e.g., how an algorithm scales up on larger parallel systems.

Another important social criterion for dealing with organizations is being able to find the person responsible for getting something done. When an AI system fails at its assigned task, who takes the blame? The programmers? The end-users? Modern bureaucrats often take refuge in established procedures that distribute responsibility so widely that no one person can be identified to blame for the catastrophes that result. The provably disinterested judgment of an expert system could turn out to be an even better refuge. Even if an AI system is designed with a user override, one must consider the career incentive of a bureaucrat who will be personally blamed if the override goes wrong, and who would much prefer to blame the AI for any difficult decision with a negative outcome.

Responsibility, transparency, auditability, incorruptibility, predictability, and a tendency to not make innocent victims scream with helpless frustration: all criteria that apply to humans performing social functions; all criteria that must be considered in an algorithm intended to replace human judgment of social functions; all criteria that may not appear in a journal of machine learning considering how an algorithm scales up to more computers. This list of criteria is by no means exhaustive, but it serves as a small sample of what an increasingly computerized society should be thinking about.

Artificial General Intelligence

There is nearly universal agreement among modern AI professionals that Artificial Intelligence falls short of human capabilities in some critical sense, even though AI algorithms have beaten humans in many specific domains such as chess. It has been suggested by some that as soon as AI researchers figure out how to do something, that capability ceases to be regarded as intelligent—chess was considered the epitome of intelligence until Deep Blue won the world championship from Kasparov—but even these researchers agree that something important is missing from modern AIs.

While this subfield of Artificial Intelligence is only just coalescing, "Artificial General Intelligence" (hereafter, AGI) is the emerging term of art used to denote "real" AI. As the name implies, the emerging consensus is that the missing characteristic is generality. Current AI algorithms with human-equivalent or -superior performance are characterized by a deliberately-programmed competence only in a single, restricted domain. Deep Blue became the world champion at chess, but it cannot even play checkers, let alone drive a car or make a scientific discovery. Such modern AI algorithms resemble all biological life with the sole exception of Homo sapiens. A bee exhibits competence at building hives; a beaver exhibits competence at building dams; but a bee doesn't build dams, and a beaver can't learn to build a hive. A human, watching, can learn to do both; but this is a unique ability among biological lifeforms. It is debatable whether human intelligence is truly general—we are certainly better at some cognitive tasks than others—but human intelligence is surely significantly more generally applicable than nonhominid intelligence.

It is relatively easy to envisage the sort of safety issues that may result from AI operating only within a specific domain. It is a qualitatively different class of problem to handle an AGI operating across many novel contexts that cannot be predicted in advance.

When human engineers build a nuclear reactor, they envision the specific events that could go on inside it—valves failing, computers failing, cores increasing in temperature—and engineer the reactor to render these events noncatastrophic. Or, on a more mundane level, building a toaster involves envisioning bread and envisioning the reaction of the bread to the toaster's heating element. The toaster itself does not know that its purpose is to make toast—the purpose of the toaster is represented within the designer's mind, but is not explicitly represented in computations inside the toaster—and so if you place cloth inside a toaster, it may catch fire, as the design executes in an unenvisioned context with an unenvisioned side effect.

Even task-specific AI algorithms throw us outside the toaster-paradigm, the domain of locally pre-programmed, specifically envisioned behavior. Consider Deep Blue, the chess algorithm that beat Garry Kasparov for the world championship of chess. Were it the case that machines can only do exactly as they are told, the programmers would have had to manually preprogram a database containing moves for every possible chess position that Deep Blue could encounter. But this was not an option for Deep Blue's programmers. First, the space of possible chess positions is unmanageably large. Second, if the programmers had manually input what they considered a good move in each possible situation, the resulting system would not have been able to make stronger chess moves than its creators. Since the programmers themselves were not world champions, such a system would not have been able to defeat Garry Kasparov.

In creating a superhuman chess player, the human programmers necessarily sacrificed their ability to predict Deep Blue's local, specific game behavior. Instead, Deep Blue's programmers had (justifiable) confidence that Deep Blue's chess moves would satisfy a non-local criterion of optimality: namely, that the moves would tend to steer the future of the game board into outcomes in the "winning" region as defined by the chess rules. This prediction about distant consequences, though it proved accurate, did not allow the programmers to envision the local behavior of Deep Blue—its response to a specific attack on its king—because Deep Blue computed the nonlocal game map, the link between a move and its possible future consequences, more accurately than the programmers could.

Modern humans do literally millions of things to feed themselves—to serve the final consequence of being fed. Few of these activities were "envisioned by Nature" in the sense of being ancestral challenges to which we are directly adapted. But our adapted brain has grown powerful enough to be significantly more generally applicable; to let us foresee the consequences of millions of different actions across domains, and exert our preferences over final outcomes. Humans crossed space and put footprints on the Moon, even though none of our ancestors encountered a challenge analogous to vacuum. Compared to domain-specific AI, it is a qualitatively different problem to design a system that will operate safely across thousands of contexts; including contexts not specifically envisioned by either the designers or the users; including contexts that no human has yet encountered. Here there may be no local specification of good behavior—no simple specification over the behaviors themselves, any more than there exists a compact local description of all the ways that humans obtain their daily bread.

To build an AI that acts safely while acting in many domains, with many consequences, including problems the engineers never explicitly envisioned, one must specify good behavior in such terms as "X such that the consequence of X is not harmful to humans". This is non-local; it involves extrapolating the distant consequences of actions. Thus, this is only an effective specification—one that can be realized as a design property—if the system explicitly extrapolates the consequences of its behavior. A toaster cannot have this design property because a toaster cannot foresee the consequences of toasting bread.

Imagine an engineer having to say, "Well, I have no idea how this airplane I built will fly safely— indeed I have no idea how it will fly at all, whether it will flap its wings or inflate itself with helium or something else I haven't even imagined—but I assure you, the design is very, very safe." This may seem like an unenviable position from the perspective of public relations, but it's hard to see what other guarantee of ethical behavior would be possible for a general intelligence operating on unforeseen problems, across domains, with preferences over distant consequences. Inspecting the cognitive design might verify that the mind was, indeed, searching for solutions that we would classify as ethical; but we couldn't predict which specific solution the mind would discover.

Respecting such a verification requires some way to distinguish trustworthy assurances (a procedure which will not say the AI is safe unless the AI really is safe) from pure hope and magical thinking. One should bear in mind that purely hopeful expectations have previously been a problem in AI research.

Verifiably constructing a trustworthy AGI will require different methods, and a different way of thinking, from inspecting power plant software for bugs—it will require an AGI that thinks like a human engineer concerned about ethics, not just a simple product of ethical engineering.

Thus the discipline of AI ethics, especially as applied to AGI, is likely to differ fundamentally from the ethical discipline of noncognitive technologies, in that:

- The local, specific behavior of the AI may not be predictable apart from its safety, even if the programmers do everything right;

- Verifying the safety of the system becomes a greater challenge because we must verify what the system is trying to do, rather than being able to verify the system's safe behavior in all operating contexts;

- Ethical cognition itself must be taken as a subject matter of engineering.

Machines with Moral Status

A different set of ethical issues arises when we contemplate the possibility that some future AI systems might be candidates for having moral status. Our dealings with beings possessed of moral status are not exclusively a matter of instrumental rationality: we also have moral reasons to treat them in certain ways, and to refrain from treating them in certain other ways. Francis Kamm has proposed the following definition of moral status, which will serve for our purposes:

> X has moral status = because X counts morally in its own right, it is permissible/impermissible to do things to it for its own sake.

A rock has no moral status: we may crush it, pulverize it, or subject it to any treatment we like without any concern for the rock itself. A human person, on the other hand, must be treated not only as a means but also as an end. Exactly what it means to treat a person as an end is something about which different ethical theories disagree; but it certainly involves taking her legitimate interests into account—giving weight to her well-being—and it may also involve accepting strict moral side-constraints in our dealings with her, such as a prohibition against murdering her, stealing from her, or doing a variety of other things to her or her property without her consent. Moreover, it is because a human person counts in her own right, and for her sake, that it is impermissible to do to her these things. This can be expressed more concisely by saying that a human person has moral status.

Questions about moral status are important in some areas of practical ethics. For example, disputes about the moral permissibility of abortion often hinge on disagreements about the moral status of the embryo. Controversies about animal experimentation and the treatment of animals in the food industry involve questions about the moral status of different species of animal. And our obligations towards human beings with severe dementia, such as late-stage Alzheimer's patients, may also depend on questions of moral status.

It is widely agreed that current AI systems have no moral status. We may change, copy, terminate, delete, or use computer programs as we please; at least as far as the programs themselves are concerned. The moral constraints to which we are subject in our dealings with contemporary AI systems are all grounded in our responsibilities to other beings, such as our fellow humans, not in any duties to the systems themselves.

While it is fairly consensual that present-day AI systems lack moral status, it is unclear exactly what attributes ground moral status. Two criteria are commonly proposed as being importantly linked to moral status, either separately or in combination: sentience and sapience (or personhood). These may be characterized roughly as follows:

- Sentience: The capacity for phenomenal experience or qualia, such as the capacity to feel pain and suffer.

- Sapience: A set of capacities associated with higher intelligence, such as self- awareness and being a reason-responsive agent.

One common view is that many animals have qualia and therefore have some moral status, but that only human beings have sapience, which gives them a higher moral status than non-human animals. This view, of course, must confront the existence of borderline cases such as, on the one hand, human infants or human beings with severe mental retardation—sometimes unfortunately referred to as "marginal humans"— which fail to satisfy the criteria for sapience; and, on the other hand, some non-human animals such as the great apes, which might possess at least some of the elements of sapience. Some deny that so-called "marginal humans" have full moral status. Others propose additional ways in which an object could qualify as a bearer of moral status, such as by being a member of a kind that normally has sentience or sapience, or by standing in a suitable relation to some being that independently has moral status. For present purposes, however, we will focus on the criteria of sentience and sapience.

This picture of moral status suggests that an AI system will have some moral status if it has the capacity for qualia, such as an ability to feel pain. A sentient AI system, even if it lacks language and other higher cognitive faculties, is not like a stuffed toy animal or a wind-up doll; it is more like a living animal. It is wrong to inflict pain on a mouse, unless there are sufficiently strong morally overriding reasons to do so. The same would hold for any sentient AI system. If in addition to sentience, an AI system also has sapience of a kind similar to that of a normal human adult, then it would have full moral status, equivalent to that of human beings.

One of the ideas underlying this moral assessment can be expressed in stronger form as a principle of non-discrimination:

1. Principle of Substrate Non-Discrimination: If two beings have the same functionality and the same conscious experience, and differ only in the substrate of their implementation, then they have the same moral status.

One can argue for this principle on grounds that rejecting it would amount to embracing a position similar to racism: Substrate lacks fundamental moral significance in the same way and for the same reason as skin color does. The principle of substrate non-discrimination does not imply that a digital computer could be conscious, or that it could have the same functionality as a human being. Substrate can of course be morally relevant insofar as it makes a difference to sentience or functionality. But holding these things constant, it makes no moral difference whether a being is made of silicon or carbon, or whether its brain uses semi-conductors or neurotransmitters.

An additional principle that can be proposed is that the fact that AI systems are artificial—i.e., the product of deliberate design—is not fundamentally relevant to their moral status. We could formulate this as follows:

2. Principle of Ontogeny Non-Discrimination: If two beings have the same functionality and the same consciousness experience, and differ only in how they came into existence, then they have the same moral status.

Today, this idea is widely accepted in the human case—although in some circles, particularly in the past, the idea that one's moral status depends on one's bloodline or caste has been influential. We do not believe that causal factors such as family planning, assisted delivery, in vitro fertilization, gamete selection, deliberate enhancement of maternal nutrition etc. – which introduce an element of deliberate choice and design in the creation of human persons—have any necessary implications for the moral status of the progeny. Even those who are opposed to human reproductive cloning for moral or religious reasons generally accept that, should a human clone be brought to term, it would have the same moral status as any other human infant. The Principle of Ontogeny Non-Discrimination extends this reasoning to the case involving entirely artificial cognitive systems.

It is, of course, possible for circumstances of creation to affect the ensuing progeny in such a way as to alter its moral status. For example, if some procedure were performed during conception or gestation that caused a human fetus to develop without a brain, then this fact about ontogeny would be relevant to our assessment of the moral status of the progeny. The anencephalic child, however, would have the same moral status as any other similar anencephalic child, including one that had come about through some entirely natural process. The difference in moral status between an anencephalic child and a normal child is grounded in the qualitative difference between the two—the fact that one has a mind while the other does not. Since the two children do not have the same functionality and the same conscious experience, the Principle of Ontogeny Non-Discrimination does not apply.

Although the Principle of Ontogeny Non-Discrimination asserts that a being's ontogeny has no essential bearing on its moral status, it does not deny that facts about ontogeny can affect what duties particular moral agents have toward the being in question. Parents have special duties to their child which they do not have to other children, and which they would not have even if there were another child qualitatively identical to their own. Similarly, the Principle of Ontogeny Non-Discrimination is consistent with the claim that the creators or owners of an AI system with moral status may have special duties to their artificial mind which they do not have to another artificial mind, even if the minds in question are qualitatively similar and have the same moral status.

If the principles of non-discrimination with regard to substrate and ontogeny are accepted, then many questions about how we ought to treat artificial minds can be answered by applying the same moral principles that we use to determine our duties in more familiar contexts. Insofar as moral duties stem from moral status considerations, we ought to treat an artificial mind in just the same way as we ought to treat a qualitatively identical natural human mind in a similar situation. This simplifies the problem of developing an ethics for the treatment of artificial minds.

Even if we accept this stance, however, we must confront a number of novel ethical questions which the aforementioned principles leave unanswered. Novel ethical questions arise because artificial minds can have very different properties from ordinary human or animal minds. We must consider how these novel properties would affect the moral status of artificial minds and what it would mean to respect the moral status of such exotic minds.

Minds with Exotic Properties

In the case of human beings, we do not normally hesitate to ascribe sentience and conscious experience to any individual who exhibits the normal kinds of human behavior. Few believe there to be other people who act perfectly normally but lack consciousness. However, other human beings do not merely behave in person-like ways similar to ourselves; they also have brains and cognitive architectures that are constituted much like our own. An artificial intellect, by contrast, might be constituted quite differently from a human intellect yet still exhibit human-like behavior or possess the behavioral dispositions normally indicative of personhood. It might therefore be possible to conceive of an artificial intellect that would be sapient, and perhaps would be a person, yet would not be sentient or have conscious experiences of any kind. Whether this is really possible depends on the answers to some non-trivial metaphysical questions. Should such a system be possible, it would raise the question whether a non-sentient person would have any moral status whatever; and if so, whether it would have the same moral status as a sentient person. Since sentience, or at least a capacity for sentience, is ordinarily assumed to be present in any individual who is a person, this question has not received much attention to date.

Another exotic property, one which is certainly metaphysically and physically possible for an artificial intelligence, is for its subjective rate of time to deviate drastically from the rate that is characteristic of a biological human brain. The concept of subjective rate of time is best explained by first introducing the idea whole brain emulation, or "uploading".

"Uploading" refers to a hypothetical future technology that would enable a human or other animal intellect to be transferred from its original implementation in an organic brain onto a digital computer. One scenario goes like this: First, a very high-resolution scan is performed of some particular brain, possibly destroying the original in the process. For example, the brain might be vitrified and dissected into thin slices, which can then be scanned using some form of high-throughput microscopy combined with automated image recognition. We may imagine this scan to be detailed enough to capture all the neurons, their synaptic interconnections, and other features that are functionally relevant to the original brain's operation. Second, this three-dimensional map of the components of the brain and their interconnections is combined with a library of advanced neuroscientific theory which specifies the computational properties of each basic type of element, such as different kinds of neuron and synaptic junction. Third, the computational structure and the associated algorithmic behavior of its components are implemented in some powerful computer. If the uploading process has been successful, the computer program should now replicate the essential functional characteristics of the original brain. The resulting upload may inhabit a simulated virtual reality, or, alternatively, it could be given control of a robotic body, enabling it to interact directly with external physical reality.

A number of questions arise in the context of such a scenario: How plausible is it that this procedure will one day become technologically feasible? If the procedure worked and produced a computer program exhibiting roughly the same personality, the same memories, and the same thinking patterns as the original brain, would this program be sentient? Would the upload be the same person as the individual whose brain was disassembled in the uploading process? What happens to personal identity if an upload is copied such that two similar or qualitatively identical upload minds are running in parallel? Although all of these questions are relevant to the ethics of machine intelligence, let us here focus on an issue involving the notion of a subjective rate of time.

Suppose that an upload could be sentient. If we run the upload program on a faster computer, this will cause the upload, if it is connected to an input device such as a video camera, to perceive the external world as if it had been slowed down. For example, if the upload is running a thousand times faster than the original brain, then the external world will appear to the upload as if it were slowed down by a factor of thousand. Somebody drops a physical coffee mug: The upload observes the mug slowly falling to the ground while the upload finishes reading the morning newspaper and sends off a few emails. One second of objective time corresponds to 17 minutes of subjective time. Objective and subjective duration can thus diverge.

Subjective time is not the same as a subject's estimate or perception of how fast time flows. Human beings are often mistaken about the flow of time. We may believe that it is one o'clock when it is in fact a quarter past two; or a stimulant drug might cause our thoughts to race, making it seem as though more subjective time has lapsed than is actually the case. These mundane cases involve a distorted time perception rather than a shift in the rate of subjective time. Even in a cocaine-addled brain, there is probably not a significant change in the speed of basic neurological computations; more likely, the drug is causing such a brain to flicker more rapidly from one thought to another, making it spend less subjective time thinking each of a greater number of distinct thoughts.

The variability of the subjective rate of time is an exotic property of artificial minds that raises novel ethical issues. For example, in cases where the duration of an experience is ethically relevant, should duration be measured in objective or subjective time? If an upload has committed a crime and is sentenced to four years in prison, should this be four objective years—which might correspond to many millennia of subjective time— or should it be four subjective years, which might be over in a couple of days of objective time? If a fast AI and a human are in pain, is it more urgent to alleviate the AI's pain, on grounds that it experiences a greater subjective duration of pain for each sidereal second that palliation is delayed? Since in our accustomed context of biological humans, subjective time is not significantly variable, it is unsurprising that this kind of question is not straightforwardly settled by familiar ethical norms, even if these norms are extended to artificial intellects by means of non-discrimination principles.

To illustrate the kind of ethical claim that might be relevant here, we formulate (but do not argue for) a principle privileging subjective time as the normatively more fundamental notion:

Principle of subjective rate of time: In cases where the duration of an experience is of basic normative significance, it is the experience's subjective duration that counts.

So far we have discussed two possibilities (non-sentient sapience and variable subjective rate of time) which are exotic in the relatively profound sense of being metaphysically problematic as well as lacking clear instances or parallels in the contemporary world. Other properties of possible artificial minds would be exotic in a more superficial sense; e.g., by diverging in some unproblematically quantitative dimension from the kinds of mind with which we are familiar. But such superficially exotic properties may also pose novel ethical problems—if not at the level of foundational moral philosophy, then at the level of applied ethics or for mid-level ethical principles.

One important set of exotic properties of artificial intelligences relate to reproduction. A number of empirical conditions that apply to human reproduction need not apply to artificial intelligences. For example, human children are the product of recombination of the genetic material from two parents; parents have limited ability to influence the character of their offspring; a human embryo needs to be gestated in the womb for nine months; it takes fifteen to twenty years for a human child to reach maturity; a human child does not inherit the skills and knowledge acquired by its parents; human beings possess a complex evolved set of emotional adaptations related to reproduction, nurturing, and the child-parent relationship. None of these empirical conditions need pertain in the context of a reproducing machine intelligence. It is therefore plausible that many of the mid-level moral principles that we have come to accept as norms governing human reproduction will need to be rethought in the context of AI reproduction.

To illustrate why some of our moral norms need to be rethought in the context of AI reproduction, it will suffice to consider just one exotic property of AIs: their capacity for rapid reproduction. Given access to computer hardware, an AI could duplicate itself very quickly, in no more time than it takes to make a copy of the AI's software.

Moreover, since the AI copy would be identical to the original, it would be born completely mature, and the copy could begin making its own copies immediately. Absent hardware limitations, a population of AIs could therefore grow exponentially at an extremely rapid rate, with a doubling time on the order of minutes or hours rather than decades or centuries.

Our current ethical norms about reproduction include some version of a principle of reproductive freedom, to the effect that it is up to each individual or couple to decide for themselves whether to have children and how many children to have. Another norm we have (at least in rich and middle-income countries) is that society must step in to provide the basic needs of children in cases where their parents are unable or refusing to do so. It is easy to see how these two norms could collide in the context of entities with the capacity for extremely rapid reproduction.

Consider, for example, a population of uploads, one of whom happens to have the desire to produce as large a clan as possible. Given complete reproductive freedom, this upload may start copying itself as quickly as it can; and the copies it produces— which may run on new computer hardware owned or rented by the original, or may share the same computer as the original—will also start copying themselves, since they are identical to the progenitor upload and share its philoprogenic desire. Soon, members of the upload clan will find themselves unable to pay the electricity bill or the rent for the computational processing and storage needed to keep them alive. At this point, a social welfare system might kick in to provide them with at least the bare necessities for sustaining life. But if the population grows faster than the economy, resources will run out; at which point uploads will either die or their ability to reproduce will be curtailed.

This scenario illustrates how some mid-level ethical principles that are suitable in contemporary societies might need to be modified if those societies were to include persons with the exotic property of being able to reproduce very rapidly.

The general point here is that when thinking about applied ethics for contexts that are very different from our familiar human condition, we must be careful not to mistake mid-level ethical principles for foundational normative truths. Put differently, we must recognize the extent to which our ordinary normative precepts are implicitly conditioned on the obtaining of various empirical conditions, and the need to adjust these precepts accordingly when applying them to hypothetical futuristic cases in which their preconditions are assumed not to obtain. By this, we are not making any controversial claim about moral relativism, but merely highlighting the commonsensical point that context is relevant to the application of ethics—and suggesting that this point is especially pertinent when one is considering the ethics of minds with exotic properties.

Superintelligence

I. J. Good set forth the classic hypothesis concerning superintelligence: that an AI sufficiently intelligent to understand its own design could redesign itself or create a successor system, more intelligent, which could then redesign itself yet again to become even more intelligent, and so on in a positive feedback cycle. Good called this the "intelligence explosion". Recursive scenarios are not limited to AI: Humans with intelligence augmented through a brain-computer interface might turn their minds to designing the next generation of brain-computer interfaces. (If you had a machine that increased your IQ, it would be bound to occur to you, once you became smart enough, to try to design a more powerful version of the machine). Super intelligence may also be achievable by increasing processing speed. The fastest observed neurons fire 1000 times per second; the fastest axon fibers conduct signals at 150 meters/second, a half-millionth the speed of light. It seems that it should be physically possible to build a brain which computes a million times as fast as a human brain, without shrinking its size or rewriting its software. If a human mind were thus accelerated, a subjective year of thinking would be accomplished for every 31 physical seconds in the outside world, and a millennium would fly by in eight and a half hours. Vinge referred to such sped-up minds as "weak superintelligence": a mind that thinks like a human but much faster.

Yudkowsky lists three families of metaphors for visualizing the capability of a smarter-than-human AI:

- Metaphors inspired by differences of individual intelligence between humans: AIs will patent new inventions, publish groundbreaking research papers, make money on the stock market, or lead political power blocks.

- Metaphors inspired by knowledge differences between past and present human civilizations: Fast AIs will invent capabilities that futurists commonly predict for human civilizations a century or millennium in the future, like molecular nanotechnology or interstellar travel.

- Metaphors inspired by differences of brain architecture between humans and other biological organisms: E.g., Vinge: "Imagine running a dog mind at very high speed. Would a thousand years of doggy living add up to any human insight?" That is: Changes of cognitive architecture might produce insights that no human-level mind would be able to find, or perhaps even represent, after any amount of time.

Even if we restrict ourselves to historical metaphors, it becomes clear that superhuman intelligence presents ethical challenges that are quite literally unprecedented. At this point the stakes are no longer on an individual scale (e.g., mortgage unjustly disapproved, house catches fire, person-agent mistreated) but on a global or cosmic scale (e.g., humanity is extinguished and replaced by nothing we would regard as worthwhile). Or, if superintelligence can be shaped to be beneficial, then, depending on its technological capabilities, it might make short work of many present-day problems that have proven difficult to our human-level intelligence.

Superintelligence is one of several "existential risks" as defined by Bostrom: A risk "where an adverse outcome would either annihilate Earth-originating intelligent life or permanently and drastically curtail its potential". Conversely, a positive outcome for superintelligence could preserve Earth-originating intelligent life and help fulfill its potential. It is important to emphasize that smarter minds pose great potential benefits as well as risks.

Attempts to reason about global catastrophic risks may be susceptible to a number of cognitive biases, including the "good-story bias" proposed by Bostrom:

"Suppose our intuitions about which future scenarios are "plausible and realistic" are shaped by what we see on TV and in movies and what we read in novels. (After all, a large part of the discourse about the future that people encounter is in the form of fiction and other recreational contexts.) We should then, when thinking critically, suspect our intuitions of being biased in the direction of overestimating the probability of those scenarios that make for a good story, since such scenarios will seem much more familiar and more "real". This Good-story bias could be quite powerful. When was the last time you saw a movie about humankind suddenly going extinct (without warning and without being replaced by some other civilization)? While this scenario may be much more probable than a scenario in which human heroes successfully repel an invasion of monsters or robot warriors, it wouldn't be much fun to watch".

Truly desirable outcomes make poor movies: No conflict means no story. While Asimov's Three Laws of Robotics are sometimes cited as a model for ethical AI development, the Three Laws are as much a plot device as Asimov's "positronic brain". If Asimov had depicted the Three Laws as working well, he would have had no stories.

It would be a mistake to regard "AIs" as a species with fixed characteristics and ask, "Will they be good or evil?" The term "Artificial Intelligence" refers to a vast design space, presumably much larger than the space of human minds (since all humans share a common brain architecture). It may be a form of good-story bias to ask, "Will AIs be good or evil?" as if trying to pick a premise for a movie plot. The reply should be, "Exactly which AI design are you talking about?"

Can control over the initial programming of an Artificial Intelligence translate into influence on its later effect on the world? Kurzweil holds that "intelligence is inherently impossible to control", and that despite any human attempts at taking precautions, "by definition. intelligent entities have the cleverness to easily overcome such barriers." Let us suppose that the AI is not only clever, but that, as part of the process of improving its own intelligence, it has unhindered access to its own source code: it can rewrite itself to anything it wants itself to be. Yet it does not follow that the AI must want to rewrite itself to a hostile form.

At this point in the development of AI science, is there any way we can translate the task of finding a design for "good" AIs into a modern research direction? It may seem premature to speculate, but one does suspect that some AI paradigms are more likely than others to eventually prove conducive to the creation of intelligent self-modifying agents whose goals remain predictable even after multiple iterations of self-improvement. For example, the Bayesian branch of AI, inspired by coherent mathematical systems such as probability theory and expected utility maximization, seems more amenable to the predictable self-modification problem than evolutionary programming and genetic algorithms. This is a controversial statement, but it illustrates the point that if we are thinking about the challenge of superintelligence down the road, this can indeed be turned into directional advice for present AI research.

Yet even supposing that we can specify an AI's goal system to be persistent under self-modification and self-improvement, this only begins to touch on the core ethical problems of creating superintelligence. Humans, the first general intelligences to exist on Earth, have used that intelligence to substantially reshape the globe—carving mountains, taming rivers, building skyscrapers, farming deserts, producing unintended planetary climate changes. A more powerful intelligence could have correspondingly larger consequences.

Consider again the historical metaphor for superintelligence—differences similar to the differences between past and present civilizations. Our present civilization is not separated from ancient Greece only by improved science and increased technological capability. There is a difference of ethical perspectives: Ancient Greeks thought slavery was acceptable; we think otherwise. Even between the nineteenth and twentieth centuries, there were substantial ethical disagreements—should women have the vote? Should blacks have the vote? It seems likely that people today will not be seen as ethically perfect by future civilizations—not just because of our failure to solve currently recognized ethical problems, such as poverty and inequality, but also for our failure even to recognize certain ethical problems. Perhaps someday the act of subjecting children to involuntarily schooling will be seen as child abuse—or maybe allowing children to leave school at age 18 will be seen as child abuse.

Considering the ethical history of human civilizations over centuries of time, we can see that it might prove a very great tragedy to create a mind that was stable in ethical dimensions along which human civilizations seem to exhibit directional change. What if Archimedes of Syracuse had been able to create a long-lasting artificial intellect with a fixed version of the moral code of Ancient Greece? But to avoid this sort of ethical stagnation is likely to prove tricky: it would not suffice, for example, simply to render the mind randomly unstable. The ancient Greeks, even if they had realized their own imperfection, could not have done better by rolling dice. Occasionally a good new idea in ethics comes along, and it comes as a surprise; but most randomly generated ethical changes would strike us as folly or gibberish.

This presents us with perhaps the ultimate challenge of machine ethics: How do you build an AI which, when it executes, becomes more ethical than you? This is not like asking our own philosophers to produce superethics, any more than Deep Blue was constructed by getting the best human chess players to program in good moves. But we have to be able to effectively describe the question, if not the answer—rolling dice won't generate good chess moves, or good ethics either. Or, perhaps a more productive way to think about the problem: What strategy would you want Archimedes to follow in building a superintelligence, such that the overall outcome would still be acceptable, if you couldn't tell him what specifically he was doing wrong? This is very much the situation that we are in, relative to the future.

One strong piece of advice that emerges from considering our situation as analogous to that of Archimedes is that we should not try to invent a "super" version of what our own civilization considers to be ethics—this is not the strategy we would have wanted Archimedes to follow. Perhaps the question we should be considering, rather, is how an AI programmed by Archimedes, with no more moral expertise than Archimedes, could recognize (at least some of) our own civilization's ethics as moral progress as opposed to mere moral instability. This would require that we begin to comprehend the structure of ethical questions in the way that we have already comprehended the structure of chess.

If we are serious about developing advanced AI, this is a challenge that we must meet. If machines are to be placed in a position of being stronger, faster, more trusted, or smarter than humans, then the discipline of machine ethics must commit itself to seeking human-superior (not just human-equivalent) niceness.

Ethics of Artificial Intelligence

The ethics of artificial intelligence is the part of the ethics of technology specific to robots and other artificially intelligent beings. It is typically divided into roboethics, a concern with the moral behavior of humans as they design, construct, use and treat artificially intelligent beings, and machine ethics, which is concerned with the moral behavior of artificial moral agents (AMAs).

Robot Ethics

The term "robot ethics" (sometimes "roboethics") refers to the morality of how humans design, construct, use and treat robots and other artificially intelligent beings. It considers both how artificially intelligent beings may be used to harm humans and how they may be used to benefit humans.

Robot Rights

"Robot rights" is the concept that people should have moral obligations towards their machines, similar to human rights or animal rights. It has been suggested that robot rights, such as a right to exist and perform its own mission, could be linked to robot duty to serve human, by analogy with linking human rights to human duties before society. These could include the right to life and liberty, freedom of thought and expression and equality before the law. The issue has been considered by the Institute for the Future and by the U.K. Department of Trade and Industry.

Experts disagree whether specific and detailed laws will be required soon or safely in the distant future. Glenn McGee reports that sufficiently humanoid robots may appear by 2020. Ray Kurzweil sets the date at 2029.Another group of scientists meeting in 2007 supposed that at least 50 years had to pass before any sufficiently advanced system would exist.

The rules for the 2003 Loebner Prize competition envisioned the possibility of robots having rights of their own:

"If, in any given year, a publicly available open source Entry entered by the University of Surrey or the Cambridge Center wins the Silver Medal or the Gold Medal, then the Medal and the Cash Award will be awarded to the body responsible for the development of that Entry. If no such body can be identified, or if there is disagreement among two or more claimants, the Medal and the Cash Award will be held in trust until such time as the Entry may legally possess, either in the United States of America or in the venue of the contest, the Cash Award and Gold Medal in its own right".

In October 2017, the android Sophia was granted "honorary" citizenship in Saudi Arabia, though some observers found this to be more of a publicity stunt than a meaningful legal recognition. Some saw this gesture as openly denigrating of human rights and the rule of law.

The philosophy of Sentientism grants degrees of moral consideration to all sentient beings, primarily humans and most non-human animals. If artificial or alien intelligences show evidence of being sentient, this philosophy holds that they should be shown compassion and granted rights.

Joanna Bryson has argued that creating AI that requires rights is both avoidable, and would in itself be unethical, both as a burden to the AI agents and to human society.

Threat to Human Dignity

Joseph Weizenbaum argued in 1976 that AI technology should not be used to replace people in positions that require respect and care, such as any of these:

- A customer service representative (AI technology is already used today for telephone-based interactive voice response systems);

- A therapist;

- A nursemaid for the elderly;

- A soldier;

- A judge;

- A police officer.

Weizenbaum explains that we require authentic feelings of empathy from people in these positions. If machines replace them, we will find ourselves alienated, devalued and frustrated. Artificial intelligence, if used in this way, represents a threat to human dignity. Weizenbaum argues that the fact that we are entertaining the possibility of machines in these positions suggests that we have experienced an "atrophy of the human spirit that comes from thinking of ourselves as computers."

Pamela McCorduck counters that, speaking for women and minorities "I'd rather take my chances with an impartial computer," pointing out that there are conditions where we would prefer to have automated judges and police that have no personal agenda at all. However, Kaplan and Haenlein stress that AI systems are only as smart as the data used to train them since they are, in their essence, nothing more than fancy curve-fitting machines: Using AI to support a court ruling can be highly problematic if past rulings show bias toward certain groups since those biases get formalized and engrained, which makes them even more difficult to spot and fight against. AI founder John McCarthy objects to the moralizing tone of Weizenbaum's critique. "When moralizing is both vehement and vague, it invites authoritarian abuse," he writes.

Bill Hibbard writes that "Human dignity requires that we strive to remove our ignorance of the nature of existence, and AI is necessary for that striving."

Transparency, Accountability and Open Source

Bill Hibbard argues that because AI will have such a profound effect on humanity, AI developers are representatives of future humanity and thus have an ethical obligation to be transparent in their efforts. Ben Goertzel and David Hart created OpenCog as an open source framework for AI development. OpenAI is a non-profit AI research company created by Elon Musk, Sam Altman and others to develop open source AI beneficial to humanity. There are numerous other open source AI developments.

Unfortunately, making code open source does not make it comprehensible, which by many definitions means that the AI it codes is not transparent. The IEEE has a standardisation effort on AI transparency The IEEE effort identifies multiple scales of transparency for different users. Further, there is concern that releasing the full capacity of contemporary AI to some organisations may be a public bad, that is, do more damage than good. For example, Microsoft has expressed concern about allowing universal access to its face recognition software, even for those who can pay for it. Microsoft posted an extraordinary blog on this topic, asking for government regulation to help determine the right thing to do.

Not only companies, but many other researchers and citizen advocates recommend government regulation as a means of ensuring transparency, and through it, human accountability. This strategy has proven controversial, as some worry that it will slow the rate of innovation. Others argue that regulation leads to systemic stability more able to support innovation in the long term. The OECD, UN, EU, and many countries are presently working on strategies for regulating AI, and finding appropriate legal frameworks.

Biases in AI systems

AI has become increasingly inherent in facial and voice recognition systems. Some of these systems have real business implications and directly impact people. These systems are vulnerable to biases and errors introduced by its human makers. Also, the data used to train these AI systems itself can have biases. For instance, facial recognition algorithms made by Microsoft, IBM and Face++ all had biases when it came to detecting people's gender . These AI systems were able to detect gender of white men more accurately than gender of darker skin men. Similarly, Amazon's.com Inc's termination of AI hiring and recruitment is another example which exhibit AI cannot be fair. The algorithm preferred more male candidates then female. This was because Amazon's system was trained with data collected over 10 year period that came mostly from male candidates.

Liability for Partial or Fully Automated Cars

The wide use of partial to fully autonomous cars seems to be imminent in the future. But these new technologies also bring new issues. Recently, a debate over the legal liability have risen over the responsible party if these cars get into accident. In one of the reports a driver less car hit a pedestrian and had a dilemma over whom to blame for the accident. Even though the driver was inside the car during the accident, the controls were fully in the hand of computers. Before such cars become widely used, these issues need to be tackled through new policies.

Weaponization of Artificial Intelligence

Some experts and academics have questioned the use of robots for military combat, especially when such robots are given some degree of autonomous functions. The US Navy has funded a report which indicates that as military robots become more complex, there should be greater attention to implications of their ability to make autonomous decisions. One researcher states that autonomous robots might be more humane, as they could make decisions more effectively.

Within this last decade, there has been intensive research in autonomous power with the ability to learn using assigned moral responsibilities. "The results may be used when designing future military robots, to control unwanted tendencies to assign responsibility to the robots." From a consequentialist view, there is a chance that robots will develop the ability to make their own logical decisions on who to kill and that is why there should be a set moral framework that the AI cannot override.

There has been a recent outcry with regard to the engineering of artificial-intelligence weapons that has included ideas of a robot takeover of mankind. AI weapons do present a type of danger different from that of human-controlled weapons. Many governments have begun to fund programs to develop AI weaponry. The United States Navy recently announced plans to develop autonomous drone weapons, paralleling similar announcements by Russia and Korea respectively. Due to the potential of AI weapons becoming more dangerous than human-operated weapons, Stephen

Hawking and Max Tegmark signed a "Future of Life" petition to ban AI weapons. The message posted by Hawking and Tegmark states that AI weapons pose an immediate danger and that action is required to avoid catastrophic disasters in the near future.

"If any major military power pushes ahead with the AI weapon development, a global arms race is virtually inevitable, and the endpoint of this technological trajectory is obvious: autonomous weapons will become the Kalashnikovs of tomorrow", says the petition, which includes Skype co-founder Jaan Tallinn and MIT professor of linguistics Noam Chomsky as additional supporters against AI weaponry.

Physicist and Astronomer Royal Sir Martin Rees has warned of catastrophic instances like "dumb robots going rogue or a network that develops a mind of its own." Huw Price, a colleague of Rees at Cambridge, has voiced a similar warning that humans might not survive when intelligence "escapes the constraints of biology." These two professors created the Centre for the Study of Existential Risk at Cambridge University in the hope of avoiding this threat to human existence.

Regarding the potential for smarter-than-human systems to be employed militarily, the Open Philanthropy Project writes that these scenarios "seem potentially as important as the risks related to loss of control", but that research organizations investigating AI's long-run social impact have spent relatively little time on this concern: "this class of scenarios has not been a major focus for the organizations that have been most active in this space, such as the Machine Intelligence Research Institute (MIRI) and the Future of Humanity Institute (FHI), and there seems to have been less analysis and debate regarding them".

Machine Ethics

Machine ethics (or machine morality) is the field of research concerned with designing Artificial Moral Agents(AMAs), robots or artificially intelligent computers that behave morally or as though moral. To account for the nature of these agents, it has been suggested to consider certain philosophical ideas, like the standard characterizations of agency, rational agency, moral agency, and artificial agency, which are related to the concept of AMAs.

Isaac Asimov considered the issue in the 1950s in his *I, Robot*. At the insistence of his editor John W. Campbell Jr., he proposed the Three Laws of Robotics to govern artificially intelligent systems. Much of his work was then spent testing the boundaries of his three laws to see where they would break down, or where they would create paradoxical or unanticipated behavior. His work suggests that no set of fixed laws can sufficiently anticipate all possible circumstances. More recently, academics and many governments have challenged the idea that AI can itself be held accountable. A panel convened by the United Kingdom in 2010 revised Asimov's laws to clarify that AI is the responsibility either of its manufacturers, or of its owner/operator.

In 2009, during an experiment at the Laboratory of Intelligent Systems in the Ecole Polytechnique Fédérale of Lausanne in Switzerland, robots that were programmed to cooperate with each other (in searching out a beneficial resource and avoiding a poisonous one) eventually learned to lie to each other in an attempt to hoard the beneficial resource. One problem in this case may have been that the goals were "terminal" (i.e. in contrast, ultimate human motives typically have a quality of requiring never-ending learning).

Some experts and academics have questioned the use of robots for military combat, especially when such robots are given some degree of autonomous functions. The US Navy has funded a report which indicates that as military robots become more complex, there should be greater attention to implications of their ability to make autonomous decisions. The President of the Association for the Advancement of Artificial Intelligence has commissioned a study to look at this issue. They point to programs like the Language Acquisition Device which can emulate human interaction.

Vernor Vinge has suggested that a moment may come when some computers are smarter than humans. He calls this "the Singularity." He suggests that it may be somewhat or possibly very dangerous for humans.This is discussed by a philosophy called Singularitarianism. The Machine Intelligence Research Institute has suggested a need to build "Friendly AI", meaning that the advances which are already occurring with AI should also include an effort to make AI intrinsically friendly and humane.

In 2009, academics and technical experts attended a conference organized by the Association for the Advancement of Artificial Intelligence to discuss the potential impact of robots and computers and the impact of the hypothetical possibility that they could become self-sufficient and able to make their own decisions. They discussed the possibility and the extent to which computers and robots might be able to acquire any level of autonomy, and to what degree they could use such abilities to possibly pose any threat or hazard. They noted that some machines have acquired various forms of semi-autonomy, including being able to find power sources on their own and being able to independently choose targets to attack with weapons. They also noted that some computer viruses can evade elimination and have achieved "cockroach intelligence." They noted that self-awareness as depicted in science-fiction is probably unlikely, but that there were other potential hazards and pitfalls.

However, there is one technology in particular that could truly bring the possibility of robots with moral competence to reality. In a paper on the acquisition of moral values by robots, Nayef Al-Rodhan mentions the case of neuromorphic chips, which aim to process information similarly to humans, nonlinearly and with millions of interconnected artificial neurons. Robots embedded with neuromorphic technology could learn and develop knowledge in a uniquely humanlike way. Inevitably, this raises the question of the environment in which such robots would learn about the world and whose morality they would inherit - or if they end up developing human 'weaknesses' as well: selfishness, a pro-survival attitude, hesitation etc.

In *Moral Machines: Teaching Robots Right from Wrong*, Wendell Wallach and Colin Allen conclude that attempts to teach robots right from wrong will likely advance understanding of human ethics by motivating humans to address gaps in modern normative theory and by providing a platform for experimental investigation. As one example, it has introduced normative ethicists to the controversial issue of which specific learning algorithms to use in machines. Nick Bostrom and Eliezer Yudkowsky have argued for decision trees (such as ID3) over neural networks and genetic algorithms on the grounds that decision trees obey modern social norms of transparency and predictability (e.g. *stare decisis*), while Chris Santos-Lang argued in the opposite direction on the grounds that the norms of any age must be allowed to change and that natural failure to fully satisfy these particular norms has been essential in making humans less vulnerable to criminal "hackers".

Unintended Consequences

Many researchers have argued that, by way of an "intelligence explosion" sometime in the 21st century, a self-improving AI could become so vastly more powerful than humans that we would not be able to stop it from achieving its goals. In his paper "Ethical Issues in Advanced Artificial Intelligence," philosopher Nick Bostrom argues that artificial intelligence has the capability to bring about human extinction. He claims that general super-intelligence would be capable of independent initiative and of making its own plans, and may therefore be more appropriately thought of as an autonomous agent. Since artificial intellects need not share our human motivational tendencies, it would be up to the designers of the super-intelligence to specify its original motivations. In theory, a super-intelligent AI would be able to bring about almost any possible outcome and to thwart any attempt to prevent the implementation of its top goal, many uncontrolled unintended consequences could arise. It could kill off all other agents, persuade them to change their behavior, or block their attempts at interference.

However, instead of overwhelming the human race and leading to our destruction, Bostrom has also asserted that super-intelligence can help us solve many difficult problems such as disease, poverty, and environmental destruction, and could help us to "enhance" ourselves.

The sheer complexity of human value systems makes it very difficult to make AI's motivations human-friendly. Unless moral philosophy provides us with a flawless ethical theory, an AI's utility function could allow for many potentially harmful scenarios that conform with a given ethical framework but not "common sense". According to Eliezer Yudkowsky, there is little reason to suppose that an artificially designed mind would have such an adaptation.

Bill Hibbard proposes an AI design that avoids several types of unintended AI behavior including self-delusion, unintended instrumental actions, and corruption of the reward generator.

Organizations

Amazon, Google, Facebook, IBM, and Microsoft have established a non-profit partnership to formulate best practices on artificial intelligence technologies, advance the public's understanding, and to serve as a platform about artificial intelligence. They stated: "This partnership on AI will conduct research, organize discussions, provide thought leadership, consult with relevant third parties, respond to questions from the public and media, and create educational material that advance the understanding of AI technologies including machine perception, learning, and automated reasoning." Apple joined other tech companies as a founding member of the Partnership on AI in January 2017. The corporate members will make financial and research contributions to the group, while engaging with the scientific community to bring academics onto the board.

The Public Voice has proposed a set of Universal Guidelines for Artificial Intelligence, which has received many notable endorsements.

The IEEE put together a Global Initiative on Ethics of Autonomous and Intelligent Systems which has been creating and revising guidelines with the help of public input, and accepts as members many professionals from within and without its organisation.

Traditionally, government has been used by societies to ensure ethics are observed through legislation and policing. There are now many efforts by national governments, as well as transnational government and non-government organisations to ensure AI is ethically applied.

- The European Commission has a High-Level Expert Group on Artificial Intelligence.

- The OECD on Artificial Intelligence.

- In the United States the Obama administration put together a Roadmap for AI Policy (link is to Harvard Business Review's account of it. The Obama Administration released two prominent whitepapers on the future and impact of AI. The Trump administration has not been actively engaged in AI regulation to date.

References

- Philosophy-of-artificial-intelligence, browse: philpapers.org, Retrieved 28 April, 2019

- bostrom, nick (2014), superintelligence: paths, dangers, strategies, oxford university press, isbn 978-0-19-967811-2

- kaplan, andreas; haenlein, michael (2018), "siri, siri in my hand, who's the fairest in the land? On the interpretations, illustrations and implications of artificial intelligence", business horizons, 62, doi:10.1016/j.bushor.2018.08.004

- Ethics-of-artificial-intelligence, browse: philpapers.org Automated-reasoning, definition: techtarget.com, Retrieved 19 May, 2019

- chalmers, david j (1996), the conscious mind: in search of a fundamental theory, oxford university press, new york, isbn 978-0-19-511789-9

Permissions

We would like to thank the editorial team for lending their expertise to make the book truly unique. They have played a crucial role in the development of this book. Without their invaluable contributions this book wouldn't have been possible. They have made vital efforts to compile up to date information on the varied aspects of this subject to make this book a valuable addition to the collection of many professionals and students.

This book was conceptualized with the vision of imparting up-to-date and integrated information in this field. To ensure the same, a matchless editorial board was set up. Every individual on the board went through rigorous rounds of assessment to prove their worth. After which they invested a large part of their time researching and compiling the most relevant data for our readers.

The editorial board has been involved in producing this book since its inception. They have spent rigorous hours researching and exploring the diverse topics which have resulted in the successful publishing of this book. They have passed on their knowledge of decades through this book. To expedite this challenging task, the publisher supported the team at every step. A small team of assistant editors was also appointed to further simplify the editing procedure and attain best results for the readers.

Apart from the editorial board, the designing team has also invested a significant amount of their time in understanding the subject and creating the most relevant covers. They scrutinized every image to scout for the most suitable representation of the subject and create an appropriate cover for the book.

The publishing team has been an ardent support to the editorial, designing and production team. Their endless efforts to recruit the best for this project, has resulted in the accomplishment of this book. They are a veteran in the field of academics and their pool of knowledge is as vast as their experience in printing. Their expertise and guidance has proved useful at every step. Their uncompromising quality standards have made this book an exceptional effort. Their encouragement from time to time has been an inspiration for everyone.

The publisher and the editorial board hope that this book will prove to be a valuable piece of knowledge for students, practitioners and scholars across the globe.

Index